T5-BYY-536

Everything Happens for the Best

BOOKS BY THE AUTHOR

And Always Tomorrow
Everything Happens For The Best

*(Recorded as a Talking Book for the
Library of Congress for the Blind and
Physically Handicapped)

Everything Happens for the Best

by

Sarah Winston

Thomas Yoseloff
New York • South Brunswick • London

Thomas Yoseloff, *Publisher*
Cranbury, New Jersey 08512

Thomas Yoseloff Ltd
108 New Bond Street
London W1Y OQX, England

498 06809 9
Printed in the United States of America

For Rose and Keeve . . .

Contents

Everything Happens for the Best

1

Anything for a Quiet Life

Mama was blessed with a philosopher's calm and an uncanny talent for plucking proverbs out of the air to cover every situation from a hangnail to a major disaster. Her tranquility did not develop in a day, however. It took years for her to realize that nothing is so bad but what it could be worse. And this she learned firsthand, since Papa was a young inventor struggling to support a wife and two children and a third on the way (this at a most unsuitable time). A new idea was in the process of fruition and Mama, poor soul, suffered dual labor pangs—her own and Papa's.

"Every dog has his day," Mama would say to comfort Papa on one of his bad days. But bad days were mercifully few when he was plunged into deep thought and, usually, ethereal oblivion. And as far back as I can remember Papa was usually happy. However, when a dark, despairing day arrived he could count on Mama's apt sayings and they buoyed his spirits immeasurably.

He often called Mama "Sweet Estherel," for he was affectionate by nature and grateful in his way for Mama's special indulgence. Mama countered with "Hreshcoo," an endearment in their native Rumanian tongue. With such a combination their marriage was probably, as Mama insisted all marriages were, "planned in heaven."

When Papa was caught up in a new idea he persisted with the soul of an artist, giving it his all through the day and night, often until daybreak. During these periods his income, meager at best, came to a standstill. And Mama, besides developing a stoic calm, became an expert at stretching the family dollar; however scarce money became she was determined her children would not feel the squeeze.

One of her regular maneuverings was a standing order with the neighborhood butcher—a half spring chicken weighing about a pound. This was earmarked solely for my sister Rose who was two, and my brother Keeve, six. Mama's share of the nourishment involved the soul rather than the body. Merely to dwell on this festive meal and its health-promoting nutrients replenished her strength, and nothing short of illness would induce her to forgo this weekly ritual.

The chicken was cooked into a delectable, aromatic soup, crammed with celery, onions, carrots, and root parsley. Mama absorbed energy by sniffing the savory odors and sampling for taste. To take more would be unpardonable despite a gnawing, prenatal craving for food.

Each Friday at noon, the moment Keeve returned from school, the soup and chicken were served. The day was always the same, the taste always the same. The routine never altered and Mama beamed with good humor which lasted well into the next week.

When one day in the late spring Keeve expressed a desire to eat his portion out-of-doors it pleased her out of all proportion. At last her little man was growing up fully realizing the benefits of pure, fresh air. Keeve wasted no time finishing his lunch and almost before

Mama could turn around he was back, his plate licked clean as a pup's. Week after week Mama's little man repeated this performance, returning his empty plate to proud Mama.

"Don't eat so fast, Keeve," Mama warned, "it's bad for the digestion." And Keeve, dear obedient child that he was, agreed and stayed out ten minutes longer. Mama hummed happily as she fed the soup and chicken to Rose.

Then one day Mama made a discovery. She sat down to rest a moment before feeding Rose, as she was heavy with child. Sitting behind the curtain out of sight, she watched contentedly as Keeve carefully juggled his lunch and sat down on the back step. He sat quietly for a few moments and Mama prided herself on her little man's behavior, congratulating herself for rearing such a fine, obedient boy. As Mama so often said, "A young twig is twisted easier than an old tree," and she sat gazing wistfully, feeling within her the stirring of a new life.

Suddenly she started as Keeve's voice broke the noonday calm. He called to the neighbor's dog in a strange, muffled voice, then looked furtively about him. "Here, Sport, come and get it!"

Sport got it. So did Keeve. And the extravagant Friday chicken dinner disappeared until times were more prosperous. That was soon to come, for after I was born Papa sold one of his devices and we moved to fashionable East 17th Street, a few doors away from Stuyvesant Park, where we could breathe the "good, fresh air." Mama insisted I brought luck to the family, as that was our first taste of good fortune.

I can still see Mama and Keeve huddled over the real estate section of the Sunday newspaper—a weekly ritual that we looked forward to as much as the colored funnies. Mama was a fiend for fresh air—her favorite topic of conversation with whoever would listen was "a little home in the country with pure air for the children to inhale in their lungs." Since Papa's business was smack in the heart of the city the odds against our moving were about ten to one. But that never stopped Mama from dreaming and planning.

Chief perpetrator behind the scenes was Keeve, now twelve, who passionately longed to move from the city. He scanned the Sunday ads carefully, circling, underscoring, snipping and filing every possibility. When he hit on one that appealed to his young enthusiasm he'd say breathlessly, "Listen, this sounds good. Six-room dwelling, back barn, poultry house, laying hens, apple orchard, stream. Price for quick sale, $5800."

"Where is it?" Mama would break in excitedly.

"It's too far"—Keeve's fervor would wane,—"it's near Erie, Pennsylvania. It's too far."

"You're right. It must be close to New York so Papa can take the train each day. Maybe there's something in New Jersey or New York, Keevie?"

And Keith would fine-tooth-comb the ads again while Rose and I and sometimes two-year-old Franny would gather closer tingling with expectancy. The funnies never measured up to this.

Week after week we went through the same routine. I suspect Mama realized it was wishful thinking, but it was thrilling and exciting and kept us in a state of hopeful anticipation. In time it got to be like a game and we never once doubted that something would eventually turn up. The mere fact that Mama wanted to leave the city was good enough for us.

Rose and I continued the game during the week as we made secret plans about our home in the country. Where we got our extravagant ideas I don't know but they included a full retinue of gardeners, cooks and cleaning women. The trees dripped with luscious black-red cherries, huge red apples that grew with that fancy fruit shine we saw on push carts, golden-ripe bananas and California thick-skinned oranges. The matter of climate was incidental.

Occasionally we spent time in the library, accompanied by Keeve who seemed to know just what books to borrow and where to get them. We thumbed through books on fruit culture, gardening and lush green lawns. The more pictures the better. Keeve would read quietly, consuming all the facts he would later tell Mama. Rose and I were entranced with the vivid illustrations; the fruit and vegetables looked delectable and enormous as the pictures we later saw in seed catalogues.

We pictured every country home a horn of plenty where you walked out in a straw bonnet—it had to be a straw bonnet—with a basket on your arm and *plink-plonk, plink-plonk,* the most luscious, ripest specimens of fruit would drop down into it. With such an abundance you could distribute the surplus among the neighbors, and if you so chose, you could sell a little to keep you in pin money. Our fanciful ideas of life in the country were a mixture of fertile imagination and dearth of facts.

Once we spent a summer on a farm in the Catskill Mountains, but I was too young to remember that. All the shade trees in my young life were confined to Stuyvesant Park. Between wide walks of concrete, a reasonable facsimile of green grass bravely appeared each spring. In a few weeks even this bit of verdure succumbed to children's play. "Keep Off the Grass" signs placed strategically throughout the little park, and low-spiked iron fences created no obstacles. Even the friendly cops turned the other way.

To us the park symbolized good health and fresh air, country, picnic grounds, and with a stretch of imagination, even beach. A granite fountain sent sluggish sprays of cool water to tickle our sweaty, outstretched palms. The more daring of us waded in the shallow pool beneath. Mama kept saying how lucky we were to live so close to a park, and to us it was the world's most beautiful one until the day we passed the incredibly lovely Gramercy Park. The grass was green and velvety, like plush carpet. No cops were anywhere to be seen and no one played on the grass. Strangely, we hardly ever saw anyone there at all.

"Let's go in," I said to Rose, my constant guide and mentor.

"We're not allowed," said Rose in a hushed voice.

"Why?" I whispered back.

"See that big iron gate? Do you see that big lock? Well, only rich people who live in Gramercy Place have keys to unlock it."

Intrigued, I turned and looked closer through the iron bars of the spiked gate. A woman dressed in snowy white was reading a book while a little girl played beside her. Another woman, similarly dressed, was adjusting a large-wheeled baby carriage. "Nurses," whispered Rose. Hardly half-a-dozen human beings inhabited the entire park. No scrap of paper littered the walks. There was something grim and forbidding about this uninhabited sanctuary in the midst of a city teeming with people.

"Only very wealthy people live on Gramercy Place," repeated Rose as she pointed to the fashionable row of apartment buildings silhouetted against the sky. "They all hire maids and nurses to care for their children. The park is private."

I said, deeply awed, "But how do you know?" Before Rose could answer, a nurse walked up to the massive iron gate and unlocked it with a huge black key. It was like watching a character out of a story book suddenly come to life.

After that eventful day, Stuyvesant Park, though not comparable in beauty to Gramercy, seemed even warmer and friendlier. Children laughed and played and romped all over the grass. There was little grass but plenty of vibrant life. Mothers, not nurses, sat beside baby carriages and the sight was warming.

During the summer Mama packed our lunch and off we went to the park each day, sometimes with her and Franny, sometimes just Rose and I. Mama walked us to the Avenue to watch us cross, then returned home to take care of the chores that await a mother of four.

We owned no encyclopedias and few books of information. Our font of knowledge was my brother Keeve, who was a source of comfort to Mama even at the age of twelve. He displayed a resourcefulness and a capacity for understanding that both delighted and dismayed us. A composite of mature grownup and impish boy, he generally kept the family in good spirits.

It was Keeve who gave moral support and backing to Mama's campaign to move to the country. Papa was too busy assembling machines or working on a new idea to pay any mind to the family's little conspiracies. "If it gives you a little pleasure, why not?" he would say, "but don't forget, we're still fighting a war." I used to wonder why he kept reminding us of the war. Young as I was, I sensed it all about me, but what had the war to do with us, I wondered? My only experience with war was with the neighborhood kids. The games generally assumed the dimensions of a small-scale battle.

"Bang, bang," the kids would cry, "let's go over the top and shoot the dirty Huns," as small bodies tumbled over each other in mock warfare. The immediate drawback to fighting a full-scale war was the city street. "Let's jump into the trenches," they shouted as they cowered behind stoops and alleyways, pop guns reverberating through the streets.

The constant war play terrified my doll-and-carriage set. The boys delighted in tormenting us. "Huns," they shouted, and bang-banged away at us with the venom of an enemy. We were alerted to war since most of the battles were fought on our small street, with the little girls singled out as arch-antagonists.

On Sundays when Papa drove the family to Brighton or Manhattan Beach, we came in glorious contact with real soldiers. The Model-T Ford sagged and wailed with the weight of Mama, Papa, four children, baskets of food, blankets, inflated rubber tubes, and extra clothing. But we always found room for a doughboy thumbing a ride. "There's a handsome one, Papa," Rose would say, and Papa would stop and pick him up. Once a soldier tickled me under the chin and I almost died with pleasure. Undoubtedly I was helping to win the war. Just exactly how, I didn t know until we returned in the evening and Rose, without batting an eyelash, would regale the "foe" with stories about real soldiers who killed thousands of Huns—soldiers we had met only that day.

When she was convinced they were softened to just the proper turn she threw one in about our Uncle Joe fighting in France. If they were brazen enough to retaliate with their uncles, she was ready with our Uncle Joe, Mama's brother, one of Teddy Roosevelt's Rough Riders, who won the Spanish-American war single-handed—well, almost single-handed. With the enemy hot on his tail he bolted over land, forded threatening rivers; all about him men fell stiffly like ducks in a shooting gallery. He alone emerged triumphant, charging his valiant steed. Uncle Joe *was* really a Rough Rider and much that she said was true, but a few gory details with the proper embellishments were always on hand to lend credibility to some of her more outrageous whoppers.

When the Army was at ease, the Allies and Huns would converge to sing little ditties like "Johnny, Get Your Gun, Get Your Gun, Get Your Gun," "Over There," and "Oh, How I Hate to Get Up in the Morning." Two or three years younger than the rest, I was drafted into the ranks as the sole buck private. The others were top sergeants and captains and their orders vied with the best. Once they commanded, "Go home and bring back a bag of cookies. And be quick." Fearful of the consequences—the Army's, not Mama's, I scurried home. A trembling Trilby, I obeyed every command; as a reward for loyalty I was raised to the rank of corporal—until the day Mama found me pilfering and I could bring no more peace offerings. I was demoted right back to buck private.

One morning I was wakened by a gibberish of excited voices . . . a frenzied mixture of Yiddish, English, and Rumanian. Words tumbled over each other. There was happy excitement, tears glistened in Mama's and Papa's eyes. "Thank God it's all over. Let us pray our children will never know another. Amen."

I was curious with wonder at this rare display. "What's over, Mama?"

Still misty eyed, Mama seemed not to hear.

"The war is over, Sarala." Papa came over and hugged me. "The armistice is signed and now all the soldiers will come back to their families . . . . well, nearly all. If this war was fought to end all wars, maybe it was not in vain. Amen." Papa was solemn. Every sentence was like a prayer and the "amens" equaled the "ands" and "buts." Never had I seen him and Mama so stirred up.

Through a haze of tears Mama said, "You're right, Henry, everything happens for the best."

"Let's go up to Fifth Avenue and watch the parade," said Keeve. "There'll be thousands of soldiers marching and bands playing.'' Somehow Keeve knew—via grapevine, newspaper or sheer intuition.

Papa and Mama hesitated. Mama said she was glad it was over and wasn't interested in the hooraying. But Papa yielded to our pleading and we walked over to Fifth Avenue.

The streets were filled with happy panic. Strangers hugged and kissed one another. Papa picked me up in his arms to protect me from the wild excitement; we were brushed along like confetti by the delirious crowds, and I burst into tears though I didn't know why.

The bizarre, feverish camaraderie was more than a parade; it seemed like a symbol of peace and hope for the future.

2

All Is Not Gold That Glitters

Soon after school was out for the summer, Papa drove carefully down the street in his Model—T, loudly honking all the way. The familiar hollow wheezing sent the children scattering to the curbs, partly in fear and curiosity as Lizzie wound its way around and through the bolder ones.

The street offered a safe area for the youngsters—the games stopped only when pushcart vendors and horse-and-wagon teams passed through. A major annoyance was the frequency of such interruptions. No sooner had a game started, than a horse would come plodding down the street, forcing the players to scatter. But games sprang quickly back to life until the next horse lumbered through.

The kids on our block were blissfully unaware of playgrounds. With the park, the sidewalks, and the street we were kept busy. If there was organized play we never heard of it and obviously we were not too much in need of it. The kids were an average healthy lot reared in low-income families. We were the heart of the melting pot with at least one of almost every religion and nationality. And no one seemed aware of the differences.

We heard Mama speak of Harry Goldman who won a scholarship to Juilliard; or of Jimmy Quirk, the quiet boy who supported his widowed mother by working in the corner grocery; or of Tony Petrone, the valedictorian of his class. We heard many stories like these but very few relating to reform school or hoodlumism.

Almost every hour of the day someone was practicing scales on a violin, piano, flute or clarinet. In the evening the instruments blared discordantly from every part of the tenement building; in self-defense you learned to play an instrument.

Juvenile delinquency was a phrase confined to a dictionary. If the tendency was there it was stifled by homework and music practice. Little time was left to work at mischief. Except for the nickel movie there were few places to entice roving youngsters; we generally stayed close to home.

Papa held the distinction of owning the first automobile on our block, and all the neighborhood kids were in awe of him, but mostly of the car. The moment he parked in front of the four-story tenement we called home, the kids came flocking. They left their baseball, stoop ball, potsie, hopscotch and tag and surged around the gleaming black oddity on wheels.

During the school year the attraction was even greater. We lived a few doors away from P.S. 16 and when Papa drove home for lunch, youngsters swarmed around the car like maggots around a carcass. The depredations of these Lilliputians whacking away at the tires, opening and shutting doors, sitting on fenders, jumping on runningboards, climbing over the radiator hood, forced Papa to devise a method for prolonging the Ford's longevity.

Slowly but noisily he came stomping out of the house, pretending to see no one in sight. Two hands behind his back clutched a six-foot length of pipe that managed to make itself visible a foot above his head.

"Keep sitting, children," he said, juggling the pipe vigorously behind him, "I want a few words with you." But as the menacing pipe came closer, the car rattled loudly as the boys hopped down and ran in all directions, flying down the street in panic.

It was unusual for Papa to drive down the street in the mid-morning; he honked his horn a little longer and louder than was his custom, as if to mark the occasion. Sensing something was up, I left my two friends, Birdie and Laura, and ran home just as Papa pulled up to the curb. We walked in the door together, startling Mama who was bathing little Franny. In the same tone he might comment on the weather, Papa broke the news that was to change the course of our lives.

"Estherel, you have your home in the country."

Mama looked up quickly. "What do you mean, Henry?"

"In two weeks you will be in Coventry, Connecticut." Mama looked at him blankly, speechless.

"Herman Black's place, Estherel."

Mama kept looking at Papa, still incredulous. Papa's dry sense of humor often kept us in a state of suspense, but this time his voice underlined a sense of urgency. "It's true, Esther, it's true."

"But how—when?" Mama stammered. "What kind of a place is it?"

"From Herman's description it sounds good and his word is enough for me. I agreed to rent it for a few months. If you like it we can buy later."

Mama walked around in a daze. All the make-believe was starting to come true. She lifted Franny out of the tub and dried him half-bathed.

"I just can't believe it . . .I thought you were against the idea."

"Hreshkoo." Mama threw her arms around Papa and hugged him. "What about the land? Is there a little for the children to play?"

"A hundred acres. Is that enough? What do you say, Estherel?" Papa was bursting with importance but his manner remained calm and unruffled.

"A hundred acres!" The world, the sky and the moon! That very day Mama started to pack. She hummed as she worked and her happiness sparkled. Mama was never so worked up with enthusiasm and we children glowed in the fever of her excitement.

The time seemed to stretch endlessly until the day when we finally found ourselves seated on the train bound for Coventry. As the train started out the whole venture still seemed unreal; and we sat entranced as cities, small towns, and farmhouses surged by. Cattle, horses, sheep, chickens whizzed past as the train rolled on. The spectacle of cattle grazing on far-off stretches of countryside, and horses free in pasture filled us with awe and wonder. We all traveled in silence, too busy watching this wondrous new world unfold. Pictures and storybooks were one thing, but the real thing was something else again. Mama occasionally handed us a sandwich or cookie, but our eyes remained glazed and glued to the windows. After four hours we alighted at the drab little railroad station in Andover.

It was about four miles to the farm. Mr. Black had arranged for a farmer, Ed Bailey, to meet us at the station. When the train pulled in he was waiting in a two-seated black, shining buggy with a fringed canopy. Ed helped Mama in first, then Franny was hoisted onto her lap. Rose and I climbed in beside her; Papa, Keeve and Ed sat in the front. Papa arranged for Ed to return later for the luggage.

The buggy sagged heavily as it started off, the wheels squeaking from disuse. "Only use the buggy on Sunday to drive the old lady to church," said Ed.

We jogged across the railroad tracks past the trim white, Congregational church and turned right on a country road, passing a group of low-roofed factory buildings which Ed pointed out as the paper mill—the town's only industry. Thundering over a bridge of rough, loose planks we came to a steep incline. Papa and Keeve stepped down to ease the haul. Halfway up the hill the horse, sweating and snorting, stopped to rest, halting the buggy abruptly.

"Come on, Blackie, be a good girl," said Ed as he

gently nudged the horse to continue; the carriage
tottered and groaned as it continued up the hill. "That's
a good girl," he said approvingly. The horse panted
heavily until the peak was behind us. Papa and Keeve
climbed on the buggy again and we proceeded, the pace
steady and gradually quickening.

We jogged deep into the country, traveling close to
cows and chickens as we made our way down the road
which coursed through a continual stretch of stone wall.
The road, deeply rutted from the strain of wheels
through many spring and winter muds, heaved the wagon
to and fro. In the short stretches that the road ran clear
and smooth, Ed would pull the reins, nudging Blackie to
a semitrot.

As we turned a bend in the road, the driver said,
"that's the place over there." His twang made two
syllables out of the word "there." We strained to the
side of the carriage, startled to see a house that appeared
to be sitting smack in the middle of the dirt road. But as
we rode closer, the road turned sharply to the left
revealing a white frame house sitting pleasantly on a
slope. It had an open verandah half-way around, and it
was brighter and more attractive than most of the
farmhouses on the way. Ed said it was built around 1754
and was badly run-down when Mr. Black took over and
put it in shape.

At the moment all I could see was a trim, white
house; a low stone wall that stretched around the
property offering unlimited possibilities for climbing and
running; the barns and shed with their many sanctuaries
for hide and seek, and an abundance of trees. Ed pointed
out the vast apple orchard within sight of the house, the
peach trees, hickory nut and cherry trees. Happy to the
bursting point, I wondered how Papa could have kept all
this a secret for so long.

Ed took on a new importance when he saw the
respect we showed for his store of information. He
continued to enlighten Papa with a detailed account of
the place as we plodded along. "Ayeh," he said, offering

counsel, "you have a fine place there. Plenty of good farming land though it's a garl-durned shame it don't get farmed." He looked at Papa appraisingly. "Guess you ain't aiming to farm none. It's a garl-durned shame."

By the time we arrived we had a visual picture of every square inch punctuated by frequent "garl-durned shames." Papa tsk-tsked attentively, appreciating the thorough account despite his honest ignorance of farming. Mama listened happily, and by the look on her face you might think she had already bought the place. For years she dreamed and planned and now it was happening. The future could be nothing but bright and rosy.

We scrambled down from the buggy, eager to get on terra firma again. So much to explore, so much to do. At this moment I thought how lucky a family we were to know a man like Mr. Black.

Though it was early in July, the season had not taken hold, Ed said. Fearing a late, killing frost, farmers were tardy in sowing crops; but we could see the first signs of corn and potatoes sprouting through the well-manured earth. We arrived too late for the "best crop of peas in years" and the asparagus had turned to lacy seed. But it was summer and the warm sun soaked up the earthy odors, wafting them across the countryside. The air was sweet and fresh and pure and did not smell of gasoline fumes and coal soot and dirty streets. The effect was like sweet wine penetrating the senses.

Rose and I were breathless with every discovery. Each morning we awoke, hopped out of bed and ran outside, expecting some new wonderland to open up to us. The days were filled with adventure and surprises—but not so the nights, we were soon to learn.

For as long as the summer evenings provided us with light, we played tag on the wide stone wall that half-circled the farm; we explored the barn and sheds and played hide-and-seek there. We took long walks on the narrow, sharply winding road, which could present a hazard when two vehicles passed; we soon learned to jump deep into the brush when a team of horses or an automobile approached. In the long stretches where the hanging trees encased the road like a leafy canopy, our steps quickened in the eerie darkness. Out in the open again, comforted by the warming sight of peaceful farm lands and cows grazing placidly in fields, we slackened our pace and continued on more calmly.

There was still so much to do; but as the days grew shorter, we were forced to abandon outdoor play. Confined to quarters earlier, I began to feel the first waves of homesickness. I longed desperately for Birdie and Laura. It was easy to forget the endless hair-pulling match between Birdie and me after she had called me "Skinny" for the hundredth time. It was easy to forget the unpleasantness and remember only the happy days. If only Birdie and Laura could be transported by some magic carpet, life would brighten considerably. But Birdie and Laura could not be transported and I sulked because we had no nearby neighbors—our closest being a mile away—and we had no playmates.

The unbroken quiet of the day, the locusts' interminable whirring, the dull mooing of the cows in far-off pastures, the persistent chatter of the katydid all contributed to my disgruntled state. Even the cheerful rantings of the crickets began to pall.

The city became lost in a haze of nostalgia which blotted out noise and dirt and grime; only fun and friends and plenty to do remained in my thoughts. The familiar haunts and friendly faces I had left behind swiftly converged; the noisy crowds, the honking horns, the rumble of elevated trains turned into a symphony of sounds that became more musical with each passing day. Only one comforting thought remained—Papa had not yet purchased the place; the emptiness became bearable as I placed a heavy red "X" each morning on the dwindling August calendar.

3

Every Day Brings a New Light

The prospect of moving back to New York in the fall grew dimmer each day. Mama, settled too comfortably into the role of nature-lover and garden ah-and-oher, constantly extolled the joys of clean country living as opposed to germ-ridden city life. She was mesmerized by the pure, fresh air, and, sweet little darlings that we were, we would stalk off holding our noses in silent defiance.

If Mama experienced loneliness she never showed it. The way she hummed as she worked, the way she nurtured her small bed of marigolds and zinnias, the way she happily strolled through the orchards. The excited way she spoke to Papa about the simplest of things—a hickory nut, the color of zinnias, the wonderful air—always the sweet fresh air. Even the way she slept, a serene beatific look on her face.

Mama's contentment clearly raised a formidable barrier to our returning. When we protested, which we did with vigor and regularity, she dismissed our ill humor as temporary foolishness and insisted that even we would soon recognize our singular good fortune in living in so pure and undefiled a part of America. "You are young now . . . it takes time . . ." she would say patiently. "Rome wasn't built in a day."

Though Mama worked harder than ever before, she never complained. The old farmhouse was clean and in good repair but it lacked the essentials for easier living. There was no bathroom, no furnace, no running water—we pumped it at the kitchen sink. Wood-burning monsters in the kitchen and parlor supplied the heat for cooking and comfort. Cords of firewood were hauled by Ed Bailey and piled close to the house in six-foot lengths. These were chopped and splintered and fed into the stoves' hungry mouths. Our preoccupation with fuel was never-ending. It seemed as if we were always in the woods gathering dry dead limbs for kindling. The chore of chopping the firewood to stove lengths fell to Keeve and sometimes to Mama when she insisted he take turns with her. "Four hands are better than two," said Mama lightly, trying to cover her pain at watching the blisters on Keeve's hands turn into heavy calluses.

Mama nursed blisters and calluses, too, but she deftly rationalized them away. "It keeps you out in the fresh air and there's nothing like a good, healthy sweat. So what are a few calluses?" It was harder to explain the benefits of a swollen toe caused by the impact of an ax, but somehow she managed, and her determination continued as firm as the stone walls around us. "Accidents happen to everyone and it's a good thing, for it teaches you to be more careful."

We resigned ourselves to the inevitable, but neither peacefully nor quietly. Each day passed more slowly, more monotonously than the one before; and we longed hungrily for what was, goaded by our vivid inventiveness that turned our small, sooty city street into the quiet splendor of the Champs Elysées. Our morale had plunged so low that even the opening of school was good news.

On opening day Rose and I, gripping gleaming new lunch-pails, walked the two and a half miles to the run-down, weather-beaten one-room schoolhouse. We walked expectantly, eagerly, hungry for new experience and the mere sight of other small human beings.

During the summer we had walked this way many times, hoping to discover a neighbor, seeking out whoever might turn up in the way of humanity. In a short time we were familiar with every sneaking, snaring brush-filled gully, every bend and dip in the rutted dirt road. But people? Except for the occasional driver of a team of horses or a feed truck we never met another man, woman or child. And in the engulfing despair of self-styled martyrs we abandoned our walks and stayed close to the farm, shutting our eyes to the changing season and the miracle of color that was creeping over the countryside.

The day was bright and clear and the trees sparkled like a kaleidoscope, here a mass of red, there a bronze-yellow, and every blend between. Occasional masses of green stood firm as if in defiance of a new order as the leaves softly fell to earth where they lay emblazoned in color like some mammoth mosaic. Where a tree met the direct morning rays, the leaves glowed like shimmering gold. The most beautiful of all seasons was beckoning, and until this day we had been too miserable to enjoy it.

We had no awareness of nature or trees, *per se,* except for those in Stuyvesant Park, where the leaves were so laden with grime, poor things, that when they fell it was purely from exhaustion. For a brief period in the spring the leaves were bright and green but by the time they reached maturity they were encrusted with dirt. We never witnessed the change of seasons. We felt it.

Still marveling at the splendor before us, I said to Rose, "I never knew leaves were all colors."

"They're not, silly, they only turn this way in the fall."

"Did you ever see them turn before?"

"Once when Papa took us riding. It was real pretty."

"Prettier than this?"

"No, this is real pretty. So many different kinds of trees, that's why."

"Oh . . ."

"Some trees stay green longer. I wish leaves would never fall, the trees look so empty."

"Me, too."

We walked on in silence, stopping only to pluck a leaf from a low-hanging tree.

"Let's make a collection of colored leaves, Ro."

"Mmmm . . .I don't know. They don't stay colored long, they dry up and turn brown and crumble."

"Maybe ours won't if we're careful. Let's do it."

"Okay."

In the distance a patch of morning sun revealed the (very) little, (faded) red schoolhouse and we walked faster, half-running until we reached the door. We recoiled in unison as a strong smell hit us like a sharp slap on the fanny. In a corner of the partially partitioned-off cloakroom were lunches in brown paper bags, cotton sacks, lard pails, a milk can, a contraption resembling a knapsack, and a few similar hold-alls. The food odors mingled disastrously with the stale, unaired stench of dampness and last year's manure. Our brand-new lunch cans looked as much at home as a city slicker in a room of country parsons. For fear the smell might seep through in some devious way, we deposited them in a far-off corner, covering them lovingly with our sweaters.

Hammered into the walls were monstrous spikes which served variously as coat-hangers, and head gashers. I was initiated into its latter use immediately, for as I stood up

I managed to strike a low one. Instead of squealing I clutched Rose's skirt in pain. Thus we made our entrance into the eight-grade schoolroom where the smell was heightened by warm bodies and dank wood.

Any new family made big news and created considerable worry and conjecture among the townspeople. The census fluctuated by virtue of births, deaths, marriages, but rarely by the outright sale of a farm to a stranger, and especially to city folks. As we entered the room, the chatter ceased abruptly as all faces turned in our direction. We were sized up as one would be by a director organizing a new cast, and no less critically. Our appearance, dress and most of all our discomfort were properly noted; the time was not far off when we would feel the full impact of this first appraisal.

Earlier we heard about Miss Felton, the schoolteacher, from Ed Bailey. "Mebbe she'll last longer than the others. They come and go about as fast as the seasons, especially the young 'uns. This heah Felton gal is pretty as a spring picture and just as cool. Hope she can handle it. Ayeh, sure hope she can."

I thought of his remarks as the girlish teacher showed us to our seats. Rose and I were separated by four aisles. All heads turned to gape at us again until Miss Felton called the roll.

Facing the teacher was as unrelated and heterogeneous a group as ever filled a classroom. Boys and girls of all ages, sizes, shapes, from the first grade to the eighth, sat deceptively passive as each name was called. By the end of the day the façades had collapsed and the flushed Miss Felton was properly inducted into the role of country schoolma'am and law-enforcer.

The very little ones sat in the first row, which was reserved for the first grade. The rest were catalogued in aisles by grades—strapping, burly ones, buxom and bony ones, outgoing and shy ones. A six-footer sat in the sixth row and a seventeen-year-old sat in the seventh. Rose and another girl were the sole eighth-graders.

One was either timid or brazen; there seemed to be no comfortable medium. We soon learned you either bullied your way around or you made yourself inconspicuous and prayed you were lucky enough to get away with it. As a result, the meek ones, most of the girls and one or two boys, withdrew timorously and in so doing set themselves up as direct targets. If you were newcomers you were immediate quarry, and we were newcomers. As a stranger, your every word and action were suspect. Anyone who was queer enough to say "yes" instead of "ayeh," or "there" instead of "theyah," bore watching. And with our wide hair ribbons, patent-leather slippers and white stockings we were marked women even before the class had time to make up their minds.

A full week passed before we were accepted as members of the human race. Then slowly, one by one, the older girls offered their friendship though it was shy and restrained. As we came to know them better we grew to like them. But not so the boys.

From the fifth grade up, as we saw it, almost every gangling, flat-headed, straw-haired galoot seemed a ripe candidate for reform school. City boys were little Lord Fauntleroys by comparison. When these country boys herded, you gave them full clearance. I was convinced that with few exceptions, they possessed a strain of Jack the Ripper since their chief delight and pursuit was the slow torture of girls, especially frightened girls, and that meant all of us.

Ed Bailey warned us to "stay cleah" of sixteen-year-old Johnny Mitchell, a perpetual seventh grader, who seemed destined to continue there barring the school's total destruction. We were deathly afraid of this heavy-set, outsized boy who resembled a snorting bull. He blustered and bullied the younger boys until they joined him more out of fear than awe. To qualify for Johnny's club, a boy had to prove his skill in such activities as chicken-stealing or girl-baiting. Initiation involved the milder sport of lurking deep in the brush and waylaying girls on their way to and from school.

The two city girls were elected as the first trophies of the season, and one morning when Rose and I were within sight of the school we were startled by a sudden loud crackling of brush.

"Maybe it's a skunk," said Rose. "Let's run. Quick!"

Just as we zoomed past the spot, three boys tore after us in outmaneuvered wrath but they were not quite quick enough for two nimble little girls who ran as if demons were pursuing them, and they *were*. We stumbled into school in a panic, the boys directly behind twirling dead squirrels and a snake.

Until our terror wore off, Keeve walked us to school. By then our senses had sharpened like an animal's on the prowl and we never edged past a wooded or dense brush area without training our eyes on every bush and blade of grass. In due time our ordeal paid off. The same trio was ready for a return engagement, heady with pre-campaign victory. But this time the two little city girls were ready, too, and we ran as if suddenly winged. During the mad chase I dropped my lunch pail, but to pick it up was to invite disaster, so we kept running. What was the loss of a mere lunch compared to having a snake twirled around your neck? And a dead one at that!

We feared returning home even more and we appealed to little Miss Felton for protection from oafs a foot taller than she. She managed this deftly, however, by assigning chores to the boys after school, thereby assuring us a mile of safety behind us as we walked home.

Now, as I look back, Miss Felton appears not as a naïve country girl at all but as a wise woman who knew just how to handle knaves, hooligans, and semi-barbarians. After the first week in low gear, she shifted to high so suddenly that she startled as well as subdued her charges. Somehow this pink-cheeked girl of seventeen took hold and succeeded where many before had failed.

With almost as much class time devoted to discipline as to teaching, the odds were against your learning more than the basic three R's unless you were blessed with the rare combination of a keen mentality, a thirst for learning and a photographic memory. Having none of these gifts, I could easily envisage myself, years later, still dashing down the road, a step ahead of Johnny Mitchell's protegés.

Rose, on the other hand, enjoyed all the virtues of learning, would digest a textbook as readily as a chocolate soda. Within the week she was busily assisting Miss Felton with the first four grades, leaving Hattie Smith, her lone classmate as the sole occupant of the eighth grade aisle.

"I'm not missing anything," Rose would assure Mama. "Hattie is learning the same stuff I had in the fifth and sixth grades and it's so much more fun teaching. Anyway, there's nothing to learn." Mama would shake her head sadly and say, "Knowledge comes only from study. I'm not so sure that school is good for you. I'll talk to Papa when he comes home."

The novelty of helping Miss Felton was short-lived and Rose soon found the work weary and repetitious. To lessen the boredom she sought determinedly for some diversion that would speed the dragging hours. This was not hard to find. As her classmates shuffled to the front of the room for recitation she committed to memory their gestures, mannerisms, twangs and localisms. With her sharp perception for nuances of sound and expression, she was busily constructing a series of classroom vignettes. Later at home, she grandly presented a take-off of pupils and teacher à la Ruth Draper. Rose brightened many a dull winter evening for us with her hilarious mimicry.

School would have been a complete wash-out for Rose were it not for her classmate, Hattie Smith. In spite of the high-necked, long-sleeved dresses that outlined her spindly body like a silhouette, she was a pretty girl. Her skin was a blushing white, delicately peppered with freckles, and her carrot-colored hair was drawn back and hung in a tight, no-nonsense braid. Except for a mouth as full and shapely as that of a voluptuous woman, she suggested a youthful Whistler's Mother.

Hattie's real trouble began with her natural sprinting ability. When the boys saw, to their chagrin, that she could outrun every one of them without trying she became a marked woman; her height and lack of girth became their prime targets for ridicule. She was teased and taunted every day but she never hardened to it. Every time they shouted, "Skinny," or "Spindle-Legs," or "Gangle-Shanks," she turned a fiery red and broke into sobs. It was sad to see Hattie cry, she looked so helpless and lonely, and sadder still because no one was brave enough to defend her.

We had come upon her accidentally during lunch hour one day and were to become good friends from that moment on. Rose and I had nothing to do so we decided to explore the school grounds which comprised, in toto, a trampled backyard and an outhouse for both sexes, vaguely partitioned, and shielded by a magnificent, old maple tree. To arm ourselves for possible future emergencies, we decided to investigate the interior which appeared unoccupied. We walked into GIRLS. And there was Hattie placidly squatting, her elbows digging into her thighs, her hands cupping her chin, and a serenity on her face that comes only with complete dedication to the task at hand. Hattie looked at us vacantly, then tugged at her skirt in embarrassment and giggled nervously. We had no previous briefing on the finer points of a three-seater, no-waiting arrangement and what hit our unsuspecting nostrils was hardly ambrosial. When we backed away quickly, Hattie mistook our sudden exodus for delicacy.

"Didn't heah you coming," said Hattie feebly. "Come in if you've a mind to." If we'd had a mind we wouldn't have come in in the first place, I thought as we retreated. "That's okay, Hattie, we'll be back later," Rose lied.

Rose and Hattie became fast friends in a mute sort of way after that first impressive meeting. Rose began to help Hattie with arithmetic and spelling. And when Rose was appointed permanent captain of the daily spelling bee she faithfully called on Hattie. Once she dared to come to Hattie's defense when the boys were teasing her; after that the look of adoration on Hattie's face when Rose was around was that of a faithful dog devoted to a kind master.

Then one day Hattie, coloring and flustered, invited us to her house. "Come next Monday when my Ma is out cleaning." I was about to ask why, but dropped it and the next Monday promptly after school we started out together. Most of the way Rose and I trailed along in silence, moving at a sprinter's walking pace in a vain attempt to keep up with Hattie. Once Rose tried to slow her down by engaging in conversation. Panting, she proffered, "How far do you live?" and "Gee, you walk fast!" Hattie, continuing the training pace responded loquaciously with "Down yondah" and "Ayeh." She seemed so preoccupied I wondered if she had asked us without her mother's consent and was beginning to regret her earlier impulse.. But I didn't wonder long. Visions of play and fun and refreshment spiced my enthusiasm and I was content to canter along like a young colt, hot and breathlessly.

We passed a few farmhouses separated by stretches of towering woodland and freshly harvested fields. A last spurt of Indian summer provided farmers with a little bonus time to gather crops and lay in a bountiful supply before the finality of a sudden New England frost. In the late afternoon sun the fields looked serene and carefully tended like a well-scrubbed kitchen floor.

We continued in silence until we came to a decrepit farmhouse, saltbox in design and hardly larger, surrounded by hordes of dirty broiler-sized leghorns pecking away at the earth. It was hard to make out what they were eating but I began to understand why the inside of a chicken gizzard looks like so much ground-up gravel. Compounding the bleakness of this mise-en-scène were the house's small, fly-specked windows framed by limp, frayed tie-backs.

Hattie turned in the stony driveway and pronounced gaily, "Well, heah we are."

She walked in the partly open kitchen door, motioning us to follow as she routed a couple of resistant chickens out the door. If Ma was out cleaning it was obvious she had had no previous experience. Dirty dishes in the tin sink reached the nozzle of the water pump, chairs were piled high with soiled clothing, and the sizeable deposits of chicken manure underfoot were mute and aromatic evidence that the floor had probably not been swept and scrubbed since the previous December in honor of Christmas. Rounding out this cozy scene were two baskets of rotting apples swarming with flies and a pair of battered felt boots encrusted with manure.

"Heah, sit down," said Hattie, shoving a stinking load

of overalls off a wooden bench. Rose and I sat down,
lowering ourselves gingerly like Siamese twins, hoping
that our proximity might ward off any further jolts to
our nervous systems.

Hattie hastened out to the woodshed and returned
with an armload of kindling and dry split logs, which she
dumped in the woodbox behind the stove. Then with the
flair of a Boy Scout she removed the lids and divider,
carefully laid the kindling and three small logs, sprinkled
them with kerosene, and struck a match. The blaze
flared to the ceiling and she quickly replaced the lids.
When the fire took hold and began to crackle noisily, she
filled the remaining cavity with solid logs. "It's burnin'
good," she said by way of conversation.

We were fascinated by Hattie's movements and our
heads bobbed back and forth like spectators at a tennis
match. Suddenly Rose found her voice. "Let's go out,
Hattie, it's real nice out." "Ayeh, purty soon. Gotta
finish my chores," said Hattie, oblivious of Emily Post.
She then dragged out a mammoth wash boiler and set it
up on a low wooden bench, then she headed for the
sink, where she cleared enough room for an iron kettle,
which she hung on an extended nodule. While tugging
furiously at the balky, wheezing pump, she said, "Sure is
handy having an indoor pump," glowing, as if she were
exhibiting a prize-winning Guernsey. "My daddy set it in
last spring."

She emptied a few kettles of pump water into the
boiler and covered the stove with the kettle and a few
heavy iron pots. Then she gathered up the soiled clothing
and dropped it in the tub, "It'll have to soak awhile
until the water heats up." Then, said Hattie, her
hospitality knowing no bounds, "Wouldja like a russet
apple?" We looked at the decaying fly-covered apples
and held our breaths. "No thanks," we muttered.

My urge to get up and run could not be

communicated to Rose and I kept on sitting, Hattie kept on working and we kept on watching. Steam started to seep from the kettles as Hattie attacked the sink load of dishes, stacking them in a chipped enamel dishpan. She sliced a slab of yellow naphtha soap, and secured it in a wire holder which she shook vigorously in the water before attacking the dishes. A grimy dish towel dried them and back they went in a wood cupboard reeking with the smell of naphtha. "Look," whispered Rose, "she didn't rinse the soap off."

"Did you say sumpthin?" asked Hattie.

"No," squeaked Rose.

The dishes put away, the kitchen took on a glimmer of tidiness. Any moment now we'll be going out to play, I thought. But Hattie had other plans. She picked up a scrub board and proceeded to tackle the gargantuan washing. When Rose turned to me in silent appeal I returned her glance helplessly and we kept on sitting. Finally she said weakly, "Guess we better get started for home."

"Ayeh," said Hattie, elbows deep in suds. "Guess you'd better. The sun is way down low and your Ma'll be worryin'. Glad you could come." With this final gesture of hospitality we took leave and walked home in silence. Until we moved, we never complained about the farm again.

4

He Who Hesitates Is Lost

Come rain, come storm, Mama walked to the village station every Friday night to greet Papa as he alighted from the train. Walking in the dark was eerie and lonely but she never entertained ideas of subjecting Papa to face the elements alone; the treasonous thought never clouded her mind as she floundered in pitch blackness with only a flickering oil lantern for company.

All too soon the weekend flew past and Papa was leaving for work and New York City again. Suddenly the house turned still and empty. We dreaded his leaving when the days grew shorter and the first bite of autumn charged the cooling summer air; during those long nights as I lay in bed listening fearfully to the old joists creaking and groaning, I would pull the covers tightly around my head, stifling sobs into the pillow and wish hard for some miracle to transplant us back to New York again. Failing that, I quickly settled for Papa to return and fill the house with a little life again. Not only did we miss the exciting surprises he always brought for each of us, but we longed for that feeling of security which suddenly vanished when he left.

Life is crammed with unanticipated circumstances that can at some completely unforeseen moment reinforce or destroy many careful plans. Happily one such vagary of fate descended on our household when we were all plunged in such misery that moving again was all but

41

despaired of.

Any sign of animal life, be it man or mule, brought us racing to the windows hoping that whatever it was would turn into our drive. And one day it happened—Ed Bailey halted his Sunday buggy out front and we almost flew from the house in our excitement. The front seat was piled high with shiny, tan leather luggage and in the rear sat an unfamiliar, stylishly dressed woman, a boy, and a girl. The girl appeared to be about six and the boy no more than twelve. This in itself spelled good news.

I nudged Rose. "Who's that?"

"Never saw them before," she said as we rushed back into the house to call Mama. When Mama recognized the urban entourage her face lit up happily. "Mrs. Black! What a wonderful surprise," she said and meant it. She laid out the welcome carpet, plush and thick, and kept insisting how pleased she was to see them and that she hoped they planned on a long visit. Apparently that was precisely what Mrs. Black did plan. She glanced about with a weary, bored, so-this-is-what-I've-come-to look, and proceeded to get straight to the point of her unannounced visit.

"My nerves . . .the doctor ordered rest . . .you know at my age . . ." She threw Mama a knowing wink and Mama tsk-tsked appreciatively. "I didn't want to come...school, you know—but Herman insisted. So here I am," she purred, "ready to gobble up the fresh farm air and all the farm milk and eggs. That should put me back on my feet."

"You came to the right place," said Mama, who accepted as a personal tribute any reference to fresh air. "This air works like nerve tonic and will put plenty of color back in your cheeks," she added softened and off guard.

I wondered about that. Mrs. Black looked the picture of health, and as for color, she had plenty, although it apparently hadn't fooled Mama one bit. Her fashionable clothes, modish coiffure, her soft, pink manicured hands and exquisitely made-up face enhanced her very healthy pallor. By comparison, Mama appeared in need of rest.

A child is quick to sense the unreal, the grandstand display, and I fidgeted and squirmed in her presence. On the other hand, young Adeline and Benny were definite signs that things were looking up and I left Mrs. Black and her stratagems to Mama.

We liked Benny at once in spite of a kind of impenetrable quality that put us off. His large, dark eyes reached out hungrily, yet at the first sign of response he retreated like a terrified cat, arched and ready to pounce. This was the side of Benny that shied from us, resisted us; but in a few days he began to reveal another side, the side that bubbled with fun and mischief.

Benny's mind worked like a computer—fast and precisely; he could think of more things to do and more places to go than anyone we had ever known and the first weeks of his visit were filled with unexpected fun and adventure. Having summered at the farm before, Benny was familiar with every stretch of land and woods within a five-mile radius. He was on friendly terms with every farmer in Coventry.

At the farm, though, he withdrew to himself and walked about with a dark, burdened melancholy that stretched his thin face like a taut bowstring. Any attempt to solace him seemed to push him deeper into retreat, and resulted in making you feel like a sneaking keyhole peeper.

Once I came on him unexpectedly in the parlor and found him in tears, blubbering into a handkerchief. My eyes puddled quickly with unvoiced rapport and a strong desire to comfort him, though I could not say a word. I tiptoed clumsily away, the old floors wheezing like a rubber doll. When he turned and saw me I froze solid like a transgressor caught in the act.

Instead of avoiding me he smiled when we met the

next morning after that embarrassing encounter. That smile on his grave, young face was as startling and unexpected as the sun glistening through a summer shower. It brightened with concealed mischief, it glowed with boyish enthusiasm.

After breakfast he beckoned furtively, his finger crooked secretively close to his knee.

"Y o u   a   b l a b b e r? Going to tell anyone about yesterday?"

"Oh, no," I said, overcome with joy that he spoke. "I know how it is. It takes a while to get used to the country. I used to cry a lot at night. I hated it here for a long while, too."

"I like it here a lot," said Benny softly.

"You're kidding, aren't you?"

"No, I mean it. I wish I never had to go back to New York."

"Then—then, why were you crying? Weren't you lonesome?"

"Yeah," said Benny evasively, "but not for the city."

"Then why?" I persisted, my interest suddenly fanned. Benny looked away, his thin hands fumbling in his pockets. When he spoke it was as if he never heard me. A sudden hint of the old melancholy crept back in his voice.

"You like it here now?"

"Yeah, especially since you and Adeline came."

"Aw, I bet." Benny's brow tightened and he looked at me curiously, suspicion filling his huge, dark eyes

"H o n e s t   t o   G o d," I said earnestly, sensing Benny's need for vigorous and absolute assurance.

"You mean it?" Benny said softly, his saucer-like eyes lighting up like an incandescent lamp. A smile hovered about his lips but he said nothing. Then, convoluting his young body awkwardly, he smiled outright as if a spring had been released and he had suddenly found the Truth. His smile was profuse and eloquent. Suddenly we were pals, our friendship sealed by mutual confession, voiced and implicit.

Slowly the sadness lifted from Benny's face, especially when Mama was around. The mother in her wrapped around him like a soft comforter and one day he started to call her Mama as if he had done so all his life. He was now one of the family and he responded with all the emotions of a natural youngster, eagerly at times, rebelliously at others, sometimes happy, angry, boisterous, quiet, teasing. What we did, Benny did, where we went, Benny went. Most of the time, however, the reverse was true; wherever Benny went, we went. His change was slow but steady, like the sun creeping from behind a cloud; something you couldn't see, like a bud bursting into flower. It began the day he volunteered to rake the apples that carpeted the orchard like a vast Chinese checkerboard.

"Let's clean them up," he said unexpectedly, "it won't take long." Then, as if we needed inducement, "It's a swell place for scrub ball but we'd break our necks playing there now."

And it continued with his boyish excitement when he revealed his soberly drawn plans, rolled carefully like a draftsman's blueprint, for a tree house to be built on two mammoth hickory tree limbs that were each as thick as the trunk itself.

After that it was one project after another. Ideas streamed steadily, methodically, like papers off a press. First the scrub ball diamond, then the tree-house, followed by monkey bars built from supple raw tree limbs and finally a seesaw and swing, for Adeline and Franny. His deft mind, his nimble fingers kept us wide-eyed, puffing.

Benny smiled and laughed easily now; impish mischief lurked behind his smiles and his laughter was real and deep as if oozing from every thwarted fiber of his being. This was a carefree boy who might have been a transplant from East Sixteenth Street.

He lapsed into glum silence only when Mrs. Black appeared or if she called him in her shrill, piercing voice, "Ben-nee." When she railed at him with an assortment of abuses and accusations it was always in front of the family. "Look how you neglect me, look how you disrespect me—all this after all I've done for you." Look how - look what - look - look. Always the same record, replayed and replayed. "Mark my words, nothing but bad will come from you," she whined in self-pity.

During her shrill harangue Benny would cloud up suddenly like the dark before a squall, the old harassed look on his face, his thin body writhing with embarrassment. What kind of help Mrs. Black expected of Benny we never knew. But we did know that Mama cooked, cleaned and washed like a hired maid, without Mrs. Black once ever offering to lift a dainty, manicured finger. Mama never complained; her silence was sufficient indictment for she was warm and friendly from her genes outward.

It got so we all tried to avoid Mrs. Black. We would turn away suddenly at the sight of her or pretend not to hear when she yelled to us, but we never quite made it. Our attempted evasions resulted in nothing more than louder complaints to Mama and ear-piercing diatribes at Benny. When she spent herself (and this was no minor feat), she cooed with saccharine sweetness over Adeline. "My dear, darling child, only *you* understand what your dear mother goes through and how she suffers. But please don't worry, dear, innocent heart, you are much too young to bear my heavy burdens." But innocent heart, having no intention of bearing her Mother's burdens, would squirm deftly out of her arms and run off to play with Franny or her dolls.

The thing that irked Mama most about Mrs. Black was her weird sense of comedy. One of her favorite diversions was to pick up the potatoes as quickly as Mama peeled them, and roll them across the porch like marbles. It was so ver-ee funnee and she laughed, doubling her hands over her stomach until the tears rolled down her cheeks. Then staggering dramatically she would say, "Oh Esther, my dear Esther, I get such pains from laughing but it's so fun-nee, ha-ha-ha, it's so ver-ee funny, ha-ha-ha." Mama thought it was so funny she would ease cautiously out of her way and into the house wondering no doubt what she ever saw in the Black Farm and the pure, fresh air.

It was Mama's and Papa's habit to break into Rumanian whenever they discussed people or confidential matters. We understood a few words like *da* and *casa* but this never endangered the security system appreciably. The times were frequent, however, when they would become so involved in their subject and so worked up with emotion that they would carelessly dip in and out of English. These lapses provided us with such choice bits of information as the fragmentary details of Herman Black's first wife, a friend of Mama's, who died in childbirth with Benny; and of his second marriage to "a pretty face but nothing else."

When they caught us eavesdropping they pitched back into Rumanian, but what we didn't hear could easily be augmented by the vivid nuances of voice and expression. A Phi Beta Kappa key was no requisite for understanding "all sweets are not wholesome," which Mama found easier to quote in English, or Papa's soulfully muttered, "That's how life is, Estherel, that's the way the world goes." Then back into a heated Rumanian observation which Papa ended succinctly with the good old English word "bitch."

We were able, then, despite some language handicaps, to piece together a picture of Mrs. Black. And now that she was here I developed a deeper respect for my parent's judgment.

It wasn't long before Benny launched us into the Big Venture. One day after the mail arrived he appeared more hopped up than usual, signalling us to the "ways and means department"—the apple orchard. Benny waved a letter and, cryptically pointing to it behind Mrs. Black, we all made off for the orchard where he passed it around with the gravity appropriate for the germination of a brand new enterprise. The thick contents outlined in glowing terms the rich rewards of trapping fur-bearing animals. "Make Big Money in Your Spare Time," "Trapping Paves the Road to Comfort," "You Trap—we Buy."

"It's true Keeve, there's big money in pelts."

"But I don't know the first thing about it."

"You don't have to. I used to hunt and trap with Ned Parsons and I learned all about it. Boy, there sure is money in pelts. Ned said that John Jacob Astor made his fortune in fur-trading. All you do is buy the traps, the rest is all profit."

"That easy?" asked Keeve, interested. "How much do you know about it, Benny?"

Benny assumed an air of authority. "There are three kinds of traps. One, a snare, catches the animal without hurting it; another grips the animal and holds it but doesn't kill it; and the third will kill it with a blow from a lever. You got to know which one to use, depending on the kind of animal you want to trap. And another thing, animals are pretty smart. If they smell a human scent they'll stay clear of it. There are chemicals to cover the human smell."

We listened, impressed with Benny's information. "What animal could we trap in this part of the country?" asked Keeve.

"Muskrats, raccoons, squirrels, skunks. Some animals

are caught with scent and others with bait. Muskrats are easier to find because they leave marked trails and live in dens. It's real exciting. Are you game?"

The next day Keeve and Benny returned from the village laden with steel traps, cookies and candy, and groceries for Mama. They rushed to the woods, set the traps, then came home flushed and tired to await destiny.

Benny said to Rose, "If we trap any minks you can have a fur coat made of them but you'll have to pitch in with the hauling." He forgot to add that we'd have to move to Alaska first to find them. He also forgot to tell Keeve about the small detail of skinning.

Rose either fell for the mink coat bit or was overcome with curiosity. One day she returned from the woods dangling a chipmunk by the tip of its tail at arm's length, her neck twisted in the opposite direction like a ventriloquist's dummy. "Maybe we'll have better luck next week," said Benny dismally when the week's catch netted exactly three chipmunks and a rabbit. Keeve looked glum and said little until he saw Benny open his penknife and begin to skin the rabbit.

"What's that?" asked Keeve, startled

"Skinning. The skin is the pelt. You have to be careful not to damage it."

"You never said anything about *that*."

"I thought everyone knew that."

"Maybe they do but I never thought about it. And to tell you the truth I don't like the whole stinking business."

"We're sure to have better luck, Keeve."

"It's not that, Benny. I get the creeps killing small, helpless animals. It sort of makes you feel like a murderer."

"I don't like it either," said Rose.

Benny looked down at his smelly, bloody hands and

shuddered. "Neither do I," he muttered making it
unanimous. "Anyway, I guess it ain't the right country.
Now if we were in Canada . . ."

While the woods refused to yield mink and chinchilla,
it teemed with hickory trees, awesome trees whose
towering limbs outlined the vertical peripheral of the
woods and from its gaunt vantage point hovered gently,
protectively, over the more leafy but fruitless
arborescence. Its peeling shagbark trunks soared fifty and
sixty feet skyward, goaded by claustrophobia or space
designs, before spreading its sparse but fecund arms.

For days at a time, after school and week-ends, we
gathered hickory nuts, ate hickory nuts, dreamed hickory
nuts. We garnered them like squirrels; large nuts the size
of walnuts, and pigmies, small as hazel-nuts. Bucket after
bucket was filled and poured into large burlap sacks as if
readied for market. At night we sat around the kitchen
table, cracking, eating them. First we shucked the
four-quartered husk. When brown and dry the meat was
ripe, delicate, succulent; when moist and slightly green the
meat was white, unripe and tasteless as straw. We soon
recognized the difference, separated the green husks and
stored them behind the stove to hasten the ripening.

Later, in Andover, to help pass the long, wintry nights
we sat in front of the big black kitchen stove, our feet
toasting in front of the open oven, noisily cracking nuts.

"A busy bee has no time for sorrow, "said Mama
obviously pleased. "You look like squirrels enjoying the
fruits of labor."

5

A Little More Breaks a Horse's Back

Benny's presence had the effect of a starting shot in a fifty-yard dash. Since he arrived a new project was brewing long before the old was finished. And in between projects he conducted tours à-la-Benny with the pompous restraint of a jaded travel agent.

"This is the Bonner house," he would say with what passed for authority. "It dates back from the Revolution and was the hiding place for runaway slaves. Now, over there . . ."

Benny wove his tales, authentic or not, around dates inscribed on old buildings and attempted to impress us with his information, imparting it with just the right tone of gravity in his voice. What he was vague about he made up on the spot; he had a rare knack for invention of all sorts.

"See that house?" said Benny, pointing to a square, robust dwelling with a lean-to kitchen added to the rear. "They're called salt boxes because they're the shape of the salt boxes the early pioneer woman used."

"And this is a Cape Cod," said Benny as we passed a farmhouse with a deep, pitched roof stretched over severe, rectangular lines.

"The salt box and Cape Cod homes were some of the first to be built in the country." To say we were not duly impressed with Benny's capacity for facts would be violating the truth.

Each time we returned from a Benny Tour he would say, as if dangling a reward for good behavior, "Someday I'll show you the Nathan Hale homestead." We looked forward to this trip with the same relish as a child to his first circus, each of us conjuring up a preconceived notion of the famed, hallowed ground. There would be thousands—well, hundreds—of curious sightseers straining at a cordon gripped firmly by spangled mounted police; at the very least, there would be a graphic re-enactment of historical incidents, like the stiff-necked sentries guarding the Tomb of the Unknown Soldier. Outside, dressed in colonial attire, sentinels would be guarding the doors and would solemnly lead us into the house to view its well-preserved interior in the manner of Valley Forge.

When the big day came and we were heading toward the Hale homestead, Benny kept saying, as if we didn't know by now, "Boy, that place is loaded down with history."

"It makes you feel so sad," said Rose ruefully, "he was so young and handsome." On this somber note we walked in silence until Benny said excitedly, "There it is!"

As we came closer, I said with no small sense of dismay, "There's no one around. Maybe it's not visiting day."

"Visiting day!" said Benny, piqued at our incredible naïveté! "Are there visiting days at cemeteries?"

Limply, we looked at the old house in a farm setting no different from other old farmhouses built during the Revolutionary period. If difference there existed it lay in the sad mantle of abandonment, the spreading desolation born of mildew, decay and rust. Faded and bleak, the farmhouse's sad emptiness emphasized the grim aura of its sacrificial past. The doors were locked securely, giving silent utterance to its stark loneliness. They seemed to say, "Do Not Disturb." We walked off, more saddened than disappointed.

A week after our visit to the Hale homestead, another Benny Tour brought us to the edge of the old dam.

The sun shone high and bright after an all-night downpour and the swollen river rose to the rim of its banks, the overflow cascading and swirling wildly over the dam and down the stream. The trees sprinkled us as lightly as a summer shower when we passed under them. And the whole countryside luxuriated with sudden lush growth, virginal and untrammelled. The dirt road still was puddly, and as Benny led us across an empty field the earth streamed with warm vapor and squished noisily underfoot like leaky galoshes. When we protested that our shoes were soaked, he said lightly, "It's only a short cut, we'll be out of here in no time flat."

The only blemish on the countryside was a rough unfinished structure perched precariously high on stilts close to the water's edge in sight of the dam. It looked like an architectural blunder that had been slapped together for instant refuge from disaster, and then had somehow gotten out of hand. What it lacked in design, construction and security, the crude monstrosity made up in size and vulgarity. The slight tilt which accentuated its proportions, defied such tampering as accidentally leaning against its latticed underpinnings.

"What's it for?" asked Rose.

"Supplies and tools. The workmen keep them there."

"It sure looks rickety. I'd be scared to step into it."

"Aw, it's not so bad. It's a lot stronger than it looks," said Benny. "Come over, I'll show you."

"Not me. It gives me the creeps. Anyway, it's getting late and we'd better start back."

54 Everything Happens for the Best

We never expected to set foot into the structure, but inadvertently one night Rose and I did, through a careless lapse of Benny's.

Sometimes without warning Benny would suddenly yield to impulse and take off for a neighboring farm to visit for hours at a time. This practice would have been maddening were it not that it offered us a little free time to recoup from the outpourings of his overactive and exhausting imagination. By the time he would return home gassed and oiled with local news and chatter and eager to plunge into some new enterprise, we were ready and waiting.

Shortly after he took off one Saturday morning the air roared thunderously like an erupting volcano. Earlier in the week this same shattering noise had exploded in a series of one violent and three milder blasts. When the fury subsided the resulting lull was strange and spectral; our recent visit to the Hale homestead still fresh in our minds, we even entertained the fascinating thought of cannon fire. But despite the possibility of its romantic or heroic origin the booming had startled us all. Even Mama.

When the mailman drove up that morning she hurried out to meet him. "Did you hear the explosion, Bill?"

"Ayeh. Gets more rackety each time, don't it!"

"You know what it is? Where is it coming from?" asked Mama quickly.

"From the old dam. They're blastin' away at tree trunks and boulders tryin' to widen it some," said Bill. "Sure got a little job in front of 'em but I reckon it'll pay off when the old dam is turned into power again."

Mama showered thanks on the surprised mailman as if he'd just handed her the deed to the property. "It's such a relief to know what it's all about. When you hear such a racket you begin to wonder . . ."

When Benny returned that evening he announced to

Rose, "There's a Halloween dance at the Pavilion next Saturday night. Want to go?" (Want to go? Does an anchovy like salt water!)

"Let's dress up in costumes," said Rose. "It's fun."

"If you want to rig 'em up it's okay with me," said Benny.

Somehow I wormed in on the invitation and when Saturday night came we started out despite a raging northeaster which flooded the countryside that morning, making the roads muddier, the ruts deeper, the night blacker. As if in silent warning the flashlight batteries were dead as a cadaver and the lantern wick flamed, spurted and died in apparent sympathy.

"It's such a bad night, children," warned Mama, "you won't see your hand in front of you."

"We'll be all right, Mama. It's not very far," pleaded Rose. "Anyway, we'll take candles and there'll be plenty of light."

"And we're in costume," I wailed, rebellious at the thought of staying home.

Mama softened despite her better judgment and we walked out before she might change her mind. Benny picked up a fistful of matches and several candles, lighting one as we started out, but a strong breeze snuffed it out before we reached the road. Hunching his shoulders he lit another, keeping it alive by cupping the dancing flame with his hand. We walked but a few steps when the wind scooped around and blew it out again. We tried other ploys, like linking our arms and walking backward trying to outwit the stiff breeze, but with sinister regularity it swooped up and around, throwing us in darkness. Fortunately we were within sight of the Pavilion when the last match was struck.

The pitch dark obliterated the lines of the building but something about the landscape suggested the dam site.

"This looks a lot like the dam," I said naïvely.

"It sure is," said Benny. "The lights are coming from the Pavilion. We've just about made it!"

"The Pavilion!" said Rose in dismay. "That old shack is the Pavilion?"

"Whaddaya think? The Woolworth Building?"

"It sure looks about ready to cave in; I'm scared to death to get near it."

"It's not that bad, Rosie, they hold lots of socials there."

"Maybe so but I'm not stepping a foot in it. "Well, I am," said Benny, ruffled. Then he added quickly, his tone conciliatory, "Aw come on, Rosie. Be a good sport."

"Yeah, Rosie, be a good sport," I parroted. "Let's go in for a little while."

Rose said nothing and Benny rambled on trying to placate her. "Boy, you should see that floor when it's waxed for dancing . . . you'll get a bang out of watching those square dances. You'll get a chance to meet all the neighbors—you'll—"

Suddenly Rose blurted, "Oh, okay." I suspect the combination of Benny's gentle urging and, perhaps, the thought of Mama's (not to mention Cleanthe's) aphorism, "Fate leads the willing, drags the unwilling," won her over and we started for the Pavilion.

The prompter, more loud than persuasive, could be heard clearly as we neared the shack.

"Just one more couple," he barked, "just one little lady and her gent. Step up to the middle and we'll start 'er swinging. How about it, young feller, don't be scared to bring your little lady up. Then he broke into song, "Take your little girlie by the arms, give her a squeeze and feel her charms!" The ditty pleased him enormously and he yelled "Yippeeeee!" and all but burst a blood vessel.

We walked in at that tender moment. The caller spotted us.

"B'jeezus, ask for it and the good Lord listens!" he roared with boisterous delight as he sashayed over to unsuspecting Rose and Benny. Circling them with reeking, damp shirt sleeves he propelled them over to the tittering, red-cheeked couples assembled on the floor. Rose tried to protest but it was like beseeching Niagara Falls to stop falling, and there she stood, in place, facing Benny where the prompter had shoved them. He signaled the fiddler to ready the dancers; a weird sawing of the bow started them curtsying and swaying and readying for action. When the music, or rather a series of agonized scrapings started, the caller broke into action.

"Grab your pardner, one and all, swing 'em short and swing 'em tall . . .lift your girlie once around, swing 'er hard and swing 'er sound!" The once demure girlies clung to their partners like tipsy spinsters on Sadie Hawkins Day. Rose and Benny were shuffled out like a deck of playing cards, fumbling, spinning, tripping. Twice the caller rushed over to disentangle them without skipping a beat and the dancing continued and repeated until every couple in the quadrille took their turn as head couple.

Still standing inside the door I watched the proceedings with fascination. Three sets of dancers pounded the floor and it put me in mind of a three-ring circus Papa once took us to in New York. You never really enjoyed watching one performance while you knew you were missing out on the others.

Most of the dancers wore costumes that obviously were created at home, a hay wig, a corn-stalk suit, a newspaper suit, (shredded after the first dance), and similar home-made outfits. A few costumes, frayed but lovely, had obviously been exhumed from old trunks in attics; there were authentic, winsome eighteenth and nineteenth-century fashions, which were probably as common to the assembled group as overalls and mackinaws. Nearly every attic corner stored at least one trunk filled with faded reminders of the past—velvets, taffetas, calicoes—willed down from one generation to the next, and these priceless hand-me-downs aroused less excitement than a dime-store bunny costume.

Even Hattie Smith, who arrived later with her mother, wore a slim, high-necked, knife-pleated beauty that looked like a morning wrapper beside the others. Ironically, the costume that attracted every eye and caused the most comment was a daring, above-the-knee, many-layered tulle skirt and strapless-bodice piece of froth worn by a visiting niece who took weekly ballet lessons in Willimantic. The men openly admired it but the women divided into camps—those who jerked their chins an inch upward and those who fingered the "boughten" costume fondly.

With a jolt of memory I thought of the Paul Jones mixer when the entire group joined hands in a huge circle, waiting for the fiddler's cue before tearing wildly around like Apaches at the peak of a war dance. The whip-blade momentum reached such a high pitch that when the signal came to halt and change partners, the sudden release of grips hurled two men against a stack of wooden cases lined up against a wall. The floor had begun to heave after the first quadrille, battered by tons of unrestrained humanity. Now loosened by the sudden charge, two cases edged and jiggled out of position threatening to crash to the floor. Their contents were of no particular interest—they probably held supplies for the dam project as Benny had explained earlier.

Standing but a few feet from the protruding cases I felt impelled to walk over and prevent them from falling. I backed up against them and with all my strength I managed to push them in a few inches.

When the dancing stopped Rose signaled me to join them on the other side of the room.

"Whew!" she said, panting like a Labrador retriever, her fears of a few moments ago forgotten. "It's lots of fun!"

"Yeah," said Benny, fanning his face with his hand.

I had seen everything I came to see—the dancing, costumes—and now I was ready to go. "Let's go home," I said as only a small kill-joy sister could say it. "It's stuffy in here."

"Go home *now*! It's still early," said Rose, her voice prickly like nettles.

I kept my silence, thinking of future junkets, but my face grew long and sour as rhubarb. Rose became angry. "I didn't ask you to come, did I? You're always tagging after me like a puppy dog and then you beg to go home."

Though I knew she was right, I still glowered. In an effort to keep me quiet and happy she said, "They'll be serving refreshments soon."

That did it. I waited almost patiently as two quardrilles, a Birdie-in-the-Cage and a Halfway Round, whooped it up before the prompter announced a short intermission.

"Come and get it, folks! There's plenty of good grub to stick to your ribs and plenty of cider and coffee to wet the whistle." He pointed to a corner of the room where several women were busily arranging food, while on a small kerosene stove a huge kettle steamed with aromatic coffee, misting up the windows warmly.

Even as he spoke, wooden horses appeared on the floor, and in minutes were converted into one long table covered with overlapping, starched tablecloths. Piled high on plates were sandwiches —chicken salad, egg salad, home-cured ham, peanut-butter-and-jelly—apple and pumpkin pies, and a variety of tempting cakes, each a masterpiece of culinary perfection. Thick mocha frostings settled exquisitely in rich peaks; creamy, boiled icings gleamed with studded nuts and fruits. Spice cakes trimmed with orange frosting and hobgoblin faces completed the festive holiday note.

Not a store cake was in sight. The ladies vied with each other for producing the lightest, tastiest cake with a fierce pride that was exceeded only by their envy. "Boughten" cakes were hinted at in the same hushed tones used to discuss prostitution and sin, and only in the I-wouldn't-tell-another-soul moments of intimacy.

On the smaller table were two bushels of juicy eating apples and a barrel of cider which the fiddler siphoned out generously. "Eat 'em or drink 'em," he said in a voice that resembled his fiddle.

The line now reached around the room as the prompter repeated, "Come and get it, folks!" And the folks went and got it, everyone waiting delicately to plunge into the food, leveling it in mere minutes. Even the ladies piled their plates greedily, juggling and balancing back to their seats like high-wire performers.

Benny made two trips; the first of which ended in disaster. Preoccupied with balancing his mug of cider, which threatened to overflow, he inadvertently tilted his plate and the food slid to the floor. In a clumsy attempt to salvage the food he spilled the cider. Everyone laughed good-naturedly and three ladies came forward to help clean up the mess, but Benny looked the picture of dejection.

In moments it was over. The table vanished as quickly as it had appeared—horses, planks, cloths, remnants of food. The prompter walked to the center of the room a bit unsteady, belched into the megaphone—it became evident that more than cider wet the male whistle that evening—and proceeded to call, "One more lady and gent! Just one more li'l lady and gent!" though not a single couple was on the floor.

"Let's not dance this one," said Rose, "I'm too tired."

"That goes double for me," said Benny whose spirits had rallied after he had polished off three sandwiches, a slice of six-layer cake, a wedge of pumpkin pie, store cheese and a mug of cider; the sandwiches had been urged on him by two full-bosomed ladies who insisted that good food would cure anything from spasms to the "spilling jitters," which they were sure Benny caught.

Again a "Paul Jones" was called to "socialize the folks." One by one the couples shuffled forward until the prompter called "Circle round," and everyone linked hands to form a huge circle. When the music started they tore around the room like frisky colts. It stopped suddenly—the signal to break—and minus several of the evening's casualties, the dancers wove in and out, the men in one direction, the ladies in another, awaiting the cue to snag a new face en route. The fiddler twanged out a chorus of "round music" and the couples fox-trotted or waltzed—depending on their appraisal of the beat. By the second round restraints fell away like wilted petals and the frisky colts metamorphosed into galloping horses. When the fiddler scraped to a halt, there was a mad scramble for partners. Pretty girls, disentangling their limbs from a surge of masculinity, were paired again in seconds while the plainer ones deployed themselves like troops on a front, waiting to charge at any exposed male whose field of vision overshot his dexterity. By the fourth round every trace of respectability had vanished; and one by one, grudging wives pinched their spouses off the floor.

This was entertainment, pure and simple, and we watched, fascinated, until it was over. My earlier desire to leave was forgotten. During a short lull provided for couples to form a Grand Square, Benny plied us with questions and stumpers. When we exhausted every riddle

in our repertoire, I resorted to a question about three
letters of the alphabet which had caught my eye earlier.

"What do the letters TNT stand for?"

"Aw, that's easy," said Benny, "it's dynamite."

"Not *real* dynamite!"

"Whatdaya mean, not real dynamite. Dynamite is
dynamite—the stuff they use to blow up rocks at the
dam."

"It couldn't be," I managed to say, "because all those
boxes have TNT marked on the side." We looked over at
the cases which were slowly dislodging again.

"By God, they do," said Benny jumping to his feet.
"Let's beat it out of here quick." On the way out Benny
shouted, "Danger! Dynamite!" pointing to the cases, and
we ran as if Johnny Mitchell had suddenly torn out of
the bushes. The warning had had a lightning effect. By
the time we had reached the bend in the road we heard
motors sputtering, spitting, horses whinnying, and we
knew the exodus was under way.

Having no matches, we stumbled and fell most of the
way back—but we still managed the return trip in half
the time. When we reached the house Benny panted,
"Whew, what a close call. That dynamite could've
exploded with all of us in the room."

Rose clutched my arm. "Better not tell Mama," she
warned, "if you want to go with us again."

And Mama never knew—not until we were safe in
Andover.

6

Fish and Guests Smell After Three Days

Mrs. Black had settled cozily into the role of delicate house guest. She was obviously getting everything she came for; pure air, fresh eggs—and the special house bonus: free maid service.

At the end of the first week Mama said gently, "It surely takes time to adjust to the change from city to country."

"It really does," conceded Mrs. Black.

After the third week Mama observed patiently, "You can't deny it, it surely takes time to get used to a change." Again Mrs. Black agreed, pleased with Mama's rare perception.

In the fifth week Mama said, her voice shaky, "No doubt Mrs. Black is now able to take over her own responsibilities." Mrs. B. felt deeply rebuked, saying she "erred in her judgment," railing on about Mama's "bourgeois understanding."

The sixth week Mama said, her voice rising, "I don't understand *some people* who sit around all day watching *others* do their work." Mrs. B. said she refused to dignify Mama with a response, but her nose twitched, her eyes snapped, and she whimpered to Adeline, "How very little the plebeian mind understands a sensitive soul."

The seventh week Mama grew bolder; in a voice that startled us all she ordered Mrs. B. to start packing. Footnote: Mrs. B. was in no big hurry. "After all, just whose house is this?"

By the eighth week Mama, as close to violence as we'd seen her, handed Papa an ultimatum. "Henry, get us all back to New York even if you have to rent a loft." When Papa failed to find a place, Mama started to pack.

The tenth week—well, the tenth week started a little differently. On Monday morning Papa took his leave as usual.

"Be patient, Estherel, if things work out as I think they will we should have a fine apartment by next week," he said, kissing us all good-bye. Papa tried to sound cheerful but we weren't easily fooled.

Halfway down the road he turned to wave good-bye again. It was late in November and the grass was coarse and brown. Dry, brittle leaves blew everywhere in heaps; they lined the dirt road and driveway, swirling against the banks. On the way to school we plowed through mounds that crackled underfoot like popcorn. The first frost had already taken a heavy toll and farmers were working feverishly to salvage the root crops before the heavy snows came. Every fruit tree was picked bare as a plucked chicken. Sheds were filled tight with cordwood. Everyone was caught up in the race against the elements that threatened to shroud the earth and bury their labors; the race to outwit the shimmering eiderdown that would nestle thick. serene and treacherous. There would be time enough for winter pursuits during the dull, dormant season which lay brewing ahead; whitewashing, stove feeding, fowl and cattle tending, maybe a little time for loafing. "It's going to be a humdinger of a winter," the farmers whistled. And they knew.

Though the sun had risen high and bright in the sky

on the fateful morning, the chilly snap in the air prompted Papa to wear his heavy overcoat. (Our lives might have been vastly different had he chosen his light topcoat as usual.) The sun, beating through his thick, warm coat had induced a heavy torpor strange to Papa. He felt weary and drained in both body and spirit; the road seemed a little rougher, the trip longer, his briefcase heavier. Besides, a new crop of worries nagged at him like a toothache; business was less than good, the pattern-maker was balky and troublesome, and to top it neatly, Mama wanted out. he couldn't gather the courage to tell Mama the plain truth outright—that he had found no apartment he could afford. But next week was another week, he told himself, and he would try again; maybe his luck would change.

Papa was tired; only an overwhelming weariness would induce him to rest. "You rest plenty when you're dead," he'd say to Mama when she pleaded with him to slow down. But today his fatigue bordered on exhaustion. About a mile from the station he yielded to his stresses, walked over to an apple tree, dropped his coat in the spotty shade and sat down, his briefcase beside him.

He reached into his vest pocket and looked at his watch; decent time to make the train. When he looked at his watch again he got up quickly . . .twenty minutes had passed—he'd rested longer than he had planned. He made a run for the drab, little station with the high ceiling and pot-bellied stove. No sooner had he paid for his ticket than the train roared in with a deafening rumble, rattling the wooden platform and structure. He climbed aboard the awesome New York, New Haven and Hartford passenger train whose sixty-mile-an-hour speed would get him to New York in good time.

Papa could see the engine rounding the first bend, gaining normal speed. He jumped up suddenly, overtaking the conductor who had just punched his ticket.

"I must get off," he said. "Stop the train."

"Can't be done, sir, but you don't have far to go—Bolton's the next stop."

"But Bolton's five miles away. I got to get off—I left my coat back there—"

"Sorry, nothing we can do now." The conductor walked on.

You don't have to be a Cassandra to know what floated through Papa's mind as he walked the five long miles back to Andover. Nothing good comes from resting . . .if I didn't rest I would have my coat . . .I'd be halfway to New York . . .

Mama's prolific talent to capsule any situation with a pithy maxim penetrated deep in her chromosomes, and when she spoke it oozed directly from her genes. We were all weaned on her little phrases: "It had to be this way," or "You have to know how to turn something bad into something good," or "Everything works out if only you want it to"—weaned and conditioned. Life's little failures were little sheep in wolf's clothing; they plagued your life to clear the way for better things. If the silver lining offered resistence we practically dragged the recalcitrant out of the clouds; we trained our sights on eventual good fortune, as a gunner trains his sights on a target, which Mama insisted would come through for good people in good time. "It takes patience and honest effort, that's all," she said, with such conviction that we believed her; this conviction—earnest, artless, resolute—filtered through unmistakably, working for Papa as well during those rare periods when his psyche craved comfort, when he labored feverishly to bring to fulfillment a creation, then failed—well, almost failed. When a snag tormented him, when the good idea stymied him, evaded him, when he worked straight through the night, straining to clear the haze that enveloped him.

At this point Mama would step in firmly; it took a

double dose of "patience and honest effort" but she braced for it. "First thing you must have is a good night's sleep and rest your mind," Mama would say in a tone that invited no rebuttal. "Mark my words, Henry, it will all work out all right. Take my word for it." And Papa would. When again he returned to his work table the old kinks vanished and new ideas, good ideas, began to form and burst into being, establishing Mama as some sort of prognosticator. Braced by her homegrown philosophy, Papa often rationalized himself into a calm frame of mind.

By the time he picked up his coat under the apple tree, positive thoughts rushed through his head. No need to hurry now . . . .train leaves at three . . . .better go down to the General Store and call Mama . . . .everything will work out . . . .

A lively telephone conversation was in progress when Papa entered the store. Horace Fripps, proprietor, was talking into the mouthpiece on the wall. He seemed not to hear Papa opening the door.

"As things stand now I have to put my hands on $300 immediately." A long pause—a few noncommittal grunts. "Don't press me to the wall. What can I do with the land and fixtures?" A longer pause. "I'll make a deal with you. Take it all and you can have it in a week—kit and kaboodle." The party on the other end was talking and Mr. Fripps was listening. Then he said, "Ayeh— I guess so.... We'll consider it a down payment, but be sure and let me know by tomorrow so's we can draw up the papers. Be good now." He clicked the receiver on the hook, pulled a handkerchief from his pocket and wiped his brow. When he saw Papa he started.

"Good morning, sir."

Papa came directly to the point. "I overheard you talking." Mr. Fripps looked at Papa quickly but said nothing. Papa continued bluntly, "Did I understand you to say you were selling?"

"That's right, sir. Wanna buy a good establishment?" He smiled wearily.

"I've seen lots of peculiar things in my lifetime," said Papa slowly, his eyes sweeping the place, "but I never heard of a house being sold over the telephone."

Fripps chuckled. "It ain't sold yet. Mebbe you'd like to buy the place yourself. Solid building, plenty of good land.... Wanna make me an offer?"

"Maybe," said Papa, noting in one fell swoop the fixtures, merchandise, billiard room, store location.

Something in Papa's tone sobered Fripps quickly. "You're not serious are you?"

Then Papa said, suddenly remembering Mama's ultimatum, but most of all her long campaign to leave the city, "I could be." He began to tremble inside. Other times in his life he was forced into spur-of-the-moment decisions; some turned out good, some bad, but it all related to him and his business world. Today was different, even momentous; his judgment could alter the family with frightening immediacy. But if he vacillated he might lose. The urgency left no room for deliberation or even consultation, and Papa discarded his mumblings like a worn-out suit.

Suddenly, like a shower of hail, he said to the dumfounded proprietor after hearing the price, "I'll take it. I'll take the land—how many acres did you say?—the store, the fixtures, the whole damn boodle as is before I change my mind. But on one condition."

Horace Fripps stared, ready for anything now.

"The pool table must go."

"By damn, it's a deal," said Fripps still in a half trance as he watched Papa make out the $300 check that legalized the transaction.

Papa never did call the house that day; he barely made the afternoon train. Early the next morning, however, a telegram arrived. Mama's hands trembled as she turned it over and over, as if in so doing she would better cope with the shock it was sure to contain. To Mama, telegrams meant either of two things—or both—death or disaster; if God forbid it was from Papa, who wrote dutifully each day, only a catastrophe would induce him to send a telegram when a good two-cent stamp would effect the same result. His daily letter arrived with the same certainty as day and night. The mail was the high point in the day and on Saturdays we waited on the stone wall long before the letter carrier was due, though we knew, except for Papa's letter there would be little else. My correspondence with Birdie and Laura fell by the wayside the day Benny appeared, and when the mail was bulky it was usually a mass of innocuous circulars and get-rich propositions addressed to Keeve and Benny.

The telegram arrived in a shining black Ford and we all gathered around Mama expectantly as she fingered it, gathering courage to open it.

"Maybe Papa rented a new apartment," said Keeve.

"Sure! What else!" said Mama quickly. "It must be the new apartment." And she tore open the envelope.

We heard the news with a mingling of emotions. A house in the village—and a store. I felt like Hansel and Gretel outside the sugar house, drooling with thoughts of candy, ice cream, soda pop. When I found time, I had a momentary pang at the thought of forever losing Birdie and Laura, but what was that compared to a store all your own? The thought was staggering.

Rose rejoiced at the thought of new friends, a new school; and Keeve, who was startled at first, seemed pleased but noncommittal. Mama was so relieved she would have cheered if Papa had leased the county dog shelter.

But Mrs. Black smoldered like dry leaves fanning to a blaze. Her plans for a long rest were suddenly shortened, and her first response was contempt. "Idiotic! Ridiculous! Yet it's not without its element of humor, ha, ha. It all goes to show how people gravitate to their forebears. Country storekeepers! Peasants!" With one hand she wrapped her skirt close, to avoid the taint of the lowborn, the vulgah. With the other she started packing.

All legal details would be expedited in less than a week, then we would move. There was no time to wonder if Papa had done the wise thing and we were too excited to care. For a time we even forgot Benny, who seemed unnaturally quiet after the telegram arrived.

Then the morning Mrs. Black was all packed, waiting for Ed Bailey to drive them to the depot, there was no Benny in sight. We ran to the barn, the orchard and the outhouse. Still no Benny. Mrs. Black stormed out on the front porch screaming "Ben-nee" in a voice that clean forgot its "cultivated" background.

Mama said, "Maybe he wanted to say good-bye to the neighbors. I'm sure that's where we'll find him. Let's go out and try again."

Mrs. B. continued to rage and fume and give out with the searching orders like a top sergeant, though she herself remained behind to man headquarters.

"It is imperative I conserve my strength to see me through this most wretched of days," she said, her outstretched palm clutching her heart.

When each of us returned without Benny she grew even more furious and blamed it all on Mama.

"You've been very skillful, my dear friend, alienating my son's affection from the very day we arrived. Well, my friend, this is the last straw," she said, pointing a menacing finger in Mama's face. "Since you apparently find him such a delectable morsel—you can have him. I present him to you on a silver platter."

She didn't fool us by her fancy talk; this was her

chance to unload Benny and it was as clear as the painted wart she tried to pass off as a beauty mark. Mama stared at her, bewildered and shocked, but said nothing. Mrs. B. latched on to the silence and used it craftily.

"Since you stand there with nothing to say I am led to believe you even planned it this way."

"I've had enough of your nonsense," said Mama, and walked away.

"Peasant!" shrieked Mrs. B. "Wait until my Herman hears of this, my dear friend, just you wait."

Ed Bailey was turning in the drive with his Sunday buggy at this moment. As Ed loaded the baggage in the rear, Mrs. B. pulled Adeline to her and ran a comb through her hair. "We'll be gone soon, my darling. You won't be subjected to any more of this. Not if I can help it!"

And then Adeline said the unforgivable thing, "Mommy, can I stay here with Benny?"

For one paralyzed moment Mrs. B. stared at her small daughter in mute disbelief, at once turning blue and white and purple. It was a stark naked moment that sent a charge of goose pimples over my body in jerky spurts like exploding corn in a popper. To see her speechless—utterly speechless—and so soundly out of character was a strange, compelling phenomenon, and for the first time I generated a feeling akin to compassion. Then suddenly as night she broke into sobs so baleful and dismal she startled us all, especially little Adeline, who immediately burst into tears.

Mama rushed out in alarm, and curiously, Mrs. B. regained her composure and began reverting to form.

"Take a look at your handiwork, my friend," she wailed, dabbing at her eyes daintily. "Ver-ee thorough. Even my daughter has turned against me."

Mama knew better than to protest against her paranoic

attack and she stood silent as Mrs. B. continued to rail.

"It's one grand conspiracy to turn my family against me," she wailed over and over with dramatic crescendo, until she and Adeline were safely ensconced in the buggy and on the road.

All this time Benny was neatly hidden behind a thick protective hedge not fifty feet away, where he could view the road without being discovered. Even long after the buggy had safely passed, he kept hidden until the train whistled and groaned out of town. Only when he was sure it was safe to return he walked into the house, his eyes puffed, his face tear-smeared.

Mama waited through lunch before she broke the news. "Benny," she said as if it hurt, "I think you should go home tomorrow. Your mother is very upset."

Benny looked quickly at Mama and suddenly we saw the deep hungry eyes we first knew. For a long, tense moment he said nothing, then he blurted, "I won't go back and live with her . . . .I'll run away. She hates me."

Mama was pained but she persisted gently. "But your father loves you. So does your little sister. They both love you very much."

"Yeah, I guess so," said Benny, muffling the tears in his voice, "but they won't miss me much. Anyway," he added cannily, "I don't like to live in the dirty city. I love fresh air and the farm." Benny knew how to make headway; he knew the weak spots in Mama's defenses and he knew when he struck the bull's eye. He continued, his voice soft, his eyes beseeching, "I—like it here with you—if you'd be willing to have me—Mama . . ."

Before she could answer we chorused, "Yeah, Mama, please let him stay. He can move with us next week."

"All right, children, you win. I'll write your Papa today, Benny. If he agrees, it will be fine with me."

"Then I'll be able to move with you!"

"If your father agrees."

"I know he will. I know he will!" Benny shouted. And Benny was right. Two days before we moved a letter arrived from Mr. Black approving the idea until "Mrs. Black was settled."

Benny shared our curiosity about the new place, and our happiness. The day we moved Ed Bailey arrived in his haywagon; after loading our belongings in the rear he hoisted Mama, Papa and Franny on the front seat beside him and the rest of us piled on top of cases and luggage. All the way to town we jounced and lurched and squealed like a load of pigs trundled off to market. Nothing ever equaled our enthusiasm that clear, brisk day.

It took but a few days in Andover, however, to realize that life on the Coventry farm was a beautiful thing by comparison, and though we were not aware, it primed us for the rugged time ahead. On the farm, discomforts and hardships were temporary, but here in the village, which until now we conjured up as something akin to the Gay White Way, the rough life reeked with permanence. We were here to stay.

For one thing, the thirty-by-fifty-foot one-story frame structure turned out to be a bleak, stark affair and until Mr. Fripps took over, housed the town creamery. It was still cluttered with garish, outmoded equipment that looked like a holdover from a Buck Rogers strip. In the basement, oversized cylinders and apparatus that once separated milk and churned butter littered the huge room. Generators, threaded profusely with belts and gears, were strapped to platforms and bolted down to the floor. Similar crude equipment hung from the ceiling, snarling and monstrous, like Rube Goldberg contraptions.

When Mr. Fripps converted the upper floor into a general store, he abandoned the creamery and ignored the equipment. The whole weird menage was thrown "as is" into the house deal, and so quickly were the papers drawn up and signed, there could have been a still operating on the place and Papa would have been none the wiser.

Papa's big passion for nuts and bolts exceeded only his love for hoarding, but even for him this was too much, and in the end, though no one would touch it, he paid a reluctant junk dealer to remove it. "I need plenty of room for assembling machines and storing pipes and flanges and castings," he explained to Mama when she questioned his change of heart.

Off the main creamery area, large enough to house a small destroyer, were three doors, each leading to a good-sized room; one, the Delco room that housed the electric generator; two, an all-purpose room that stored the coal bin on one end and on the other a well-equiped summer kitchen. The third door, strangely, was reached by climbing three broad cement steps, and when we tried to open it, it resisted stubbornly. "Let's take turns pushing," said Rose. We pushed, we hammered, we coaxed, we kicked—to no avail. Then we attacked it collectively. It refused to budge.

"Something secret must be hidden there—maybe even a treasure chest," said Rose.

"Yeah, I bet," said Benny, "more likely to be a body. Maybe even . . .well—no . . ." The hint was as broad as his grin.

"Maybe what, Benny?" said Rose quickly, her eyes like saucers. "Maybe what?"

"Maybe it's the town morgue."

Rose and I stared, terrified. Keeve said, "Come on, Benny, come off it. You trying to scare them to death?"

"But I'm not kidding. It could be" persisted Benny.

"Yeah. Sure. Why don't you try the Royal Jewels next?"

"You'll have to admit there's something spooky about it," said Benny. "How come you have to climb steps to get in, and how come this is the only door that's locked?"

This was true; the room hinted of seclusion . . . .dank, dark inner sanctums. But why? For whom? For what? These questions we wanted answered—and at once. We appealed to Papa, who finally agreed to come with us. "All right, I'll take a look," he said, leaving more important work.

He yanked and jiggled the doorknob, at the same time pushing with the weight of his body, but the door just stood there, solid, resistant, smug, as if to say, "Keep trying, boys, I don't mind."

"This door is tough like iron," observed Papa standing back, figuring a way to budge it, "but I don't think it's locked; it would give even a little if it were. It feels to me like it's struck with dampness."

He walked over to a wooden box of tools, picked up a hard rubber sledge hammer and began to pound short, exploratory raps around the seams of the door. "It's stuck all right," he said, proceeding to hammer with the swing of a blacksmith, his strong, supple body in rhythm with the motion.

Now that we were close to discovery, Rose and I stepped back to safer ground. Papa's breath was coming hard and he rested a moment. Then he picked up a crowbar with a fine, wedge-shaped edge and began prying around the seams, making an inroad every few inches. Satisfied, he picked up the hammer again, and suddenly, with the second rap, the door yielded with an ungodly groan. Papa walked in and Keeve and Benny hurried after him. All we could make out were huge, shadowy objects in a dark, windowless room, and from the strong odor of cold, damp mold that rushed out at us we knew the walls and floor were mortared. Then Keeve's voice, hollow as an echo. "More creamery junk."

7

No Rose Without a Thorn

"Land!" cried Columbus.

"Electricity!" cried Mama, seeing light bulbs dangling from lengths of wire, stiff and ugly.

"This is more like it!" cried Keeve, spotting the Delco dynamo and solid wall of high-power batteries. And Delco, it turned out, shifted from blessing to headache. Contrary one day, affable the next, the generator seemed almost human. As if to make an impression, the first night Keeve started her up she worked slick as a top; the house blazed with light and cheer and we ran from room to room turning on every bulb. No nasty meters to warn of juice consumption. "Boy," said Benny, "if they caught me doing this at home!"

Then at bedtime—our relationship with Delco secure—she sputtered, popped, spit, and went dead as a cadaver. A week later Papa located a Delco serviceman in Hartford, and until then we burned oil lamps and candles. When nursed back to health and filled with a fresh draught of gasoline, Delco putt-putted vigorously and the lights went on again.

"Don't weaken the batteries," warned the serviceman.

"Keep her charged daily."

"Keeping her charged" meant running the motor before the lights went on and all through the evening. Running an ordinary motor was one thing, but Delco was distinctly special and different from other motors. When Keeve fueled her up and pressed a lever to turn her over she sputtered, choked, bellowed, rattled, choked, boomed, then finally caught and turned over. For miles around the noise was like a Mack truck with the cutout missing, the echo reverberating through the village like an endless volley of rifle fire; plenty of light but little peace and quiet. "There's at least one thing you can say for oil lamps," said Keeve, "they don't yak-yak-yak when they light up."

It was many weeks before we were able to ignore Delco's racket. Yet the times we were reduced to oil lamps again, the sound of her sputter, bellow and gasp was sweeter than the strains of a Brahms lullaby. There were even times when we were proud of the rackety engine since ours was the sole electric plant in an oil-lit town; and ten years later when power lines came to Andover and when heavy storms threw them out of whack—and the town in darkness—Delco came sputtering through like a seasoned soldier.

After Papa bought the store the one thing that impressed him to the point of elation was the running water and flush toilet in the basement. "The important thing is having the convenience of a toilet indoors. With good plumbing it's just a matter of time before I install a bathroom," he said, cheered by the discovery.

This was good news. In Coventry the bathtub was replaced with a bathing ritual—two basins—one for soaping, one for rinsing, and in this way we kept ourselves decently abluted. Nor was it bad in cold weather with the kitchen doors secured. While the water heated on the stove, the warm, steaming air lulled the

senses like a Turkish bath. There was Mama or Rose
waiting to scrub your back—well, insisting, and we hardly
missed the tub—especially me, who took a dim view of
bathing in the first place. But the news of an indoor
flush toilet spelled luxury.

Outhouses are hilariously funny for the next
guy—never for you. In Coventry running to the privy in
clear, mild weather was one thing—but on wet, cold days
it took on the might of a Spartan and the will of a yogi.
It was big league compared to our other deprivations.
But it was not without its creative moments; before a
mad dash to the two-seater I became so adept at
spur-of-the-moment choreography I was primed for the
Charleston long before it bounced into vogue. "It should
have a heater," I wailed again and again, thawing my
fanny by the kitchen stove.

Here in Andover the Chic Sale private, one-seater
model that stood, from sheer persistence, in a clump of
locust trees a safe distance from the house, was a sad
relic of bygone days. Porous with quarter moons and
stars and covered with years of tangled brush, it tilted
percariously like the Leaning Tower of Pisa. Hornets and
wasps found in it a sanctuary for breeding their young,
and I suspect it might have been torn down long ago if
anyone cared to volunteer as a target for a bad-tempered
hornet. Whatever the reason, it remained standing. And
lucky for us it did.

Within an hour of our arrival Papa discovered a major
break in the plumbing system. "What do you know," he
said in dismay, "I don't really think any water has
flowed through these pipes for months, maybe years. I
can't understand how I missed—" And that winter we
beat a sullen path to the outhouse after Mama bravely
exterminated the surprised hornets.

We were not completely without water. The kitchen
was piped with a separate line from a little spring a mile

away. And the faucet in the broad, shallow soapstone sink weakly trickled water.

"Everything happens for the best," said Mama again. I couldn't imagine how. But she was right. If we rebelled against running to the outhouse, Papa's fastidious nature rebelled even more. One day in early spring he called Mr. Pryor, the plumber from Willimantic; within a week the bathroom—a glistening white washbowl, toilet, and bathtub—was installed, and the first flush of that toilet was as momentous as the maiden voyage of an ocean liner. Since we were firm about bathing with hot water it was some time before we initiated the bathtub. When a gleaming, fifty gallon copper water tank was hooked to the nickel-trimmed kitchen stove and the first stream of hot water surged through the virgin pipes, the family watched wide-eyed.

Our bathroom replaced the large dining room. "We don't care," said Rose and I in a careless moment, "if we have to sleep in the attic to make room for progress." And that's just where we landed—in an attic as bleak and dismal as a factory loft. "It's not too bad," said Rose. "Just think of all the privacy we'll have . . .we can read as late as we want to." And until the novelty wore off we would keep the light on well into the night, reading, working on picture puzzles and whispering. The four-by-six reserve water tank monstrosity at the head of our bed doubled as a handy catch-all for books and games. To lessen its horror we threw a runner with orange, cross-stitched lilacs diagonally over its top. Even the rough floor planks brightened under two coats of maroon paint, and when Papa hired Mr. Raney, a retired carpenter, to enclose the open rafters with beaverboard, Rose and I set about papering the walls. We chose a delicate all-over wisteria design, and except for a few strips which we pasted wrong-side up the job wasn't too bad, especially since Mama or Papa never had laid eyes on wisteria before and no one knew they were upside down, or cared—much less we.

"If only we had some pictures," said Rose as she looked around the four newly decorated walls. "If only we had some pictures," she said again, hovering over Keeve's sacred hoard of pin-ups which he'd collected for years and personally carried up from New York City. The next day the walls came alive with screen luminaries tacked side by side—Pearl White, Harry Lauder, Mary Pickford, and enough others to encircle the room as a border. After the first shock even Keeve agreed it looked pretty nifty—like the lobby of Loew's 14th Street Theater.

"The only thing that disturbs me is the billiard room," said Papa one day. "We don't want to attract bums or cutthroats. Anyone who plays pool is a good-for-nothing gangster, a tramp." He winced when he saw the pool table still standing, though Fripps had promised to remove it; but that same evening when Mama padded down the green felt table in preparation for an extra bed, Papa admitted it was not entirely without merit.

Three rooms off the massive billiard room comprised the family's living quarters and we scarcely had room to turn around in. Keeve and Benny slept on the pool table until Rose and I moved up to the attic. Soon after, the pool table vanished and the huge room was converted into a dining-living room.

The first year in Andover served a purpose. After that anything that presented itself in the way of improvement seemed closer to luxury. When the time came for Benny to leave he seemed eager to get going though he insisted he'd rather stay. "Yeah, he'd rather stay like a pig in a hen coop," said Keeve.

Winter blew in suddenly like a sheet of frost and bedded down with the brashness of an uninvited guest. We worked hard at keeping warm, huddling around the kitchen stove, toasting our feet in the open oven—all else was cold and draughty. As a result we alternated between chills and sweating. At school it was the same. Until the second bell rang we shared the furnace grate with other children and thawing dinner pails, the warm air puffing up our skirts like crinolines as we clung to each other like survivors on a raft. Our toes would swell with penetrating heat until we took our seats; then the burning and the biting and the itching began.

Mornings when Mama kindled the fire in the kitchen stove the dry split logs spewed off a fiery leaping warmth, until with a sprinkle of coal she smothered the dancing flames, the sudden heat. Mama waited until we departed for school, then blocked the stove with coal. Each night after locking up she persisted with the losing game of stuffing the hungry cavity in an attempt to keep the heat going till morning; and each night she would tinker with the damper. "Maybe if I keep it this way it won't draw out so quickly." And "this way" was a different way every night, but in the end the coals turned to dead ashes long before dawn and the cold settled quickly and heavily. Another source of heat was the thin, sheet-metal stove in the store that devoured four-foot lengths of cordwood with the lust of a greedy seal. We were constantly padded like Eskimos-in-training which resulted in our being overheated and underventilated.

Going to bed each night was not the simple little matter of making up your mind to retire. Even after Papa installed a coal furnace to heat the store and living quarters downstairs, and built an upper floor with twelve rooms, it did nothing to alter the nightly ritual of bedding down for the night. We nursed the heat, shutting tight all doors against seepage from the frigid zone above, even the store, and then it began. We undressed hurriedly, standing on chairs around the kitchen stove;

the first one up was rewarded with the hot-water boiler and the lush sensuality of warmth from the heels upward. We changed into heavy, flannel nightgowns as Mama prepared hot stove lids which she wrapped in thick layers of the Hartford *Times* and topped with tiny pillow slips. Then with the proper note of leave-taking we put on warm winter coats. Armed with these survival reinforcements, a Spartan will, the speed of a Paavo Nurmi, a long deep breath and we were off. We took the stairs two at a clip, scuttled down the narrow hall and into our room, slid the lid between icy sheets, shed our coats and plunged into bed. Rose and I stuck together. When one turned the other turned, chancing no air pockets, and when our eyes closed we slept the sleep of the dead despite temperatures that froze water pipes and cracked jars of food.

If it was hard going to bed at night, it was far worse waking up in the morning. "It builds character," said Papa, and each day we woke to a new set of character builders. Mama was up early to start the heat in the kitchen; when the top frost was decently nipped she cued us on the ceiling with a broomstick. A few light raps meant, "Start waking up, children, it will be warm soon." It vibrated through the downy feather bedding and we came up for air. But not for long. Every breath exhaled was a cloudy vapor that seemed to caramelize mid-air and back we dived under cover. The windows did nothing for our moral fiber; they looked like freezing units on defrosting day, and just about as lucent. The second call we rarely heard through a deep second sleep but the third vibrated the floor and walls and we knew Mama meant business. Rose was the first to mobilize character. Nudging me she'd say, "We'd better wake up, it's getting late." With that she'd jump out of bed and I hopped out after her; throwing our icy coats over our shoulders we'd stumble downstairs like two animated zombies.

When Rose and I complained of the cold, which was every day, Keeve, the self-styled stoic, would say, teeth chattering, "Well, how about the Eskimos? They live in ice huts. Do they complain? Compared to them you're living in a Turkish bath."

"But we're not Eskimos!"

"Pretend then. You'll feel warmer."

Even then Keeve believed in mind over matter.

Before the garret was converted to bedrooms it doubled as a freezer. "It's a fine place to hang a side of beef," said the farmer, who convinced Mama that a steer in our attic was better than one in his barn. And the next week a huge carcass was hanging from a hook on a rafter. "It'll keep fine until spring," said the farmer, counting the bills. "See you then!"

Two days later when Mama and Keeve went up, armed with a freshly honed knife and large platter, they returned in twenty minutes, exhausted. "Boy, that cow is frozen stiff," said Keeve. "We couldn't even nick the surface fat."

"We'll have to wait until Papa comes home," said Mama, who hadn't counted on Papa's horror of anything slaughtered, even without his aid and abetment.

"Are we becoming a branch of Swift and Company? Who ever heard of a cow—even half a cow—under the same roof with civilized people? It's against the laws of nature."

"To tell you the truth, Henry, I like it even less than you but the way the man spoke it seems everybody does it. The nearest butcher is in Willimantic and there's no other way of getting meat."

"I still contend we're not butchers. Anyway, who needs meat? Are there no humanized substitutes?"

"I'm sure there are plenty," placated Mama, "but around here we can't get them."

"What alternative am I offered? None. So give

me—give me whatever you need to mutilate defenseless animals."

And Papa went up and sawed and chopped and groaned and came down with mouth-watering steaks and chops and roasts which he refused to eat on principle. But heathens that we were, we savored every whack down to the last beef stew.

8

A Thin Bush Is Better Than
No Shelter

Though Mama was born with a talent for aphorizing away disappointment, the day she took her first grim look at what was to be her home, she was strangely silent. The sight of the store, neglected, disordered, dirty, foul-smelling, would have staggered the heartiest soul, especially Mama whose fear of germs defied the best of her pithy maxims. Dismally she viewed the specter, alien and odious; like soldiers on guard, the poolroom was manned by four spittoons placed strategically in corners, and despite these precautions the floor and walls were splattered with tobacco juice in the manner of Jackson Pollock. Judging by the aimless shots of sour spittle—if shooting for spittoons was a criterion for safety—a herd of buffalo grazing in an open field was more secure than a baby in bed.

Mama wasn't scared long by the filthy prospect. She charged into the cleansing operation with buckets of boiling water, Lysol, Sal Soda, a can of Old Dutch cleanser; she scrubbed and scoured and sterilized until every board in the dingy walls and floor sparkled. Satisfied that every germ—the disease and ordinary variety—was properly annihilated, she set up house.

If she felt anxiety it was artfully stifled. Perhaps if she dared she might have said, "The thing is done, let's make the most of it." Instead she got down on her hands and knees and scrubbed and shined, telling herself and us that "everything happens for the best."

The entire stock was removed from the store and all that remained were store fixtures, counters, candy, tobacco and baked-goods cases, a food scale and an indoor kerosene pump. The long counter spread over the width of the store and was filled with deep, long drawers that slid open from the rear. Shallow glass dummies were hinged cleverly in front, displaying the contents of each drawer: coffee beans, loose tea, sugar, kidney beans, navy beans, pea beans, hominy, barely, rice, flour, soap chips, tobacco and a variety of packaged cereal dummies. It was a colorful, arresting, lively sight. More lively than we had bargained for.

"This must have been here since the Civil War," moaned Keeve as he dumped one wiggly display out after another.

As Rose and I sudsed the mountain of display cases, she said, "I can't wait till we start waiting on store."

"Me too," I echoed naively. "Especially the candy and cookies and ice cream."

It was late spring before Papa hung an "Open for Business" shingle on the door. He appeared to be in no hurry; tending to a full-time business occupied most of his time and the store was incidental. Or so we thought.

During the remainder of the winter Papa continued to commute by train, but in the spring, the roads cleared, he returned one day with the Ford. And then it began. Each week he carted from New York spanking new merchandise—one week a load of groceries; another week, tobacco, then candy, auto supplies, and it continued until the store looked like a backwoods

Macy's.

"If a thing is worth doing, it's worth doing well," said Papa. By the end of the first year the shelves groaned with a variety of items characteristic of small-town general stores. We carried just any little thing—gasoline, oil, ice cream, tires, tubes, candy, kerosene oil, cookies, tobacco, patent medicines, notions, soda, grain, shoes, socks, gloves, hunting caps, automobile accessories and hard-to-get, not to mention hard-to-sell, hardware. If you asked for it, we had it; if not, you could bet your life we'd get it. Papa drew the line at ladies' underwear and apparel. "I'm not competing with G. Fox and Co.," he'd say.

A customer might require the following items: "Fill 'er up. While you're pumping it up I'll go in for a cold sody."

In again behind the counter. "Here's your change, sir. Thank you."

"Say now, I most forgot the screw in my pocket. Mebbe you can match this size?" Match that size! Hundreds of bottles of screws on the shelves . . . .Ten minutes later, "Here it is!"

"What do I owe ya?"

"Two cents, I guess."

"Come t'think of it, you'd better put in a couple quarts of thirty oil."

Outside. . .inside again. "Will that be all?" Prayerfully.

"Reach me a plug of tobaccy and a tin of Prince Albert and here's a slip the little lady give me. Just holler if you can't make it out. Heh, heh."

"Will That Be All?"

"Ayeh, reckon it will."

"We'll have the best-stocked store in Tolland County," Papa boasted to Mama.

And this turned out to be too true.

He stocked items that no other rural store carried

within a radius of twenty miles, nor cared to carry. It started slowly with a complete line of groceries, then like a snowball rolling downhill, mushroomed rapidly. If a customer asked for a spool of thread, the next week we carried a complete supply of needles, thread, combs, toothbrushes, safety pins, scissors—just any little thing the wife might desire. When a farmer casually inquired about sneakers, unwittingly he catapulted us into the shoe business and nothing exasperated us more than selling shoes. No matter how many sizes we kept on hand, someone was bound to want the size just sold.

When school started a boy came in and asked for a notebook. Just one little five-cent notebook. The next week we outrivaled Keeney & Co., the Willimantic stationers. Papa figured it this way: if one box cost fifty cents, a dozen boxes cost five dollars—a substantial saving of one dollar. "Anyone would be a fool not to buy the larger quantity," explained Papa. "This way you hand down the savings to the customer and everyone's happy." So a dozen boxes appeared. Some items you couldn't give away. Six varieties of erasers, pen points, fancy wood-handle pens, typewriter ribbons and paper, typewriter brushes and covers. We owned about the only typewriter in town and these items sat on the shelves until we used them up or they dried out. As for the variety of erasers—how many mistakes can people make, even if they indulge in a fresh one every week?

One day a customer asked for cider. The month was October, harvest time, apple time.

"Cider?" asked Papa in a tone smacking of dismay. "Cider?"

Within a week more calls for cider came in. He called Mama from the kitchen. "People are beginning to ask for cider and I'm turning them away." Papa's distress was real. "Do you know what I'm thinking, Estherel?"

"What?" said Mama. Papa took this for vigorous

assent. "If the turnover is good it will mean constant ordering and reordering. I have an idea that would eliminate this nuisance." His face brightened like a child with a new toy. "We'll buy a cider press—that will solve our problem."

"We can't stock every single thing a person asks for. Besides, cider presses take a lot of money—"

"Everything takes money, but a sure-selling item like cider would pay the cost in the very first year.—Ask anybody. Not only that," said Papa, latching on to Mama's air and health addiction, "you can have freshly squeezed apples as quickly as orange juice—and no one knows the value of potassium more than you. Need I say more?"

In ten days dozens of sparkling gallon jugs filled with shining amber fluid lined the front of the store. On the side of the garage stood a brand-new, mammoth cider press. In one week we learned to feed it succulent, potassium-filled apples, to man the levers and clean the press, to wash the canvas strainers, to remove the crushed pulp, to bottle the fragrant, oozing liquid. Papa initiated, and the family produced.

When the flow of honey-colored juice oozed divinely, like cascading champagne into wooden barrels, we picked straws for the sheer pleasure of watching the first violent spurt gushing through—the climax to endless washing, sorting of apples, cleaning, setting up the press, laying fresh strainers and finally controlling, working the levers.

The time was smack in the middle of the prohibition era; cider, near-beer were the closest you could get to 80-proof cheer if you kept within the law. Farmers drank it and grumbled. "Ain't worth the glass it's bottled in," they'd say, downing five or six to prove their point. They kept on guzzling and they kept on growling.

Some turned to bootleg hooch that ate into the linings of their stomachs, insisting their bellies were strong as cast-iron. "Look," they'd say, clouting it for emphasis, "it's still holding up." By the looks of a few, their suspender straps deserved no small credit.

When the local supply was drained, the demand for Jamaica ginger suddenly boomed.

One day Curly Smith walked in and asked for Mama, who from the outset had earned the reputation of healer, home-style.

"My old Boshie's in a bad way," he said, his face a study in despair. "Took her to a vet and he ordered me to get a bottle of ginger to settle her spasms. While I'm here, you'd better give me a couple in case of emergency. Y'never know when a cow'll kick up in the middle of the night."

Mama agreed with Curly, handing him the two bottles, some words of sympathy and a bit of advice. "Keep them warm and out of the draught."

Suddenly all the cattle in town were stricken with the spasms; simultaneously Jamaica ginger was selling quicker than we could reorder. In a week Curly Smith was back in the store.

He called for Mama again. "B'jeezuz, Ma'am, I'm sure saddled with the jinx. My whole dang barn took to the plague and I'm clean out of ginger."

"Oh, my!" said Mama, deeply concerned. "But you're lucky today. We just received a fresh stock this morning and it's going fast. There's an epidemic in town; all the cattle seem to be hit."

Curly looked at Mama mutely. He was all concerned with the problem at hand. He said, "Better make it six bottles this time—a matter of life and death for the ailin' critters."

"Tsk, tsk," said Mama, hurrying him back to his cows with the ginger just as Cecil Coombs, a farmer from Long Hill, walked in.

Mama shook her head sadly. "You having the same

trouble, too?"

"What sort of trouble, ma'am?"

"You mean you haven't heard of all the cattle coming down with the spasms?" Mama looked at him closely. "Guess you haven't been to town lately. That accounts for it."

"Mebbe so, but my cattle are thriving like a bunny litter. Never sick a day."

"Am I happy to hear that!" said Mama. "Every one of Curly's cows are down with the spasms."

"Did you say Curly's cows?" Cecil burst into a loud guffaw. "Why, he don't own a full-sized critter. All he tends is a litter of hogs and a coop of hens."

"You must be mistaken," Mama said firmly. "He just told me so."

"I'll treat you to a steak dinner, ma'am, if old Curly didn't ask for Jamaica ginger. Will you take me on?"

Mama looked at him blankly. "What's that got to do with it?"

"Nothing much, hee hee, exceptin' it's sparked with alcohol. Don't it seem a strange coincidence, what with the law closing in on the stills?"

"Are you saying he drinks the ginger?" Mama looked at him in disbelief.

"Make up your own mind, ma'am. Looks like I know Curly for a few years now. Wouldn't put anything past that old booze-hound," said Cecil, who again broke into loud guffaws that shook him like a fit of St. Vitus dance. "Ayeh, it's mighty good medicine," he said when he came up for breath.

After that we never sold the joy ginger. For a short while things were decent, when suddenly hair tonic became a fast-selling item. Mama didn't need a house to fall on her head. Suspicious at once, she set about questioning people like a correspondence-school detective. This, too, she learned with horror, men substituted for liquor. For those who used the hair tonic for the less happy occupation of hair-grooming, we ordered vaseline pomade. Anything with the slightest alcohol content was in demand—even cake flavoring, especially vanilla. Mama warned, as she hid the bottles in a counter drawer away from thirsty eyes, "Never sell vanilla unless you know the family well."

Every weekend Papa arrived with a load of supplies and a few new ideas which he thought up en route from New York. He drove slowly, under thirty miles per hour, giving him plenty of time to think up new methods of efficiency, a new piece of equipment.

The first thing to go was the old cash register.

"There must be some way to keep account of items—to know which sell quickly, which move slow, which don't sell," said Papa one day. During the week he shopped around, and on the next trip from New York he carried a gleaming new American Can combination cash register, adding machine, one of the first to tally individual items. Not only was it a precise adder-upper but an accurate recorder of every item sold.

It worked this way. Each line of merchandise was numbered: gasoline, 1; oil, 2; auto supplies, 3; groceries, 4; patent medicines, 5; confectionery, 6, soft beverages, 7; tobacco, 8; and so on up the list. The number of the line was recorded on the left side of the slip, the amount on the right. At the end of each day we tore the little white account off the roll and tallied up the score. Thus we recorded in a formidable ledger the daily sales of our varied wares for instant bookkeeping, but in too short a time the adding machine turned out to be just another job at the end of a busy day.

We threw the "register job" back and forth at each other, "It's your turn." "No, it's your turn." Sometimes days passed and the slips piled up, but they were always finished before Papa returned on Friday. All but a few times and then Papa was thrown into a trauma. "What if the revenue agent comes this week and there's no record of sales?" The horror of it all struck us clearly as we tallied the slips, fearful of that ogre, the revenue agent, who in all our years of storekeeping never once showed up. As if the government cared what part of your income came from timers or from pickled tripe. But Papa did, and enough to make him alternately happy and angry when he glanced through the ledger.

Except for little Franny, the whole family was pressed into service. At the age of nine, I could qualify with sufficient experience for gas-station attendant, cider-press operator, bookkeeper, dishwasher, and general store clerk. I was a whiz in auto supplies. Selling gaskets, cylinders, carburetors, Bendix springs was as easy as scooping ice cream—sometimes simpler. Rose and Keeve managed even more. But Papa topped us all. He managed to learn everything but how to tend a garden, and that remained as alien to him as marijuana cigarettes. He was amply endowed with creative talent. Besides, he was an expert mechanic, plumber, electrician, buyer, clerk, boss. Washing dishes and floors were never beneath him and he worked right along with Mama. Whatever the job, he was ready. He awoke at five-thirty, retired at midnight, never sitting down except at mealtime. When Mama would say, "Henry, take a little rest, you're working too hard," he'd repeat, "Plenty of time for that after I'm dead," a philosophy he generously extended to the whole family.

Hard work and I went together like ice cream and sauerkraut. During the week while Papa was in New York I relaxed, played, wrote little stories in notebook after notebook (the stationery department had its features). A good part of the time was spent trying to evade my turn at "doing the register." My distaste for numbers is still strong.

When the weekend rolled around, however, I made up for lost time. Saturdays and Sundays were busy days, with five times as many automobiles on the well-traveled Boston Post Road, and we were kept busy from early morning till late at night. If we worked hard, Papa worked even harder; how he managed all he did defies understanding. He drove to New York early Monday mornings, rising at three, when often the fog was so thick and blinding no other car would venture on the road. During the week he tended to his business with the same intense vigor, with the same disregard for his health. Fridays, after a full week, he returned loaded down with merchandise, ready for a work-packed weekend. This was Papa's life; if it were different he would chafe. He appraised a person's character by his ability to produce a solid day's work, and for this reason we kept moving about, looking busy even when we were not.

When a job was to be done there was no question as to our ability—it was a matter of doing it, and we did. A job was expected, so we performed it. In a year I added to my repertoire, multigraph and mimeograph operator, typist (pick and pecker), sign painter, window decorator. So did Rose and Keeve. We handled Papa's advertising campaigns that involved thousands of multigraphed letters and typewritten envelopes. He would say calmly, "Look, children, I must have this finished by the time I get back from New York." And we finished it. Or he would say, "Write up a good form letter and a few slogans for blotters." When Papa said we could do it, we did—never questioning his judgment, obedient children that we were. Didn't every other household do the same? We were advertising agency and printing shop all in one, and could tell a mat from a cut any day in the week—and what's more we knew how to use them.

In the course of years, with his thirst for facts and information, Keeve became a small walking encyclopedia.

If you were in search of facts—anything from the goldtail moth to the editor of a trade magazine—Keeve would have the answer, or tell you exactly where to find it. He grew up finding out for himself, as did Rose and I. Years later I visited the old farm in Coventry and chatted with Mrs. Kernan, the woman who bought the place soon after we moved to Andover. "I'll never forget my surprise the first time you waited on me and totaled up a long column of figures," she reminisced. "You were just a little mite and I remember you asking your dad to doublecheck it. Do you know what he said? 'Check it? Why? For what reason? At your age you should be able to add without mistakes.' And do you know, he kept right on loading the shelves with canned goods. I'll confess I wasn't as sure as your dad and I went over that column myself, and sure enough your total was as right as rain. I don't think I'll ever forget that."

Whether by design, indifference or naïvité, we were put on our own and there was nothing to do but make good.

9

All Roads Lead to Rome

When Cecil Coombs referred to himself as one of the Four Hundred, we soon learned that the number represented the sum total of inhabitants, and not a clique of social snobs.

The railroad cut through the heart of town and you were separated geographically, not socially; there was no "right" and "wrong" side of the tracks. Where you lived hardly altered your social status; all relationships thrived on a first-name basis despite the mixed population of farmers, storekeepers, teachers, first selectman, a superior court judge, carpenters, the state auditor, blacksmith, insurance clerks, paper-mill workers and road laborers.

When we lived in Coventry we looked forward to an occasional hike to the "village." Isolated on the farm, Andover meant stores, post office, railroad station, library, Town Hall—civilization. The hike to the village was more than a treat, and we were well schooled on the privilege, when we could bribe Keeve and Benny into taking us. Now that we were part of it all, the glamour vanished and we saw the town as it really was.

Situated diagonally across the road from our store was

the center of activity—the Town Hall. Here, Grange meetings, Saturday-night dances, town meetings, church suppers and socials, school programs and amateur theatricals were held with regularity. School nights drew capacity crowds—two hundred people—and of these, half were standing in the rear, down the aisles and some on chairs in the entryway.

The stage was sturdy and ample, with heavy, red velvet traverse-curtains, and behind it the dressing-room-kitchen with its wood-burning stove, wood box, pump sink and huge pantry full of thick white crockery and food staples. A wing on the side of the Hall provided a dining room—and here took place the mouth-watering event of the year—the Girls' League Strawberry Supper. As members, Rose and I helped hull the crates of sweet, juicy berries that spilled red and generously over steaming baking-powder biscuits, topped with mounds of freshly whipped cream. Supper consisted of a half dozen varieties of salads, thickly sliced country ham and oven-baked beans. Plenty of hot rolls, butter, coffee—and topping it, the tantalizing dessert. Supper menus during the year were similar, minus the berries, substituted by home-baked pies and cakes. Occasionally, a New England boiled dinner was provided by the Ladies' Aid. The long tables groaned with platters of food, served family style, and you helped yourself until you were sated if you so chose. You paid fifty cents if you were an adult—sometimes thirty-five.

Living across from the Hall was not without merit. We knew something was making for the night when Johnny James hobbled up the steps and entered the Hall. When smoke poured from the chimney we knew Johnny had the long wood stove going full blast. When lights filled the windows we knew Johnny had trimmed the wicks and filled the huge oil lamps hanging from the ceiling. It was exciting to live so close to life and activity and to watch the first buggy or Model–T drive up to the Hall steps. And to hear the strains of a fiddle and the thump of a piano and the call of a prompter clear across the road. Or when the dance ended, the talk and laughter, the hushed giggles and whisperings in the dark, and on wintry nights, the coughing of cold motors, the tearing gears, the screeching horns, until the last car chugged out of sight and the last light dimmed out. Then darkness and loud silence.

The bustling grocery-post office was another center of activity. Twice a day—mornings and after the six o'clock train rumbled in—Rose and I took turns walking over to pick up the mail. We lived too close to the center of town for rural delivery and this turned out to work happily in our favor, giving us a valid excuse to take off for a little while. It was more than rewarding as we waited for the postmistress to sort the mail, distribute the letters in pigeonholes, our eyes darting back and forth to Lock Box 10, watching the gradual swell. When we arrived too soon we waited for Tony Venetti to cart the mail sacks down from the depot in his wheelbarrow; and often the sorting was delayed until a store customer was waited on. This was excitement of the best sort, the waiting for news—unexpected news, good news, not-so-good news. You could count on a group of villagers to be there sitting, waiting, chatting as the sorting went on. And the friendliest of smells to hit your nose—the mingled odors of shriveled oranges, spices, tobacco smoke, frosty mail bags. When talk died down you could browse over the WANTED signs tacked to the bulletin board and tsk, tsk over the scarfaces, desperadoes, crooks—occasionally a boyish face to melt you with pity. Or pinned up beside the criminals, hand-printed posters: Armatures turned, Lathe Work Done; DANCE; Ladies' Aid Supper; For Sale: Oil barrels with Faucets; AUCTION: Land Sale; Wanted: Someone to claim jackets, boots, dishes left at school.

The beat of the town pulsed through these notices.

It was weeks before I could walk to the post office oblivious of the abandoned cemetery fringing the road. In the winter, when darkness spread early I flew as if winged, expecting some specter to reach out and grab me. Even in the summer light, the eerie sight of unmown grass, the tall weeds, the thick poison ivy embracing the tombs sent me darting by as if the devil himself had popped up beside me, relaxing only within sight of the post office.

Rose never shared my terror, and one day as we passed the old cemetery that dated back to Revolutionary days she said, "Let's go in and read the grave markings."

"You mean for us to walk through?" I stopped, horrified.

"Why not?" said Rose coolly. "You're not still afraid, are you?"

"No, I'm not really afraid," I said, my heart thumping, "but anyone can see you'd be wasting your time. Just look at this one." I pointed to a stone close to the road. "See how faded the letters are."

"That's only one," insisted Rose. "Let's go in and look for the fun of it."

I held my breath. Mama said you only have to be afraid of the living, never the dead; besides, I could not admit to Rose how scared I really was. I stiffened and walked in beside her.

"See? there's nothing to it," said Rose.

"Sure," I lied, too. "It's silly to be more scared of a gravestone than any other stone—just because—"

"Yeah," assisted Rose. "Just because it happens to cover a corpse."

We stepped carefully from gravestone to gravestone, trying to read the weathered inscriptions. "Here's one.

Listen," said Rose. "Revolutionary War, Captain Eleazer Hutchinson." The date was not legible—only when death came—seventy-four years.

"He couldn't have died in battle at that age," said Rose, disappointment dulling her voice. She read on slowly, deciphering the epitaph:

> The grave is now my home,
> But soon I hope to rise
> Mortals behold my tomb
> Keep death before my eyes.

"Gee," said Rose, her voice curdling.

"Let's go now!" I started to turn

"Wait. Don't be a sissy, it's lots of fun; besides, it's loaded with history. Do you know this might be one of the oldest cemeteries in the country?" Rose took for assent my grim silence; she walked on. "Here's another good one," she said, reading in ghoulish delight:

> Stoop my friends as you
> Are passing by.
> As you are now, so once was I
> As I am now, so you must quickly be
> O be prepared then to follow me.

Goose pimples covered my body. "I'm leaving!" My voice left no room for doubt, and I started to run.

"Wait—I'm coming, too," said Rose, catching up with me. "But I'm coming back tomorrow to copy these poems for school."

"Not with me."

"That's okay. I'm not afraid."

Maybe she wasn't, but it took many months before I forgot the grim markings, memorized from sheer terror. There came a time, however, when the cemetery affected me less than an old barn or tree, and I was able to appreciate Cecil Coombs' oft-repeated story.

"Ayeh, in the old days there wuz ways of tellin' when a boy reached his manhood. Do you know how?" We shook our heads dutifully. "Well, I'll tell ya," he said, sucking in his lower lip. "When the lad had stomach enough to play a game of cards on the memorial tablets at midnight without accompanyin' jitters, then they called him a man."

Behind the Congregational Church was the town's small, one-room library. Here, Mrs. Foster, the portly librarian, introduced us to a world of authors, and we were soon carting home books and magazines which we devoured during the week when Papa was away—everything from *The Five Little Peppers* to the Horatio Alger stories, though we were duly warned the latter were meant for boys only. My favorite was The *Secret Garden*; my tears flowed silently and steadily as the Elbe, and I read this over and over in the privacy of my room where I could freely indulge in my great sorrow.

My first experience with libraries occurred while we were still in New York and I was in the first grade. This was to end in mild disaster.

It was bitterly cold the day Keeve, Rose, and I walked to the library on 23rd Street on slippery sidewalks covered with dirty mounds of snow. The wind pierced, almost blowing us over as we quickly covered the ten long blocks to the library, counting the crosstown avenues. My nose ran, my teeth chattered, my hands and toes numbed with cold. Then finally we were safely inside the warm, musty-smelling building. A young librarian showed us to the children's section where a printed fairyland lay waiting. Scores of books with beautifully colored pictures lined the shelves. Mother Goose in all her glory was available to anyone with a reader's card. Keeve said I could borrow two books after I received THE CARD—the open sesame to a dream world. I was in a state of frozen ecstasy, my teeth still

chattered, but now from pure excitement. Choosing two
books was a task that made King Solomon an amateur
by comparison, and after long deliberation I chose a
Mother Goose book and another called *"The Sunbonnet
Twins."* Beaming, I brought my treasures to the librarian
who explained the rules and regulations as she handed
me a card. "Sign your name here, little girl," she said.

Now, at the age of six, signing my name to an
impressive document was a milestone in my life.
Suddenly I assumed importance and was ready to take
on this grave responsibility with proper humility.

But I had not counted on the Supreme Test. The
librarian offered me a pen, and fear gripped my heart.
What would she say if she knew I had never held a pen
before? Would she forbid me to take the books? If I
couldn't write with ink, would she permit me the
responsibilities of a book borrower? I was in great
trouble—and there the librarian stood, waiting for me as
I clutched the pen, still shaking with cold.

I was ready to burst into tears and admit defeat, but I
remembered the cherubic Sunbonnet Twins, and
doggedly worked away at my name, resting between each
letter. Finally and triumphantly, my trembling fist
produced a jagged mass of letters that spelled my name
and I handed the card back to the librarian.

Though the wind cut through my body and I trembled
with cold, I was only aware of the two books clutched
tightly to my bosom as we ran home.

"Mama, Mama, see what I got!" I cried, rushing
through the door, thrusting the books in front of her
face.

But a strange thing happened. Mama did not respond
in her usual way; she took one long look at the books
and her face darkened.

"Keeve," she said, "tomorrow you must return these
dirty books to the library. God only knows what disease

germs are breeding there."

Surely Mama must be mistaken. But now, for the first time, I saw the books as they really were—torn, grease-stained pages, dirty covers, mutilated bindings, and knew that hundreds of little hands had thumbed through the pages before me. But I hardly understood Mama's fear of diphtheria and scarlet fever that raged through the neighborhood, and suddenly burst into tears that wouldn't stop.

"But I have a card, Mama," I appealed to her, sobbing. Mama said nothing, but she still looked upset.

"But, but," I pleaded, "it was so cold . . .and my hands were shaking . . .and I signed my name . . .and I love the Sunbonnet Twins." My heart was near to breaking.

Mama's voice softened and she drew me close. "I'll tell you what, Sarala. Tomorrow we'll both go down to Green Hutz and I'll buy you the same Sunbonnet Twins book, but this one will be new and clean and will belong just to you."

A trip to the department store with those shining new escalators salved my wounds at once, though I still cherish the library card that was stamped twice and used but once.

Mathematically, school life in Andover was twice as interesting as in Coventry; a two-room schoolhouse, twice the number of pupils, bigger and better outhouses. The latter were most impressive, with latticework framing a hideaway for each door; but even the fancy fronts could not diminish the stench, and we rushed home from school each noon to lunch—and to plumbing. But not without envy, however, as I watched my classmates wave the signal that released them from class and sent them outside into the open.

You never asked to go to the johnny. Instead, you crossed your index and middle fingers, stretched your hand high and forward as in grim salute, and waited. If your appeal went unheeded, back and forth went the vigorous salute until the teacher dismissed you. When even this distraction was ignored then both hands went into action until the teacher fully recognized the urgency. "You may leave," she'd say wearily as the class broke into hushed titters.

The school was divided into two classrooms and each room equipped for four grades. I entered the fourth, Rose the eight, but the term in Coventry prepared me for little more than the Fourth-of-July races. Here in Andover there was no need for my newly acquired prowess since there existed no equivalent to the Mitchell creature, and we were soon inducted to a formal, organized course of study. Each month we were visited by a county nurse and an itinerant music teacher. A definite treat was the arrival of frail but spry Mr. Johnson, whose white hair matched his immaculate white shirt. He trained our voices for Christmas, Easter, and graduation, stiffly precise, like a West Point plebe. His tuning fork reverberated loud and clear in the sudden stillness, like church chimes on a Sunday morning. All business until the lesson was over. And then he smiled approval, and that smile spoke like a roguish wink of the eye, a promise of more to come. Then out came the worn leather case of phonograph records. Fumbling for the right record, he unfolded its story, spicing it heavily with good humor.

"Now you take this Beethoven fellah who wrote this music. What a sad lot he was born to, a hard rough childhood, a drunk for a daddy. As if this wasn't enough he goes and turns deaf in his later years. Now, boys and girls, would you call him a happy man?"

"No!" yelled back the class.

"You say no and I hear you say it loud. As if you knew. As if I knew. But I'll tell you one thing I know—no man ever produced more enchanting sounds.

All his hate, all his love, all his anger, even the beautiful countryside and quiet moonlight poured into his music like a good dream come true. Did Mozart compare to him?"

"No!" thundered the class. The way he parried the question, there was no other answer.

"You're right! But you're probably guessing. How could you all know? Sure, Mozart made great music, too, but it turned out like a lovely still-life painting—great beauty but not much heart. Today I chose to play Beethoven's immortal Pastoral. Then you will see for yourselves, boys and girls, you will see for yourselves."

A sudden lull spread over the room and we listened raptly, a new awareness, a new appreciation lighting our faces. "Old Johnsy," we called him fondly, but he never really grew old despite his snowy white hair.

The narrow, steep incline that led to the schoolhouse connected the main highway to Hebron Road. In winter, on a cold clear night with the snow bedded hard and slick and only the moon above for light, it turned into the best little road for sliding parties and suicides-in-training. We boarded a rough homemade sliding contraption called a double-ripper—one twelve-foot plank, two crude bobsleds and heavy whipcord intended for gearless shifting—and along with eight or ten other dull normals, started at the peak of Hebron Road and zoomed headlong onto the Boston Post Road as the driver cut sharply to the right, missing by inches the startled sedans and trucks that passed by. Sometimes the turn tumbled us over the road like coals spilling over a chute; but barring a minor collision with a slow-plodding wagon, a few concussions and abrasions, the ride was moderately safe, if you were young and feeble-minded.

Even more suicidal was the hill that only the I'll-show-you-Harrys attempted; treacherous as the

motorcycle slope that leered at a seventy-degree angle,
close to Willimantic, it boasted extra hazards, like sturdy
oaks with ten-foot girths directly in its path. Sleds
zigzagged in and out like Swiss skiers; one false move
could make quick copy for the obit columns. Only the
super-showoffs tried it and the rest stood by, a little too
eager, to notify the next of kin.

Long Hill, the road leading to Coventry, was another
sliding dilly. "It's the safest hill around," purred Marcy
Holcomb, rounding up a few girls for an afternoon
sliding party and wienie roast. "Hardly anyone ever uses
it excepting Saturday nights."

What Marcy said was true. Long Hill was the beginning
of a dirt road veining off the main artery and used
almost wholly by local townspeople. Few strange cars
rattled over the rutted road that led to the Coventries
and those that did were all but regarded in the light of
trespassers—a carry-over from the early days when a
Yankee farmer firmly resisted a public road crossing his
property, viewing it as a crusty invasion of private
domain. To the point of harassing the traveling intruder
by planting fences across the road.

In view of this meager travel, Long Hill was considered
as safe an area as any. Still, Rose was not convinced.

"That hill seems pretty steep to me, Marcy."

"It's really not. It's safe as a bug in a rug," insisted
Marcy. "Long Hill's divided into three small ones and it's
ever so much safer than School Hill."

This was true. Three leveled crests could cut into your
speed on the way down, provided the snow was soft and
manageable. But for weeks now, near-zero temperatures
had firmed and slicked the snow until it glistened like a
glacier.

"Don't worry," said Marcy, "I'll be in charge. I won't
wave you down until each of you clears the second
hump. It'll be safe and loads of fun. Honest!"

We agreed, drooling at the thought of the wienie roast. At the appointed time, two o'clock Saturday afternoon, Rose and I hauled our sleds up Long Hill where Marcy and the others were ready and waiting.

"Gosh, we thought you'd never come," said Helen Baker, chewing her lips in disapproval. Helen was known as the girl who got to school even earlier than Annie Kenker, who arrived a whole hour before class. Together they shared this sacred bond, sneering with importance and solidly claiming the best position over the furnace register. Helen believed firmly in self-denial, early rising, early arrival, and now she waited virtuously blue with cold.

"Let's get going, I'm freezing," said Helen flapping her arms like a penguin.

And then Marcy took over and signaled us on, one at a time. Helen Baker first, perky, pretty Lil Keiser second, Rose third. In minutes everyone was launched safely, just as she said. Even safer than we expected; not a vehicle in sight since the moment we turned into Long Hill Road. Marcy was right. It really was the safest sliding hill.

"Sarah next!" signaled Marcy, and I jumped on my sled, bellyflop. Paddling the slippery ground with my hands to get a slow firm start, I suddenly scooped the first hill with startling speed. I tried to brake the slide by dragging my feet, but the road was solid, icy packing and it was like dipping them in thin jelly. There was no stopping now. I had tried double-rippers, shared belly flops, but this was my first solo and I had reason for fear. But there were Helen and Lil turning their sleds around and Rose coasting slowly and it would be seconds before I'd join her, exchanging our little excitements.

As I flew over the first hump a thunderous rumbling pierced my knitted earmuffs—a rumbling induced by a team of horses crossing the loosely planked paper-mill bridge, and speeding forward at a steady clip.

I tore on over the second hump, my breath coming in spurts like air from a hand pump. Hallelujah! This was it—and only seconds away.

On came the horses, whinnying, sliding, menacing, slipping to the left and right of the glassy road like an engine suddenly brakeless, the wagon snapping from side to side. The driver jumped from his seat, choked the reins with all his might, roaring "Whoa, whoa!" But the team moved on as if devilish prongs were piercing from behind. It now seemed a certainty that we should meet at the foot of the hill and it was up to God and me to forestall the encounter. And at once! But how?

Suddenly brave with terror I looked to the right. Barbed wire snaked along the bank, taut, ominous, ugly. Jutting out from the left bank like barnacles, hungry for small humans, were huge rocks and spearlike icicles, but here at least no flesh-ripping wire. Anyway, who had a choice? And the few seconds left on earth could not be squandered in contemplative meditation. There seemed but one last thing to do. Heaving sharply to the left with every panicked sinew in my body I dived headlong into the ice-encrusted bank.

Then oblivion. Sweet, protective oblivion.

When I came to, the farmer was pulling me out of the bank, cut, shocked, bleeding. Rose was crying, "Sarie, are you all right? Are you all right?"

The girls hovered around, pale and frightened, squealing in alarm, trying to help. All but Helen. She stood apart muttering, "Now, if she'd a-come earlier like the rest of us . . . ."

"It could have been worse," said Mama, comforting me in bed, the aphoristic gleam warming her eyes. Then, stroking my head, she murmured, "You know, Sarala, bitter pills sometimes have wholesome effects."

Mama was right. When next I went sliding it was down the gentle slope in the safe open field directly behind us.

10

Not Parties, but Principles

To learn the many faces, the many vagaries of human nature, you explored the broad field of psychology. Or you got behind the counter of a country general store.

Here, opportunities for meeting people were limitless. All kinds of people—bumpkins, sophisticates, day laborers, executives, dolts, scholars; the variety of fellow creatures entering the door each year might have proved a fertile field for pollsters covering anything from the political scene to sexual habits of the human race. Few aspects of human nature are not met over the friendly counter of a small-town general store, especially with trade as diversified as ours. Our location, directly on the Boston Post Road, the major connecting link between Boston and New York, played some little part. Transients walked in and out all day long, some to gas and oil their cars, some to stretch their legs and rest, some curious about small-town establishments and the people who managed them.

But the mainspring of our trade were the steadies, the people who traded regularly, the people who came and shopped, sat and talked, and talked and talked. Keeve, inspired no doubt by memories of the early poolroom trim, called them the "straight shooters" forum, the regulars who congregated on cold winter nights, huddling around the sheet-iron stove for hours, getting up only to spew a mouthful of tobacco juice out the door. They tolerated Mama's ban on the "disease-spreading" spittoons, but when a guy had to spit, he had to spit. In the morning the glistening white cover was sullied by blobs of brown stain and you got the queasy feeling of greasy fingerprints on new wall-paper.

When a "member" reached into his hip pocket for a plug of tobacco, it fascinated in a nauseating sort of way. And always when yellow teeth shaped a wad or when snuff was gathered up into a ball with thumb and index finger with the eye of a gourmet, then placed in a drooling mouth, you watched, magnetized.

Not all members of the forum chewed tobacco or Copenhagen snuff. Some smoked corncobs or "seegars," and sometimes one lit a cigarette, and always the air was strong and dense with acrid smoke that made the eyes smart. Before retiring, Mama threw open the doors, airing the store and freezing the house for thirty minutes.

Papa would grudgingly hand a package of tobacco over the counter. "I don't like selling this poison. It ruins your health; you're a slave to the habit, and besides, it costs you good money. If I didn't sell it, you'd find it somewhere, I suppose." Over and over again he asked, "What good do you get out of it?" A question which usually provoked the retort, "Try it yourself, then you'll see."

"Who? Me? Not for a thousand dollars." And he never did.

Around the stove they sat, each fortified with his favorite brand of tobacco or snuff, discussing the affairs of state, arguing the merits of recent legislation, newest fads, the latest town gossip. Never any lulls. Yarn after yarn unraveled like a ball of wool in the hands of playful kittens. Sitting around the stove on nail kegs, chairs, crates, cussing and haranguing and joshing, here in this small group, tinctured with native shrewdness, throbbed the pulse of New England.

It didn't take long to learn that our town was as heavily Republican as the rest of New England. "A Democrat's got no more chance than a snowball in hell," howled Jess Miller shortly after we moved in, and from the thigh-slapping glee that ensued it was clear that all Democrats were as welcome as a killing frost in June. Despite this, a small but firm core of Democrats nettled the status quo, and there were some who predicted "those damn Democrats will be giving us trouble yet."

In the small village of Andover, politics was more a personal matter than political. Many were staunch Republicans or Democrats not from deep conviction or principle, but from strong tradition, generations of tradition. Most of all from strong personal interest in the outcome of the local election. We learned this early when Papa hired a farmer to chop a cord of wood for the stove. Election time was near and the town buzzed with pre-election gossip and predictions. After splitting the last log, Homer Briggs walked in, sat down on an empty crate and slowly drew his pipe and pouch from his pocket.

"Well," he sighed, with the contentment of one who knew a good day's work was behind him, "ain't long now to election time."

Without waiting for Papa to answer he said with a forgiving, knowing wink, "I heard you joined up with the Democrats."

In small-town politics you had no political privacy; everything was thrown out into the open like the Monday wash. No closed doors or secret party affiliations. If you aspired for a job, the town knew it as well as your name or your trade; you knew where your neighbor stood whether you liked it or not and the air was cleared as by a cool, fresh blast of wind.

Papa looked up, surprised. "That's the way I've been voting," he said.

"Ayeh"—between pleasurable puffs at his pipe—"I always say every man's a right to his own thinkin'. Suspect it don't make much difference anyways. Take my family, we're Republicans from way back—every garl-durned one of us—that is to say, every one exceptin' my brother Tim in Tolland. He didn't get nowheres in the party so he went and switched to the Democrats. He says they's a cinch to carry the town this year. Never can tell, though. Polytics is a funny business," he said plainly as if commenting on the weather.

In our town with a census of four hundred men, women and children, the chances of your name being mentioned at caucus were better than good; the stronger the Republican inclination, the better your chances. Politics, like the morning milk, was bound to get into your kitchen. It had smug familiarity, personal importance; it was part of your life like Grange and church and square dancing. The party slate was set up. You voted your man in at caucus and you voted him in on election day. The man was your party, by God, and you were as loyal to your party as to your spouse.

Instead of deep thought, perception, clear vision, a split ticket often indicated pique, rebellion. "You bet I'm a Republican but that don't mean I'm going to vote for that lady-chasin' cattle thief." Personal hostility was stronger than party loyalty and those who broke the lines completely and switched parties were more angry than informed and eventually denounced as party traitors. Shifts were rare, however, and always guaranteed a lively session, generally winding up with a vendetta on socialism. "You can't tell this horse-shoein' farmer that he ain't a black masqueradin' Socialist."

One evening tall Chris Gilbert, better known as "Buckteeth" Gilbert, walked in and sat down abruptly on his favorite nail keg. Chris owned an eighty-acre dairy farm, large enough for him to rise at dawn and keep working until sunset but not large enough to keep him out of politics. He worked hard in the party, talked to all the neighbors, kept his dairy farm clean, and for this the town bestowed on him the title of Justice of the Peace ever since he was able to vote. "It's a good title," admitted Chris wryly, "but I ain't had the chance to put it to use." He was good-humored, honest, and as long as he stuck to dairy farming twelve hours a day he offered no major threat to the community.

"What d'ya know," he said, carefully inserting a wad of Copenhagen in his protruding jaw. "I hears there's a bunch of females who started something they call a league for women voters or some such outlandish handle, and I hear it said they's both Republicans and Democrats joining. Now I ask you, what kind of monkeyshines is that?"

"Don't make good sense to me," said Jeff Miller, bored with any talk short of the latest debauchery, to which he contributed more than anyone. He wooed and courted girls from neighboring villages, and in due time wound up in soft hay lofts, not matrimony, then hurried back to boast of his conquests.

"They says they's non-partisan," said Chris.

"Non-partisan? What's that?" Jeff slicked down his fresh-cut pomaded hair with the back of his hand, obviously interested.

"From the piece in the Hartford *Times* it appears they aim to give folks a full-dress account of a man's record when he's runnin' for office. Demycrats, Republicans, alike. They don't tell you none who to vote for, figgerin' once you get the lowdown about a man you got a better chance to make up your mind."

"Sounds like a lot of Bolshevik talk," said Jeff, still smoothing his hair.

"Well, I dunno," said Chris. "By the looks of the lady members, lots of 'em Republicans, it don't appear so to me. They be aimin' foremost to educate women-folk about votin'." Chris grinned and his mouth stretched wide as a tarpon's. " I was tellin' Essie it don't sound harmful but there's no sense in her gettin' all mixed up in it. I figger she got all the education she needs bein' hitched up to a milk farmer like me. Just as long as she's lookin' in I don't have no bother, but brother, just you start educatin' 'em enough to run the show, then boy, you can sit back and watch the sparks flyin'."

There was solid unity on this issue. Every man liked his woman "in her place." "By God, they got too many newfangled notions already," said Cabe Johnson, adding his bit for the first time. Cabe's rows with his wife Ermie were no secret. Ermie had lots of time on her hands, no children to hinder her, and with the farming chores done, the washboard put away, she was ready for more pleasurable pursuits. Nor was it a secret that plump but shapely Ermie enjoyed more than a little neighborly feeling for her fellow man. Often we would see Ermie driving by in a touring car with the top drawn back, sitting close to a stranger at the wheel, her short, bobbed hair blowing over her face, and waving heartily just as if it were Cabe sitting beside her.

It wasn't long before Ermie's accelerated activity provided an open season for town gossips, though strangely, her true love lay with Caleb. We heard it first from Jeff Miller's overpious, garrulous mother.

"That Cabe Johnson oughter horsewhip some sense into that sportin' wife of his. "It's a downright shame

the way that hussy carries on behind that fool Cabe's
back."

"She should talk," said Chris Gilbert. "Why, she's just
tryin' to cover up for her no-good, lady-chasin' son. He's
probably the one that made her wayward." This was
months ago.

Chris looked at Cabe thoughtfully. "You're right,
Cabe, next thing you know women folk'll be wearing
britches."

"When my woman does, by God, I'll put a plow in
her hands, and if I know my woman she'll take off them
britches quicker'n the time it takes to holler uncle," said
Cabe.

"Haw, haw, your Ermie's experienced in taking off
britch—" Jeff stopped short. Cabe's face had paled, his
eyes slit like steel blades and he rose abruptly as if he
suddenly thought of plowing into Jeff. The rest looked
on in frozen silence. There was no mistaking their
sympathy for Cabe, yet they sat, grimly fascinated, their
faces all but saying, "This looks like the makin's of a
good fight and no town worth its salt should be without
one."

"You know I was jest horsin' around, Cabe. I didn't
mean no harm in it." Jeff forced a weak smile. "You can
take my word for it," he said placatingly.

Cabe spat contemptuously out the door, strode back
to the counter, his face now a feverish red, and paid
Papa for a can of Union Leader. "Take your word for
it!" he growled. "Take your word for it!" He walked
quietly to the door and turning around he said, "I'm
givin' you fair warnin', Jeff. Jest you be careful with
your loose 'n easy talk." He added slowly, a new fury
threading his words, "That is, if you don't want your
stinkin' hide full of buckshot," and lunged wildly out
the door.

"Goddam now! What did I say that every other

uprighteous citizen in town ain't sayin'," whimpered Jeff, losing the old gay-dog bravado. He looked expectantly around the room, waiting for the good word, for someone to come to his defense. No one did.

"What the hell! Y'might've figgered he never heerd it before," said Jeff. The men cast their eyes floorward and shuffled uneasily in their seats. Chris got up and bought a tin of Copenhagen, Cecil Jones tore a long, protruding splinter off the orange crate, and Homer Perkins harrumphed loudly. Then Chris returned with his snuff, arranged his rump neatly on a nail keg, wadded a firm ball, and then said quietly, "Well, as I sees it, Jeff, you're mighty lucky you didn't get your brains bashed in." He looked straight at Jeff, adding, "If it'd be me, I'd sure've done it."

"Listen to the man talk!" said Jeff, his voice a hollow bluster. But no one turned and no one listened. The men were getting up and moving toward the door, and Chris followed. Outside we could hear the sound of gears grinding into first, then the sputter of Model T's taking off. Jeff kept sitting silently, his face a mask of livid anger. Then he got up suddenly and said, his voice a sickening rattle, "Goddam 'em, they can go to hell, one and all," and tore blindly out the door.

Staunch Republicians rarely split their ticket to put a man in office, but it did happen. It happened the time Dr. Dixon ran on the Democratic slate for state senator. Though he insisted the good Lord did not endow him with special talent or ability for politics, the county took to him like a bird to singing. Nor did it matter when he stood on rostrums at political rallies and declared with honest fervor, "Folks, there's one thing I don't know nothin' about—and that's polytics." Folks in the audience howled and applauded.

"Just listen to that man talk," they said, with the

conviction that no candidate enjoyed a better sense of whimsy. Here was a man with humor, a man so smart he could afford to tell you he wasn't; better still, he was a man who spoke their language, lived their problems. Every farmer in the county knew Doc and knew him well, and no amount of political shenanigans could sway them.

Everyone who entered the store felt the same. "He stood by me many a time," said Chris Gilbert, "and I'll never forget when my prize Guernsey came down with Bang's disease. It sure worked the devil in poor Boshie's udder and I figgered she was good as done for, but I called Doc anyway, and he came a-runnin' like a greyhound. Unless you seen the gentle way he nursed her, tender, worried, like he was nursin' a child of his own, you wouldn't believe it. In a couple of days she was good as new."

"Ayeh, that's old Doc Dixon himself," said Cecil Jones. "He's patched up many a sore, bleeding hoof in my barn, and it got so when the hosses'd see him comin' in they'd give out with a whinnying chirrup like he was one of 'em."

"Nobody like him," agreed Cabe Johnson, "I can tell you that. One summer every cow in my barn was ailin' with mastitis, and no sooner'n Doc tended 'em they was back to their normal output. Nope, their ain't nobody like him." Cabe shook his head in tribute.

Relief and gratitude welled in the milkers' hearts when ailing cows returned to their yield of warm, foamy milk. Everyone had a kind word for Doc Dixon, even Lem Merrick, who never agreed with anyone. "The way I sees it," he said, his chair propped against a wall, chewing an El Producto cigar with the air of a Rotarian. "If these here polyticians don't do no burnin' up in the world, what's the harm of puttin' in a man who's honorable enough to admit he don't. I get the feelin' there's somethin' dead honest about the way that man's mouth wrinkles every time he smiles. Y'can't miss it."

Tall, lanky, kindly Doc Dixon was in before the votes were tallied.

Then there was old Doc Wiggins of Coventry, the only doctor this side of Willimantic and Manchester. When Doc couldn't be reached, some "city doctor" was called in, but only in dire emergencies. City doctors charged four dollars per home visit, while Doc only asked two no matter how far he drove. But the price was not important; there was something warm and healing, something reassuring when Doc drove up in his old black Chevrolet sedan. It wasn't the color that struck you—in those days you could get any color as long as you chose black—but the high lustrous finish that made the old Chevvy look like all was well with the world.

"Y'might think he was one of those high-priced healers by the looks of his slicked-up car," said Lem Merrick as Doc drove by one afternoon, his car sparkling in the sun. "But thank the good Lord there ain't no other similarities."

"Ayeh," agreed Chris Gilbert, nostalgia creeping into his voice. "Doc's been around so long he's like a part of the seasons. He brought me and my kids into the world, he's tended my Ma and Dad ever since I can remember. He's got a God-given gift for rememberin' faces, names and ailments—everyone's stored safe and tight in his head."

"Why, these city doctors don't even know your name till you tell 'em. Then they pulls out a card from a steel file stacked with thousands of others," said Lem. "If your ailment ain't to their suitin' they sends you to a specialist. Not Doc. When you're ailin' he mends you whether it's the grippe or a broken leg or bringin' a baby into the world—he'll mend you, b'God. No matter what time of day or night you calls him, you know he'll git there. Never any phony excuses, he just gits there."

"It's the truth, ayeh, every durned word of it," said Cecil Jones, plugging his mouth with a wad of tobacco.

Only once did Doc Wiggins call at our house and that was the time Keeve came down with a bad case of poison ivy. Mama knew none of the local remedies and she was baffled by the sight of his bloated hands. Any other time when one of us was foolish enough to come down with a cold or the grippe, Mama took over at once—and that meant the works. She was a natural when it came to doctoring up the family, always relying on three of her favorite remedies: an enema to "clean out the lower bowels," gallons of hot lemonade to rout the "poisons in the system," raspberry tea to "sweat out a fever," and ipecac syrup to bring up anything that had the effrontery to remain down—and once in a while a dose of castor oil if she could catch us. Mama was at it every hour on the hour. "You can't give it a chance to take hold," she insisted, "you got to work steady at it." And Mama did.

"You can't even be sick in peace around here," Rose would grumble under the covers. But, somehow, under Mama's relentless purifying program we were soon well and out of bed. And when Papa was home we got up even sooner. He didn't say much but he walked around with that "plenty of time for resting after you're dead" glint in his eye and that said enough.

When Keeve's hands blistered and swelled to twice their natural size Mama called Doc Wiggins. Poor Keeve. It was a sight to see him pace the floor with his arms held high on either side, apelike, a look of agony on his face. And when Doc Wiggins arrived, twenty minutes after he was called, he started right off to heal Keeve's hands.

"You girls hurry out in the field and pick a passel of nice broad plantain leaves," he ordered quietly as he removed his jacket and rolled up his shirtsleeves. When we returned he was fixing a baking-soda solution in a large basin, dissolving the lumps with his fingers.

"Those are mighty purty leaves," he said, examining them carefully as he walked into the kitchen to wash them. Then, lining the basin, he said, "It's nice and cool. Put your hands in there, son."

Keeve thrust his swollen, itchy hands into the basin. "Oo-oh," he squealed, rolling his eyes in relief.

Doc felt it, too, and smiled. "How's it feel boy?"

"Good!" Keeve's voice quivered.

"Sure it feels good," said Doc Wiggins, placing his hands in the pan and gently applying the solution. For a full thirty minutes he patted the soothing mixture over the bloated sores. Every time the phone rang it was for Doc, but he continued to work on Keeve's hands as if he were free for the day.

"Just take their names and tell 'em I'll be toddlin' along as soon as I can," he told Mama, after the second call. And when he was satisfied the itching and the pain had diminished he said to Keeve, "Well, son, guess we can dry our hands. Now we got to get rid of that trouble-makin' pus before your hands'll heal up," he said, opening his bag and selecting a needle. "It won't hurt but a mite, but if it does, just you holler loud and I'll put a stop to it. You'll promise to do that, won't you?"

Keeve nodded his agreement and held out his hands as Doc pierced the blisters one by one, tenderly, fatherly, his face a study in concern.

"Guess y'won't be pitchin' baseball for a day or two, son, but t'won't be much longer than that. I give you my word on it."

The itching eased now, the pain relieved, Keeve looked up at Doc and smiled like an adoring mongrel, and Doc responded by rumpling Keeve's hair playfully. "Y're comin' along fine, young feller," he said, his eyes crinkling with humor, "y're coming along just fine!"

Mama, in her gratitude, stuttered her thanks, bestowing on him her highest tribute, nothwithstanding her success as a rival healer. "If we ever need to call a doctor again, God forbid, I'll know who to call!"

That's how most people felt about him, yet now and then there was a little grumbling. "My Ma'd be livin' today if t'weren't fer him. She passed away and him jest sitting beside her, not aimin' to do another blasted thing."

"What was ailin' your Ma?"

"He said her heart give out, but y'can't tell me she didn't have a few good years in her yet."

"That so! How old was she when she passed on?"

"Jest a mite beyond her ninety-second birthday. Ayeh, jest a mite."

Then one day Doc announced he was running from the second district on the Republican ticket for the United States Congress. This was the first big news the town heard, and word got around fast. Chris was the first to bring it to the stove forum.

"Didn't surprise me none too much, what with his gettin' on in years and workin' himself sick, nursin' and tendin' to folks from early mornin' till late at night. I reckon that old Doc figgered gettin' up in the pitch of night was for younger fellas now, and it was high time he was gettin' a little rest. Like as not when these polyticians asked him to run for Congress, he musta figgered it was the right sensible thing to do."

"Makes good sense to me," said Cabe Johnson. "Leave it to old Doc. He's got a good streak of Yankee in him!"

However, as time went by, the old doctor was eased out of the forum, slowly and unmistakably. Other events, other topics, hardly as notable, began to fill his place.

But one night when everyone had said what he had to say and an awkward lull ensued, the talk turned back to the Honorable Theodore Wiggins.

"Anyone heerd from the doctor since he became a distinguished citizen?" asked Cabe Johnson.

"Just a little hearsay here and theyah, hardly accountable and mostly rumor, I reckon, but if what I hears is the truth," offered Jeff Miller willingly, "old Doc ain't blazin' a trail of glory. I hear it's said around Washington that as a polytician, Doc's makin' a mighty good physician. The rumor is—and y'know the wicked way rumor starts spreadin'," added Jeff, well schooled in the art, "that Doc Wiggins holds some kind of record as bein' the only congressman who never once got up to make a speech on the floor o' the House."

"Well, if that ain't like the old Doc himself," said Cecil Jones, smiling broadly.

"Ayeh, that's Doc all right," chuckled Lem Merrick. "I can picture him settin' back, lookin' like he had all he could handle, jest listenin'." Suddenly aware of his shrewd perspicacity, Lem snapped his fingers. "He ain't nobody's dummy, no, b'jeez, he ain't."

The Democrats' choice for Governor, a sixty-eight-year-old retired dean from Yale, created more than a little stir among the stove forum's regulars. One night Lem pulled out a crumpled newspaper column.

"He might be a Democrat but you got to hand it to him. He's campaigning strong for pulling Connecticut out of the mud. With the back roads as they be now you might's well be drivin' through a sea of lava," he said, passing the newsprint around.

"Why not?" said Jeff Miller, now married to one of his hayloft playmates after a bit of gentle persuasion at the butt of a rifle held by Poppa. Four months later their first-born came into the world. "Ain't he runnin' for guv'nor of the state? When election time comes creepin' up you hears all kinds o' fancy idees."

"You call 'em fancy?" Lem looked up in surprise.

"Sure, they's fancy. We been travelin' these same roads for years. My old man traveled 'em, and his old man before him. What's good enough for them is good enough for me."

"Well, Jeff," said Lem, carefully tamping the tobacco in his pipe, "it's this way with me about them back roads. Havin' 'em or not havin' 'em ain't no skin off m'hide. I happen to live on the good old state road." Lem lit his pipe, puffing vigorously, and looking hard and straight at Jeff, he said, "And come to think of it, Jeff, so be you. It don't hurt none to sit here and shoot off when you don't much need to use 'em, but I reckon you'd be speaking from the other side of your mouth if y'was needing 'em.

"I ride 'em now and again."

"Ayeh. When you choose to ride 'em. Do you ride 'em fust thing in the early spring when the heavy snow's melted? Do you ride 'em when you're clean out of grain and feed or when the vittles is low?—Do you ride 'em when you got to get to town with yer twenty-gallon cans o' milk that gives you yer livin' if the road's passable or not? I reckon not. I'm tellin' ya, Jeff, it's like tryin' to s k a t e   o n   w a t e r e d - d o w n ,   ankle-deep c h e e s e. I know better'n most folks. I know because my team of hosses has pulled 'em out a-plenty and I don't get no spark out of money like that."

Lem continued to speak his piece and the men listened intently, with mixed feelings, getting up only to spit, order a bottle of soda or tin of tobacco. While it was evident they shared Lem's stand, first of all they were good Republicans; endorsing Dean Cross was tantamount to heresy. But they were honest men, forthright men, and Henry Talcott, a nearby chicken farmer, spoke for all when he said, his blood rising to his face, "Jeff Miller, if it was up to you, we'd still have the old Indian trails with its sloughs and boulders and stream crossin's. As fer me, I'm one good Republican that's votin' for Wilbur Cross. Trumbull's been around for three terms, and what good has he done the farmer? None, as far as I know and I ain't aimin' to give the Party another try. And let me tell'ya something else." Hank paused to refill his pipe. The men waited mutely attentive. "I heerd this here Wilbur Cross talking. I been to a couple of rallies over to Mansfield and Tolland, and y'shoulda heerd the way the folks whooped it up every time he come up fer air. I'm tellin' ya, boys, he ain't no Johnny-come-lately, he ain't no city boy professing his undying love for the farmer; he comes from good farming stock dating back to the old settlers, and b'God he stands up and talks like a good dirt farmer without no fancy airs, neither. It pushes right through his fine eddication like grass sprouting in the spring, an' I figger it this way. Here's a man that knows the farmer's cricks better'n anyone I know of, and he talks like he's aiming to do something to help out. I tell'ya we'd be fools not to—"

"I hear say," broke in Jeff, "that his only ableness lays in milkin' a cow or breakin' up a settin' hen, and nothin' more."

"Why, that's a mess of horse dripping's." Hank continued, as if uninterrupted. "Yes sirree, we'd be damn fools not to vote a man like him in office. We got to shake up them polyticians and they's hokey-pokey and we got to put in a man that'll do it, Demycrat or no."

The men sat silent as the air filled with acrid smoke. This was no Democrat speaking. This was Hank Talcott, vigorous Republican, steadfast Republican, coming from a line of Republicans dating back to Lincoln's day. And now Hank was the first to speak out for the Democratic candidate, Cross. There was no sound other than the awkward shuffling of feet, chairs scraping, the early fall winds whining outside.

Then Jeff Miller spoke again, carefully sidestepping Hank Talcott's declaration. "Mebbe y'got me wrong, Hank; I like good roads and good guvenment same as the next, but jest you put these Demycrats in and fust thing y'know they'll be levyin' head taxes and road tolls to pay for they's fancy notions. Good roads takes good money, y'can't deny that."

"Sure it takes money. Anything good takes money but y'can't turn back the clock of progress as easy as switching from Daylight time to Standard. And what's more, I'd like ya to name me one grangin' farmer wuth his vittles that wouldn't be glad to pay up when it means a saving of time and extry money in the long run."

"Could be y'got somethin', Hank," said Lem walking to the door. "Ayeh, could be y'got somethin'. We got a bellyful of the Roraback rubber stamp and it's clean time a few new faces come into the picture. Ayeh, Hank, wouldn't be surprised if I was with ya all the way." Lem winked his eye in approval and walked out the door.

On election day the state winked their approval and voted Wilbur Cross in office. And breaking all precedent, for three succeeding terms.

11

After Winter, Spring Will Come

That year spring came suddenly and sweetly after the long, cold winter. When Thoreau suggested, as a cure for melancholy, the first sight of brave spears of skunk cabbage pushing through the earth, he couldn't have known more rapture than I. The tight swirls slowly unfolding into broad green fronds were among the first signs of green life, and as welcome as an oasis in a barren desert. Fine, new grass, soft as baby's hair, was pushing through the moist earth, throwing a tinge of green over the countryside. Here and there a patch of dead, brown grass persisted, as if defying the new generation.

Spring came swiftly, fresh and full-bosomed. All about, the trees were pregnant with budding life, the air fragrant with perfume as if a mammoth atomizer of apple scent had been sprayed over the village from above. It intoxicated, it stimulated as champagne stimulates the senses and I burst inside with an unknown mysterious pleasure. At dusk, the overture to spring was augmented by a weird chorus of toads and crickets.

We had seen Coventry after the first flush of summer but never before had we witnessed the miracle, the vast wonder of nature unfolding day by day before our eyes.

It was strange, it was alarming, it was beautiful; it loosened awesome, fearful, wonder-filled sensations. It was an awakening, like falling in love, and I was left a little giddy by it all. Even the house seemed almost beautiful when the budding sugar maples draped their soft, leafy boughs about the stark outline of the old frame building. Even today the miracle of spring each year will never replace the utter magic of that first spring in Andover when my eyes all but popped from their moorings at each new discovery.

Keeve was excited, too, but in a different way.

"This is the life," he told Mama. "You can be self-sufficient, grow your own food, tap on nature's endless resources like the early pioneers and not have a worry in the world."

Keeve couldn't wait to begin tapping on nature's bounties and his first generous move was aimed at relieving the trees, which almost drooled their impatience, of their cumbrous store of sap.

"You start with your own crude materials," he said as he lost no time boring small holes in massive trunks big enough for reedlike spouts and bucket supports. "Now, Rose, Sarah, it's your job to hunt up every pot and pail in the house and hang them on the spouts. No use wasting time."

Rose and I scrambled into the house, dislodging every cooking utensil in the cupboards. Even Mama helped, and we all hurried out to fasten the pots and pans to the spouts already beginning to ooze sweet, watery, white liquid.

"This doesn't look or taste like maple syrup," said Rose wryly, licking her fingers.

"Of course not, kiddo, this is only the raw material. What we do with it makes the syrup."

The next day we collected several gallons of sap, which Keeve promptly poured into Mama's new wash boiler.

"Another day and we'll have enough to fill the boiler," said Keeve, hanging the empty vessels on the spouts again. "Old trees are the best sources of sap; they practically ooze with it. Y'know, it's hard to believe but we'll be getting sugar in its purest form right here on our own property," said Keeve, carried away with the thought.

Later, when all the sap was poured and the lid clamped on the boiler, Keeve said to Mama, "Now, all we do is let it boil and forget all about it. Gradually the water will evaporate and the sap will begin to thicken. When that happens the crystallizing stage has set in and that's our cue to let it cool. Then you get your sugar. It's as simple as that. Now—when we're ready to produce our own maple syrup, all we do is remove the boiler from the stove before crystallization sets in. It's so simple, any child can do it."

"Is that so," said Mama, duly impressed. "You can learn something every day."

We were never to know why, but we never did get our sugar. The sap boiled for hours and hours and in the end we salvaged less than a pint of watery syrup. Keeve shook his head dismally. "I read the directions carefully, but something must've gone wrong and I can't understand what."

"Don't worry, Keeve," consoled Mama. "Nothing ventured, nothing gained." And Keeve, buoyed by her understanding, said, "Anyway, I heard the trees dry up if you drain 'em every year."

Keeve avoided the subject of self-sufficiency from then on, and when we used maple syrup it came from bottles neatly stacked on the store shelves, labeled "100 percent pure" Vermont maple syrup.

A world of wonder had opened up that first spring. When we moved in it was late fall and too late to explore the thirty-two acres that came with the house.

But as soon as the snow vanished and the ground was firm underfoot, we set about exploring the land with hardly less fervor than a troop of Scouts on a treasure hunt. And as we tore our way through a maze of tangled vines, almost stumbling headlong into a rushing stream fully fifty feet wide, swollen with the weight of melted snows and spring rains, we felt the exultation Columbus knew when he saw the first dim signs of land. Trees and bushes and dense growth hid the stream from sight as if shielded from some unknown hazard. In our wildest imagination we never dreamed of a brook where we could wade and swim on hot summer days. Papa never referred to it. If he knew this in the beginning it must have slipped his mind, for he seemed fully as confounded when he came down to view our discovery.

Papa's eyes widened with pleasure. "We'll dam it up with stones to make it deep enough for swimming, and when the water is low enough, children, pick up all the little stones from the bottom and it will be smooth and comfortable just like Brighton Beach. When Grandma and Aunt Mary and the rest come out this summer, will they be surprised!" The thought filled Papa with an unaccountable source of pleasure.

We had dug into the grab bag and pulled out the prize of the season, we were certain. We were eager to cross the stream, but the swollen, tumbling waters made this impossible. Even the low bank areas were partly inundated and we were resigned to wait until the waters subsided to normal level. Instead, we headed in the direction of a wooded area adjoining the lower end of the stream. Another vast world of discovery lay in wait and we lost no time exploring it. Here, the woods were a gay profusion of wildflowers burgeoning sturdily in the shade of the towering locust trees, but what held our thirsting eyes was the abundance of delicate white petals on leafless stems, swathed in round, thick-lobed greenery, their stark delineation much like a Rousseau painting. Quickly, greedily we swooped down to pick them. But just as quickly stopped. An orange-crimson, sticky liquid spilled from the stems, sticking fast to our fingers.

"We got to be careful," warned Rose, "it might be poison." The next day at school, however, we learned with relief this scentless, exquisite wildflower, known as bloodroot, was the Indian's answer to a drugstore complexion—and quite harmless.

We kept on picking wildflowers, fascinated by the adder's tongue, deftly encased in long, tapered, speckled leaves, and its mustard-yellow blossom that looked like a tiny lily. Everywhere, like a blanket of rich velvet, violets in hues of white, lavender, deep blue and shades between, grew thick as grass and we could pluck a bunch with one frisk of our scooped hands. We picked hepatica, anemone, arbutus, forget-me-nots, spring beauties till our sweaty hands could hold no more and we returned home. Arranging them lovingly in small bowls and tumblers, we set them around the rooms like prize entries at the state fair. Mama was so overcome with delight, that every spring after that we filled her bedroom with flowers on her birthday—which obligingly came in May—until it looked and smelled like a funeral parlor. "It's the best birthday present in the world," said Mama happily year after year.

Another day we came to a thicket of tangled growth. "Wonder what's on the other side," mused Keeve as we tore our way through a maze of wild underbrush, Keeve tearing and breaking through the sedge until we passed through from behind. We continued onward for about ten feet, pulling twigs and leaves out of our hair and ears, when Keeve stopped suddenly.

"Just look at that," he said, his voice hushed with awe. Directly in front of us was a scene straight out of fairyland. A little brook no wider than a country road,

dabbed with sparkles of sun stubbornly pushing through
the shield of growth, rippled, no—gurgled quietly along.
Distinct, if faint music, spilled capriciously over stones
and pebbles as it made its way leisurely around the bend.
And above, gangling trees formed a protective overhead
like a huge mother hen. The whole picture was like a
scene out of Mother Goose; the crooked brook, the
storybook air. We watched, bursting with discovery,
knowing we would return one day to investigate the
quiet mystery lurking around the bends.

And we returned one day in late June when buzzing,
whirring locusts warned the heat of summer was upon
us, when the sun steamed down, drawing the fetus of
earth to life. Though planting was held up warily from
late April to early May when the ground would be safe
from killing frost, the earth was already bearing its
abundant yield, ready to be plucked by late July or early
August. Farmers knew when to ready the soil for
plowing, to begin cultivating acres of produce, or when
to water down miles of fecund soil.

In the early summer the heat was strong and the
plowing and the tilling and the sweating went on
rhythmically as the dawning of day and the falling of
dusk. On such a day we ran for relief to the gentle,
shaded brook. Tearing off our shoes and socks we
proceeded, slowly at first, to dip our toes cautiously
while our feet sought soft earthy masses along the
stony bottom, the coolness firming our wilted bodies at
once. Timidly, one behind the other, we waded upstream
expecting any moment our little world of mystery would
suddenly dissolve into the wide stream we called the
River. With every step, sharp little stones cut into our
tender, shoebound feet but we pretended not to notice
and continued on, following the bends and turns and
later, to our delight, wound up diagonally west of the
River.

"I'm sure no other human being explored this brook before," said Rose. "We're discovering it, I'm positive."

"Yeah," said Keeve, balancing a poise on a rock, "just like Ponce de Leon."

The sharp pricks, cheerfully endured as the excitement carried us past another turn, led us to a stretch of natural beauty. We stood there gaping, wanting for words. Before us, covering one side of the bank, grew a velvety deep green moss, as smooth as plush carpeting; on the other side, solid masses of lacy, feathery ferns, adorning the bank like a church altar. Around and above it, the rare jack-in-the-pulpit sprouted as commonly as field arbutus in the spring. Shielding this splendor like a line of defense was a succession of trees, an endless, winding corridor of trees.

Keeve broke the silence. "We'd better start back now," he said, his voice strangely soft. I promised Mama I'd hoe the garden today."

Turning back was not easy when every manifestation of nature offered new wonder, new promise, like sticking your hand in a ten-cent grab bag and pulling out a dazzling surprise. The peculiar, total effect of this beauty and symmetry was to instill in me a mysterious churning that vented itself absurdly in a bold flash of bravado. "Watch me," I said suddenly. "I bet I can walk back, stepping from stone to stone, without once touching the bottom."

"You'd better not try it," cautioned Keeve, "the stones are pretty slimy. I almost fell in a couple of times."

"Yeah," agreed Rose, "you better not try any fancy stuff."

"Who's afraid?" I airily proceeded to hop from one rock to another as Rose and Keeve walked determinedly ahead in an effort to ignore me.

Drunk with my prowess, I managed to keep directly

behind them, deftly spanning the wide gaps between rocks. The heavens, the sun, the air were but a pace behind me; the world and I were one. It was fun, it was exciting, but it was not easy. It took rapid appraisal of every slippery stone, instant decisive judgment; it took more nerve than fortitude and each jump left me breathless and panting. But I kept on, propelled by some vast hidden motor until we were but a few yards from the crude clearance where we entered. And just as I was about to hurl myself onto the last rock, the home-stretch rock, my foot slipped on the slimy moss beneath and I fell face forward, landing on my stomach in a most inglorious manner. I was seized with such pain I was sure the end had come. Not quite the end, for there was still sensation. Every pointed, jagged stone in the world had suddenly converged into the area of my fall and there I lay as flat as an Indian fakir on a bed of nails, convinced that every bone in my stupid body was either crushed or broken. I lay there too hurt, too stunned to move and then Rose and Keeve were beside me, hoisting me out of the brook, soaked and dripping. I glanced quickly at both hoping for an ounce of pity, of compassion, even brotherly, sisterly fear for my life. But not a trace of tender sorrow or pathos or sympathy.

All Keeve could say was, "Come on, trapeze artist, let's go." Rose said nothing but her look said enough.

I tried to walk, but a sharp pain in my ankle brought me down. "I can't stand up," I cried. "I think my foot's broken."

"Okay, then, hold on to our arms," said Keeve magnanimously, pulling me up again.

Mama watched this little trio in dismay as I hobbled into the house, my cotton dress plastered so close it was like being naked. To justify her panic, and perhaps to extort a bit of compassion from all, I was beginning to hope I had really broken something. But hope is not

often reality and the whole thing turned out to be one
big fiasco after all. It was only a strained ankle, and not
too bad at that. Rose muttered something to Mama
about "some kids" who were too smart for their own
good and my head buried itself just a little deeper into a
book.

A strained ankle hardly spelled finis to our
explorations. We owned thirty-two acres, at most we had
covered only four or five, and when the River subsided
to normal level and we could cross without hazard, we
ventured to the other side. We waited long for the
crossing but the long wait was not without its rewards. It
was like opening a gift box that arrived early with the
warning "Do Not Open Until Xmas." All about the earth
was fresh with virginal, natural splendor. There were no
roads or pathways to indicate human passage, and except
for a little wildlife—busy chipmunks darting from tree to
tree, rabbits scampering in and around bushes, birds
flying, nesting, singing—the land appeared untouched,
untrammeled. In the distance a wooded slope cascaded
ever so gently into a ravine like a Constable painting, and
we approached it with awesome respect.

Keeve was flushed with eagerness. "Just look at the
spread of those branches. Boy, what beauties! It'd be
a cinch to build a treehouse there." The old Benny gleam
shone in his eyes. "How about it, Rosie?"

Rose didn't share his enthusiasm. "How would you
haul the lumber across the River? It would take ages to
float and cart 'em."

"Maybe you're right. Anyway, we couldn't cross it in
all kinds of weather." Keeve shook his head wistfully.
"It sure is a swell spot, though." The thought of a
treehouse simmered for months and when he finally did
build one it was high in a maple tree so close to the
house you could stick one foot out and climb through a
bedroom window.

We walked past the woods onto a clear stretch of meadow, hurdling a stone wall and landing in a small orchard dotted with low-spreading juniper and wild cherry trees, its fruit green and raw. We could hardly envision the magic that would take place; that in a few weeks the limbs would swell with plump, winey cherries ripe for plucking. And that one day in August we would fill bushel baskets with this fruit, which Mama would empty into hand-sewn gauze bags, crush and tamp gently until the black-red juices siphoned off thickly into wooden casks and earthenware crocks where it remained until properly fermented and ready to taste.

Another day we followed the River bank and found it lush with swamp-apple blossoms. We broke off huge limbs of the fragrant, spice-scented blooms for Mama, who could be counted on to break into raptures over any growing thing from a bunch of wild mustard to a single, delicate rose. Perhaps the fervor was not always warranted but we basked in her warmth like a plant in the sun and kept on deluging her with new surprises.

We picked bouquets of a lacy, golden flower and rushed home to adorn the house and store with several vases of this strange growth that grew abundantly in the fields. When we learned, however, that this treacherously dainty weed called Goldenrod was the cause of the current hay-fever epidemic we abandoned it like the plague.

Climbing up a steep bank we came across a stretch of open field as smooth as a teeing green. With the scenic woodsy bank as background, it seemed the ideal spot to build a summer retreat. The thought simmered for years and shortly after our marriage, though green with inexperience, my young husband and I hauled mammoth twenty-foot-long six by sixes on a beat-up contraption that always jammed, and at long last laid the foundation. Willing and eager though we were, building a cottage

required more know-how than the book shelf my
husband built in his dormitory room at school. Not to
mention that final beam that laid me up in bed with a
sprained back for two weeks.

"Every man to his own trade," said Papa. "When you
can afford to build you'll hire a carpenter." It didn't
take much persuasion to make us abandon the venture
and leave the job of pioneering to those of more hardy
stock.

After the first two trips, Keeve's ardor for Nature
suddenly subsided. We then enlisted Mama to accompany
us on these exploratory excursions.

"Walking is the best way to exercise every muscle in
your body," she'd say, tripping over fallen trunks
spanning the river. "Follow me," she called as calmly as
if paring an apple, and we followed like ducklings after a
duck, awkwardly trying to keep pace with her nimble
dexterity. Only on the other side did we look back and
quiver.

Before that first full summer came to an end we had
explored every acre of land and found each square foot
of soil crammed with stirring natural beauty—woods,
fields, streams, brooks, rolling hillsides, wildflowers,
stone walls—everything suggesting the virginal
phenomenon of New England was concentrated right
smack within our thirty-two acres.

If there was blight it was man-made, and flowed down
from the paper mill into the stream. Pulp wastes
channeled directly into the adjoining river polluted the
waters with its reddish acids, and on those deceptive
days when the water seemed clear we plunged in for a
swim only to loosen rustlike particles clinging to stones
and rush them to the surface. We emerged like russet-red
Indians. During the summer, however, there were weeks
when the mill shut down, and then once again the waters
flowed clear and sparkling.

12

Live and Learn

By the indigenous nature of its stock and trade, the country general store seemed to exude a familiarity that drew people as to a warm hearth—good solid townspeople, passing transients. But there were others that would have a comedian collecting customer material had he clerked in our store for just two weeks. The horse trader, loafer, eager beaver, shrewd buyer, soft-talking welsher, the mark-it-down-on-the-ice-ha-ha deadbeat, the I-can-get-if-for-less haggler.

The Sunday customer who was a steady for a single loaf of bread after church, the kind that spent his paycheck in Willimantic the night before, then barked if we were sold out, "What kinda store *is* this—runnin' outa bread?" Or the customer with no place to go, "Jest moseying around," namely, the three thousand glass jars of assorted bolts, nuts and screws—only to decide he didn't need "nothin' much except mebbe a tin o' tobaccy. Got off early—no sense in rushing home, ha, ha."

Then the hilariously funny jokester, the violent

thigh-slapper who roared out windy blustering jokes with b'God's for punchlines. And outdoing the funnyman in brashness was the "familiar" type—the big boy who quickly made himself one of the family by virtue of bottled near-beer. Clutching the watered-down spirits, he'd burst into the living room with a breezy, "Hi'ya, Sarie, howdy, Rosie darlin', how be the world treatin' ya this fine morning?" This specimen was good for two or three hours of unadulterated boredom until we developed a system of bouncing. Rose would say, with no pretense at subtlety, "Hurry, Sarah, we'd better finish that job upstairs before Papa gets back."

"Oh, yes," I'd shout, "I almost forgot."

"Well, so long, Ed, see you again," we chorused, and as we flew upstairs Ed suddenly remembered the barn needed a coat of whitewash and he'd better get started on home.

Then there was the cookie gorger. "Wonder whut that tastes like," he'd say, prying open every hinged cookie window in the showcase. "Mmmmmm, mighty good-tastin' biscuits," he managed to chortle through a mouthful. "Sure makes a man wanta wet his whistle, sure brings on the thirst. Be a good girl, Sarie, and fetch me a nice cold birch-beer sody."

And the sampler. "Mighty nice crate of oranges y'got theyah. They's Californias, ain't they? Don't mind if I sample one, do ya?" He proceeds to peel and gulp one in seconds. "Can y'beat that! Y'never can tell a book by its fancy cover. It were tart and flat—not so good after all. But them peanuts now—they looks mighty fresh and temptin'." He shells a handful, wolfs them voraciously. "Yes sirree, they's purty good just as I had 'em figgered. Bag me half a pound."

Even worse was the deadbeat—the scourge of our business—who would pull to a halt at the gas tank and honk his horn noisily.

"Whew! Jest about made it. I clean run out. Might's well fill 'er up." And when we pumped the last gallon of gas into his wheezing contraption, he'd fumble in his pockets, first one, then the other, his jacket, the floor, the seats, under the seats, the side pockets, his face a mask of woe.

"Goddam if I didn't leave m' wallet in m' other britches. Now don't that be a durn fool thing to do! Guess there ain't no other way but t'put it down on the book until Wednesday. I'll come around then and clean it up." This kind was generally vague about the year.

"Charging" items where a reasonable profit was involved was one thing, but gasoline sales even over busy weekends continued to be a losing affair and until the day Papa discovered the parasite he blamed it on bad bookkeeping, a leak in the tank, evaporation, deadbeats.

Then one week the Gulf truck arrived on schedule with a full load of gasoline. Mac, the driver, hopped off as usual and walked into the store, and after a few pleasantries—he'd been delivering gas for years and was an old friend of the family by now—walked over to the door. "I'll fill the tank now, be back in a minute."

This time Papa followed him out. "Do you have a full load, Mac?" he asked quietly.

"Absolutely, Mr. Gallagher, positively, Mr. Sheen," quipped Mac. All three tanks ready to spill over!"

"You're sure?"

"Sure as I'm standin' here. God, Henry, you know me from way back. I've been treatin' you good and prompt all these years."

"That's right," said Papa, "but sometimes the best of us make mistakes." And then he did something he had never done before. He walked to the truck, hopped over the steel rail studding the tanks, unscrewed a lid, and inserted a long stick until it hit bottom. He pulled it out, looked at it carefully, then unscrewed another lid, this

time discarding the stick, and peered into the small
opening. He passed over the third. Instead, he jumped
down and walked slowly over to Mac, whose right foot
was busy building tunnels in the dirt. Papa waited,
speechless, as the driver put the last delicate touch on his
creation. He waited until Mac blurted, "I'll make it up
t'ya Henry, I swear to God almighty I will. Just give me a
little time."

Papa looked balefully at Mac, faltering for words. Not
a stranger, not a deadbeat, but a friend of many years
had betrayed him. "I trusted you like one of the
family . . .that you could do this to me . . . ."

"I don't know why, Henry, but give me a little time
and I'll make it up to you. Just give me time." Mac's
face was sickly white; rivulets of sweat ran down his
cheeks. "First it was Jenny's doctor bills, then shoes for
the kids, then my sick mother. Once I got started I
couldn't stop. But I'll make it up t'ya, b'God, if it's the
last thing I do." He wiped his face with the back of his
hand, then suddenly turned to Papa.

"Henry, I know I don't got no right to, but I'm going
to ask for your mercy. If the company hears of this I'll
be bounced on my ear . . . ."

"You don't have to worry about me." Papa extended
his hand and Mac clutched it, tears filling his eyes. After
that Papa complained no more of gas shortages and
everyone was happy to forget about the whole thing.
Especially Mac.

It took years for Papa to realize that sinking money
into the store was like trying to siphon a bottomless
well. Every dollar he earned in New York went to the
local creditors. And back he went each week to labor for
money he quickly spilled back into the store. The chief
reason for our insolvency was the person who charged to
the hilt, then suddenly stopped buying; the ledger was
full of such dead accounts. It worked this way. A

customer would order a week's supply of groceries.

"Y'better mark this down on the book." He fumbles in his dirty money sack. "Reckon I jest got enough to pay off last week's bill. This occurred week after week and somehow "this week's bill" never got paid. And Papa, always trusting, figured that one day the reckoning would come and extended more credit. Sometimes it came, most times it didn't and sad experience taught us the signs of a deadbeat. He'd appear one week, buy double the usual quantity of food, merchandise and gasoline, brandish his money sack flamboyantly as he paid last week's bill, and that was the last we'd see of him. The signs were clear, as clear as the scheming droop of his eye, but credit had been open to him and we watched, helpless to ward off the threat.

There were other reasons the store suffered, and here Mama was the chief offender. If a customer was out of work she'd supplement their meager food order with a "few little things for the missus"; a few little things like canned corned beef, canned salmon, a fresh ham, coffee, cocoa, canned milk, beans, rice, "chocolate for the kiddies," and whatever else happened to be within reach. "Pay when you can," she'd insist, shoving the merchandise into his arms. "Rome wasn't built in a day."

Keeve would scowl his disapproval. "No wonder we can't pay our bills on time. You hand out all the profit."

"It could be worse, Keevie. Maybe someday you'll realize that when people don't have enough to eat you stop figuring in profits and dollars and cents."

Providing free groceries was one thing, but the real scourge of the business was the phony who could pay and didn't, the type that thrived on Papa's reluctance to dun people. "If they can pay, why wouldn't they," he'd rationalize. "And if they can't pay, what's the use in hammering them? Give them time, they'll come around."

This remarkable attitude endeared him to every deadbeat, though in most cases Papa's faith in human nature failed to pay off. But sometimes it did.

One of the steadier delinquents who shopped regularly but paid rarely suddenly became the beneficiary of a modest legacy. We never classed Harry Ward as a deadbeat. He worked hard and long each day on the farm, and when he shopped we knew in advance he couldn't pay. But we extended credit anyway. Mama, no doubt, was the founder of the welfare state, for when it came to subsidizing, no one could beat her, insisting all the time that one day it would all even up. Even Mama was surprised by the news of the windfall.

When his creditors got wind of it they swarmed around his house like flies on a dungheap.

"Y'better go up and collect, Henry, while they's still somethin' left," advised Lem Merrick. The money's flying 'round thick as leaves before a northeaster. Better ketch some before they all blows away."

"Harry will come around now that he has it," said Papa. "He's a good man."

"Hah! Wouldn't bet on it if I was you."

A few weeks passed and Harry didn't show up, not even for his weekly order.

"One of the good boys," muttered Keeve. "When he's got money he stops coming to the store."

Papa was quiet but we could tell his faith was starting to waver—yet he stood firm and refused to hound him. When pressed for action he'd say, echoing Mama, "There's a time for all things."

And then one teeming wet day, when the fuss of the legacy had subsided, in strode Harry grinning as big as life and ordered his usual supply of groceries and staples. Little was said as the large order filled the counter, and when Papa tallied up the total Harry dug into his new money pouch. "Whut's it all come to, friend? Whut's this and everything else I been chargin' come to?"

Papa seemed startled at first, then he lit up as if a shaft of light had suddenly struck him. Slowly he pulled the worn ledger out of a counter drawer—no mistaking the relief, the satisfaction, as only a few minutes earlier the tobacco jobber left with a promise instead of a check. On this dark, dreary day Harry entered as if in answer to a prayer. Mama was right again. "Every day brings a new light," she so often said, trying to buoy Papa's spirits, and maybe her own.

Papa nervously flicked the ledger pages, added up the totals on the machine, tore off the stub and handed it to Harry.

"I didn't forget you, Henry, and I'm mighty glad I still got some to pay you off," he said, pulling out a sheaf of brand-new bills. "This is one account I enjoys settlin', I swear to God above. You was the only man in town decent enough to hold off badgering me." Harry's voice was low and husky. "No, sir, I'll never forget it." He shook Papa's hand, picked up his supplies and walked out.

"What did I tell you!" Papa rushed into the kitchen breathless. "People are decent human beings if you give them a chance."

"Well . . .I'll be danged," muttered the stove council.

We could count on a few out-of-towners to stop by regularly. By nature Papa was friendly and gregarious. He enjoyed being around people when he wasn't thinking up new ideas. All kinds of people; he liked everyone, saw good in everyone; a customer could count on a warm welcome plus a bonus account of Papa's latest invention, if he stayed long enough to listen. This irritated a few who stopped at a gasoline station solely for gas and oil and not a lengthy dissertation on flanges, elbows, ball-bearings and pattern-makers. However, there were

many who enjoyed it and these kept coming back for
more.

Whether a customer stopped in to consult his map,
pump air into his tires or make a purchase, he was
greeted by a one-man reception committee, the days
Papa was home. And he could buy or not; this was
incidental, but in most cases they filled up on gas and oil
and watered their radiators. Some came in and bought
tobacco, candy, sundries. Many transients we came to
know by name, like Ernie and Sally who stopped in
every other Saturday en route from Manchester to
Storrs—and by far the best-looking couple that set foot
in the store. Ernie's face was the kind that peers
seductively from Arrow-collar ads, tall, handsome,
immaculate, with a crop of thick blond hair just wavy
enough to make any girl's heart turn a double back-flip.
Not only handsome, gentle and well-groomed, but a
disposition as sweet as pure honey. Ernie had
everything—including lucky Sally, and in a few months
they were to be married. Sally was sweet and lovely, too,
but in a shy, quiet way. She never had much to say but
her smile was alight with warmth and friendliness.
Between them they made an irresistible pair.

In our household Ernie was the favored one. He never
commented on the weather, or resorted to dull questions
about school. Instead, he jumped to the heart of your
interest, which he managed to root out the first night he
came in.

"What's the new step today, Sarah? How's it go?"

If no other customers were about I proceeded,
bursting with pleasure, to show them the time step, the
double shuffle, a new ballet turn, or whatever I had
learned the week before. The floor bounced, candy jars
rattled, showcases heaved, but there we were, Ernie,
Sally, Rose, and I, tripping merrily "off to Buffalo" to
the jazzy strains of "The Darktown Strutters' Ball," or

executing ballet steps to the tune of "Nola," hoping desperately that no one would show up to spoil our cozy dance session.

When it was all over we laughed and gasped for breath. Ernie would say, "Girls, this calls for a treat," as he walked over to the counter to choose the best box of candy in the case, and the four of us gorged on chocolates until they disappeared. Before they'd leave he'd buy another for Sally, a ritual I looked to with sheerest delight.

Papa was in the store one warm Saturday evening when Ernie and Sally walked in; this time things were a little different. A swarm of youngsters were congregated in the living room viewing a silent cliff-hanger projected by cameraman Keevie. From the store, Ernie and Sally watched the movie, decently impressed.

The whole idea started some years back in New York when Papa returned from the movies one evening with a gleam in his eyes, an idea in his head and a strong determination. Within a few weeks a thirty-five millimeter camera, a projector and screen were delivered to the house. He explained the extravagance to Mama.

"See, Estherel, in this way I can demonstrate my machines intelligently for prospective customers. It replaces the valuable hours of labor I spend setting up machines and tracks for trial demonstrations." An exasperating thought for Papa who dreamed up ideas for the sole purpose of saving labor.

Keeve was enterprising even then, though he was still in knickers. "We could buy a dozen reels of film and start a moving-picture house."

"What kind of nonsense is that? I have enough headaches right now," said Papa firmly, and the venture was ended. But he did concede to buying a few old reels. "It's better than going to public movie houses." In due time he picked up several rusty reels removed from the market for months, maybe years, at a ridiculously low price—six films which we played over and over until they were as familiar as favorite tunes. We never tired of them and by now we had memorized the printed dialogue in every scene.

Word has gotten out and every youngster this side of Bolton Notch and Columbia was lured by the free movies. And on "movie nights" the store was jammed—the kids loudly demanding their favorites—Charlie Chaplin in "The Star Boarder" and a melodramatic thriller titled "The Bangs Burgler." Boos were loud and long when the faithless, scheming heroine appeared—boos that lasted throughout much of the reel, between splices.

Every break in the film—and this came every two or three minutes—added to the fun. "Here it comes, here it comes," they cried gaily, and Keeve was ready with his splicing equipment to mend the torn film with some obnoxious glue smelling of banana oil. Occasionally the mending held firm and the kids cheered as if he'd batted in the winning run in the World Series.

After each performance the kids yelled for the pièce de résistance, a formidable family production entitled "The Family Picture," which Papa filmed soon after he purchased the equipment. This unique tidbit drew the most laughs and sometimes the youngsters doubled up on the stairs, holding their sides—simply because it was so grim and unfunny. It was, as the title implied, a family picture, with Papa running off with triple honors as cameraman, director and producer. He carefully posed the family and a visiting uncle who plastered his hair for the occasion. Mama combed her pompadour ever so neatly, finishing it off with a jeweled comb; she knew what was coming. So did Uncle Joe and Keeve, but they forgot to let the rest of us in on it. Rose and I stood rigidly as if posing for a snapshot—a "cheese" smile frozen on our faces for most of the agonizing reel. I couldn't imagine what was wrong with Mama, who kept bouncing two-year-old Franny on her lap while she laughed and talked with Uncle Joe. Keevie, too, kept moving foolishly, drawing himself up stiffly to a militaristic position, first saluting Mama, then Uncle Joe, an action which unleashed a playful fervor in my uncle who suddenly started to tickle me under the chin in an obvious attempt to make me laugh. I obliged by giggling nervously, for by now it seemed that everyone was acting strangely—worse yet, was going stark raving mad. And so it went through fifty feet of film. Except for one shot—an adorable, full-screen closeup of blond, curly-haired Franny laughing joyously—the entire reel was a fiasco.

This classic produced the usual spontaneous hysteria and it was no different the night Ernie and Sally walked in. Boys and girls were piled three deep on the stairway that led to our attic bedroom. Others crowded around the banister. At least thirty kids were enjoying the family spectacle, noisily supplying dialogue, direction. "Salute now, Keevie," "Tickle her under the chin," "Make her laugh." When at long last THE END was flashed on the screen and the lights went on, in walked Ernie with two cartons of Hershey bars and passed them around to the squealing kids. He slipped two bars in Rose's pocket, gave her a little hug and walked back to the store and Sally.

Perhaps not as glamorous, but just as steady were the two fishermen from Columbia who never failed to stop on their way home with a trunk load of fish.

"Here comes Mutt and Jeff," Rose would say, spotting their Durant convertible and a miscellany of rods dangling from both sides and the rear. One was tall and thin, like a prize Texas stringbean slightly tapered at the ends. His hip-length boots fell halfway between his knee-cap and crotch and he looked like a leaning flagpole divided down the middle. The other was short and squat, his rubber boots halted by the sudden jut of his buttocks. His arm muscles, in harmony with his well-defined rear, bulged as if continually flexed; his general appearance was one of enormous strength and he walked about heavily like a stunted Goliath. But they differed only in stature; when it came to creating yarns about the big ones that got away they were alike as identical twins.

Each week we heard a new story and we listened patiently, politely but unbelieving.

"I tosses my minnowed cane pole into the water, waitin' there as usual for a nibble when suddenly—ask Ben here if it ain't the truth—there's a jerk on the line. I starts in to reel and reel, and mind you, at the end of that hook is a black beauty a good four foot long. I calls to Ben who laps it over and collars me from behind so's I don't fall flat on m'face. I keeps on sweatin' and reelin' an' haulin' for a good twenty minutes, yes sir, it was fish agin man, when all of a sudden I'm flat on my face and Ben here atop o' me. That sleek beauty outdone us jest when I'd swear I had 'er. Y'never seen anything so purty . . . .Ayeh, she sure was a beauty—mebbe five feet—"

"Do you like fish, ma'am?" Jeff asked Mama the first time they stopped in.

"Oh, yes, it's good brain food," said Mama. "If I could get it fresh we would eat it often."

"Ma'am, if you'll step outside a minute, mebbe we can accommodate ya." They brought Mama to the rear of the car, opened the trunk to a mess of trout—shining, sparkling, sweet-smelling. Mama drooled. "What beautiful fish—and so fresh!" There was nothing that Mama liked better than fresh fish—that is, before the new order set in. In New York she rarely bought it, but she never stopped trying. First Avenue fish vendors regarded her exhaustive inspection as a personal slur on their integrity. "Wattsa mad, Lade? Puta down, puta down. Alla de fisha fresha today—if you no like, no buy." Indignantly, Mama would drop the limp, green-gilled flounder and leave, her nostrils burning with the stench of decay.

"I brought home too many spoiled fish before I learned my lesson," she'd tell Papa. "Now, before I buy I smell it, then I look under the ears. If the gills are firm and reddish I know it's fresh."

When Mama viewed the gleaming mess of fish her face lit up like a boy with his first catch.

"How many can you spare?" she asked quickly.

"As many's y'can handle."

Mama looked again at the long, plump, glistening trout, and hesitated, like the little boy who was offered as many ice-cream sodas as he could do away with at one sitting, knowing well his capacity.

"If you could spare three . . ."

"Only three? Ain't enough to choke on, ma'am," said Mutt, baling out eight slick beauties over Mama's mild protests. "Jest be sure to store 'em in ice."

When Mama offered to pay they laughed heartily. "We give it all away, anyhow."

"You give it *all* away? Don't you eat any?"

"Eat it! Truth is we hate the stuff."

"You hate fish—and you go fishing?"

"Whut's eatin' fish got to do with fishin'? Best sport there be."

When Mama insisted on paying, Jeff agreed to accept it in trade. "Guess we could do with a bit of refreshment. A coupla plates of ice cream'll do it." And when Mama augmented this on their way out with two well-packed quarts of ice cream Jeff said, "We're gettin' the best end of the deal." But Mama insisted she did and everyone was happy.

It always pleased Mama when Tony Venetti stopped in. Tony barely spoke English but his warm grin spread eloquently over his face and into his eyes, and when he had something to say he managed it with the help of expression, deep laughter, earnest gesticulations and a word thrown in here and there for show. Always, in his husky way he'd begin, "I no spikka good Eenglessh buta you know watta I mean," and he'd continue to laugh and grunt and slash the air with his short brown hands until we guessed what he meant.

The early part of one summer Tony told Mama a long story about "chamotz" and "cabooch," and each time he came in he'd gesticulate and shake his head and say, "Ah, the chamotz and cabooch—ah—ah" and laugh his pleasant throaty way. We never understood what he was talking about but we knew it was important to Tony and we agreed knowingly and said it was fine and we were happy he had it, hoping desperately he wasn't complaining about his gall bladder.

Then one day in August Tony walked in with a small basket of superb tomatoes and a mountainous head of crunchy, green cabbage—the luscious seed catalogue variety. He was beaming from ear to ear—and that was a good distance—as he gently removed the vegetables from the basket and placed them on the counter. He chuckled softly. "How you lika de chamotz and cabooch?" he said, proud and shy like a small boy, his chin sweeping his chest back and forth.

"Beautiful! I never saw anything like them before. How do you grow such fine vegetables?" And Tony smiled gratefully, knowing she was speaking the truth.

"Hada good luck, a lidda horse manure, a lidda rain and sunshine—and uppa dere." Tony pointed to the heavens as he made the sign of the cross. And though Tony worshiped at no cathedrals, a more devout man there never was.

"Take!" he said pushing the produce toward Mama. "Is for you." And Mama took and made the mistake of offering to pay. In a tone, quiet with hurt and dignity, Tony said over and over, "No, no, no; is for you"—vigorously fanning his hand in front of his sober face.

Tony lived by himself in a little shack close to the depot and worked as a track walker for the New York, New Haven and Hartford Railroad. In all kinds of weather Tony started his lonely vigil at midnight—to Bolton Notch and back—alerted for loose ties and fallen debris, his eyes glued punctiliously to the tracks. This was Tony's main job but he took on two others at the same time—carting mail sacks from depot to post office—and never in all the years that he worked there did he miss a train. The third was more a labor of love than a job and he drew no pay. Every night before taking off as vigilante of the tracks Tony was on hand to help his crippled neighbor, Charlie Foster, over to the little depot where he worked the night shift as station agent. In the morning he was back, wide awake and smiling, ready to help Charlie back to his house. When Tony slept, nobody knew. "Issa notting," he'd say in his husky, kindly way, "issa notting."

Tony worked a worthless, hilly piece of New York, New Haven and Hartford Railroad property by special permission. It was a steep hill close to his shack that the kids used for sliding in the winter. When the rains came in early spring his seeds were washed away as quickly as he planted them. Yet he persisted in sowing, spading and cultivating the hilly rows, sweating and straining like an overworked horse until one day a bit of magic started to take root.

When Mama saw this piece of land she was dismayed. "Work our field, Tony, the ground is good," she said over and over until he consented. And the next summer

his "chamotz" and "cabooches" and red-hot peppers
grew and thrived even more in our fertile field. "Itsa
good, itsa vera good," beamed Tony.

Everyone knew why Tony worked so long and hard;
everyone knew he was saving his money to build a house
so that he could send for his wife and children in Italy.
Tony labored many years for the fruition of this great
event and one day his grand plan started to take form.
He bought a small triangular slice of land directly across
from the railroad depot—the scorched remains of the only
hotel Andover knew—and there Tony began to mold his
dream into reality. The plot was small, and smack in the
center of town, the bulk of it stone foundation, and the
local wiseacres defied him to build anything but a
monstrosity atop it. But Tony heard nothing and day by
day he put his sweat and heart and money into that
house until it turned into an edifice of love, down to
the last shining coat of white paint. There it stood,
waiting for the warmth of a woman and a strange, grown
family to bring it to life.

While Tony was building the house he took time out
to work on the pint-sized plot surrounding it. In a few
months, tangles of grapevine crept along ugly, massive
railroad ties forced deep into the earth, as poles, and in
little more than two years the grassless plot took on a
bit of lush of old Italy, spiced by a piece of rugged
America—namely, the New York, New Haven and
Hartford Railroad.

One day when the monstrous six-by-sixes were softly
hidden by vines hung heavy with leaves and clusters of
superb, winey grapes, Tony was seen walking up to the
door stuck from disuse. His strong body, buoyed with
unconcealed well-being, heaved vigorously and the door
jerked wide open. But Tony was not alone this time.
Beside him, like a scene from a movie script, were his
three grown children and full-bosomed wife. Tony waited

until they entered the house, looked heavenward a
moment as if in prayer. Then he walked in slowly behind
them, closing the door softly but firmly . . .as if he'd
done this a thousand times before.

We were settled in the creamery for more than a year
when one day Mama went down to charge Delco. But
she didn't get far. When she reached the middle landing
that turned into the basement she stopped short—the
cement floor was flooded. Mama knew at once that zero
temperatures had frozen and burst the water pipes—and
Papa had just left for New York that very morning. She
hurried back up; there was nothing to do now but locate
a plumber in a hurry. As she was thumbing through the
telephone directory George Merton walked
in—good-humored, ruddy-faced George who was equally
endowed with good health and good old-fashioned
know-how, and all the town knew it. He stopped in
often with his lovely wife, Sara, who was beautiful on
the inside as well, and we got to know them better than
most.

At the sight of him Mama dropped the telephone
book and smiled with relief. In a few minutes George
was down in the basement working away at the water
line. There was no shortage of tools and pipes since Papa
had equipped it as a second workshop for idle
moments, and two hours later he walked up, his rubber
boots wet to the ankle.

"Guess you'll have no trouble for a spell. Lucky the
mister had plenty of pipes and flanges around," he said.
"Now just be sure to turn off the water every night. It
gits mighty cold down there in the cement basement."
And as an afterthought, "no, ma'am, they'll be nothin'
to worry about."

Mama was brimming over with good feeling. She
thanked him over and over, blessed him and his entire
family, and for the occasion threw in a couple of fitting

proverbs like "As you sow you shall reap," and "Virtue is its own reward," then got down to essentials.

"Now what do I owe you, George?" Her relief was so great, if he'd named the contents of the cash register she'd have turned it over happily.

This wasn't the first time he helped out when Mama was alone. When a car pulled up for gas on a cold day he'd rush out to the pump, urging Mama to stay inside and keep warm. "This weather ain't for women-folk," he'd say, turning up his collar. Or when a customer would walk in with an empty five-gallon kerosene can, he'd snatch it from his hands and fill it at the hand pump near the door. And many a time when a farmer drove up for a sack of chicken mash or cracked corn, he'd help hoist the hundred-pound feed bags on his buggy or truck. He was known to leave his work, his fields, if help was needed in a hurry and he could be counted on as sure as the coming of day. He was a gentle man and his earthy breeding shone through like a new suit of clothes.

"How much do I owe you for all your trouble?" Mama repeated.

"Well—" said George as he looked about the store appraisingly, "guess a nice bag of cookies'll do."

"Bag of cookies?" echoed Mama. "Sure! Now figure out what I owe you."

"I did, ma'am," the farmer said in his high robust voice. "A nice bag of cookies'll do me fine."

"You don't mean that!"

"Ayeh, I reckon I do," he insisted cheerfully. "While you be fixin' the cookies—mix 'em up if t'ain't no bother—I'll go out and warm Lizzie. She takes a heap of crankin' these days."

I was behind the tobacco case stacking up a fresh supply of cigarettes. Mama quickly looked around, figuring out some way to pay him. She then picked up a twenty-pound brown paper sack, filled it with the choicest variety of canned goods, packaged candy and tobacco we stocked.

She waited as George walked up to the counter, his breath steaming from the cold, and then she pushed the bag in front of him. "Thank you again," she said, her warmth exuding like an open hearth.

George picked it up, felt the weight, looked inside the sack and slowly laid it down, a smile lighting up his sky-blue eyes. "Whut in God's name you got in theyah?"

"Just a few little things for you and the wife."

"That's mighty kind of you, ma'am, but that ain't what we bargained for. Just a bag of cookies. That be all. And as mama looked on speechless he proceeded to empty the sack of everything but the cookies. "Much obliged," he said walking out, "they's a mighty fine mixture in theyah."

"A fine man," said Papa when he heard of it. And for Papa a fine man meant the ultimate in human virtue. If at that very moment George had chosen to ask the supreme test, to see the blueprint of his latest invention, which he regarded as the United States government guards the Mint, he would have agreed, albeit wincingly.

13

A Spade's a Spade

One bright Saturday morning Judge Younger walked in the store and went directly over to Papa, who was checking stock in auto supplies. A visit from the Judge was a rare occasion.

"Henry, raise your right hand." Puzzled, Papa did as he was bid. The Judge continued slowly, the lines about his eyes wrinkling with good humor. "Do you solemnly swear to uphold the Constitution of the United States, so help you God?" Papa was still puzzled, but who would refuse to uphold the Constitution? He said, "I do." Stroking his little Vandyke beard thoughtfully, the Judge shook Papa's hand.

"Henry, you are now qualified to hold court." This was Papa's swearing in as justice of the peace. No one was more surprised than he.

In a weak moment Papa agreed to have his name put on the ballot for justice of the peace—the only nonpolitical office in Andover—and your name on the ballot pretty well meant victory. But soon after election he'd forgotten all about it. A new idea was brewing and his energy was diverted into sketching designs for the pattern-maker. Politics was a minor concern.

Word of the swearing-in got around and that evening when the stove forum congregated the talk got around to Papa's sudden new calling.

"I only hope I don't make too many mistakes." Papa's tone was sober and concerned, the burden of justice heavy on his shoulders.

"What would you really do if a thief was brought up before you?" Rose's face sparkled with mischief.

Papa was silent a moment. "I'd give him another chance. Everybody deserves another chance."

"Ayeh, Henry, that they do," agreed Lem Merrick, "every sinner deserves another chance."

Then the talk turned to Judge Younger. "Ed's the best garl-durned judge in the state," said Cabe Johnson, "even if he be a Democrat. What's true is true."

"That's a fact," said Lem, "why, he was head of his class at Trinity College and the best man with figgers they ever turned out. I hear nobody since equaled his record as a mathematician."

"It's mighty true," broke in Cecil Jones. "The college asked him to stay on and teach but he was set on reading the law just as his daddy did before him."

"It ain't no secret he refused plenty of them honorary degrees because it'd cost him ten dollars to rent a cap and gown." Cabe shook his head fondly. "Never was a man for cermony, no sireee."

"And he never took a fancy to automobiles neither," said Cecil. "Fought them off for as long as he could get away with it and then he got what he calls a "one-lung" Cadillac. Says it took him anywhere he wanted to go but hardly ever got him back." The men laughed heartily. "Sounds like Ed Younger all right."

"He's got a powerful sense of humor. Don't know where he gets his ideas. Imagine calling his cats Remus and Romulus and Simeon P. Baldwin."

Cabe looked amused. "That what he calls them? Now who but Ed would of thought of that?"

Homer Briggs spoke up for the first time. "It sure tickled me when I heard about his pet squirrel. Florence, he named her. Slept in his trouser pocket most of the time and one day when he was entering court he put on his official black robe, reached in his pocket, and there was Florence sleeping peacefully. Think it bothered Ed? Not a whit. He went on and held court as usual, extra careful not to wake her."

The stove forum concurred completely in their respect and admiration. There were no dissenters when it came to Judge Younger, Democrat or no.

A week later his daughter, Ruth, invited me to her home. I went filled with expectancy, for I was deeply in awe of anyone lucky enough to live in a trim white clapboard house unattached to a store—especially unattached to a store. Once before I had stopped in briefly and my eyes widened at the sight of floor-to-ceiling bookshelves. Only in libraries had I seen such an abundant display of books, and when Ruth offered to lend me her treasured *"Oz"* books my day was complete.

Today I would be visiting Ruth again and maybe I'd be invited to select another *Oz* book to take home and read. I arrived early in the afternoon and there was Judge Younger in his bare feet reading aloud to Ruth from what looked like a massive volume of history, and Ruth listening intently. Whatever he was reading came alive with immediacy and I too found myself listening until Ruth saw me. She jumped up from her chair. "That's all for now, Daddy." But Daddy didn't hear and kept on reading.

Again Ruth protested, but her father continued, pretending no one had spoken. Crooking her finger for me to follow, she ran outdoors; but the Judge, still

reading, trailed after her. This little tableau was
enchanting and I giggled with delight. The Judge winked
at me and went back to his reading. Then Ruth
scrambled up an appletree and the Judge perched himself
beside the trunk, raising his voice so she could hear. It
was so dear and so funny Ruth laughed and called down,
"Oh, Daddy, you're crazy!" Daddy feigned
disappointment and walked away.

We all looked forward to the fall after the apples were
harvested, when Judge Younger would order a fresh
barrel of cider from Mr. Kimball who owned the cider
mill. The cellar was lined with wooden vats in all stages
of fermentation—sweet apple fresh to cider vinegar—and
the Judge was known to taste with savor from several
barrels before drawing a pitcher that had just the right
degree of sharpness.

Before the ritual of rolling the fresh barrel of cider
into the basement he drilled a hole in the bung and Rose
and I and all the neighboring children queued up on
his back lawn to sip and suck from straws of dried
day-lily stalks growing profusely along the stone walls.
We reached from a pile of varying lengths, short ones for
the full barrel and longer ones as the cider drained,
formed a line, sucked until we were sated, then took our
place at the end of the line waiting for another round.
This went on until we could drink no more, and with a
flourish of mock ceremony the barrel was rolled into the
cellar.

A few townspeople appeared rarely, maybe two or
three times a year. These were farmers who kept close to
the land from sunrise to sunset and only showed up
when their produce was ripe for trade, or to stock up on
"victuals" like flour, tea, sugar, spices, coffee, tobacco.
They produced their own supply of milk, butter and
eggs and there was plenty of chicken when the hens

stopped laying; they grew their fruits and vegetables for year-round storing and smoked and cured at least the sides of two pigs each fall.

Ollie Wesson was one of these. Anyone could spot her way off in her one-seater buggy as it plodded slowly up the hill from the underpass. She was short and heavy with more muscle than fat and her dress never varied, always the same beat-up, wide-brimmed straw hat, the same stained cotton sweater buttoned up no matter what the weather. In the spring she wore men's felt boots encased in rubber; in the summer she eliminated the felt.

Ollie was well in her sixties, yet her skin was firm and leathery, not soft and crepey as with other folks her age— more a mummy-like parchment that almost crackled when she spoke. The only deep lines were in her neck and these were made deeper by ingrained dirt, especially in the summer when she reeked of stale sweat and essence of barnyard. If we learned one thing from Ollie it was a new kind of breathing control.

But that wasn't all we learned. If Ollie was short on cleanliness she was long on profanity. She wasn't our only source but she deserved a four-star rating. We heard many choice words from motorists changing flats and pumping tires—free air was something new and few supplied it—but Ollie needed no motivation, it was part of her vocabulary like "and" and "but". The first time she reeled off a few expletives, Mama said no decent person, not even a stevedore would talk that way. The second time Mama said nothing, and after awhile we'd listen with more amusement than tolerance.

Ollie never showed up during the winter season, but three times each year when the vegetables were ripe for picking she'd arrive in her one-seater piled high with seasonal produce. Her first trip was in the early spring when the peas were ripe and the asparagus was ready for cutting. The stalks were packed upright and tight in her

willow basket. Not stringy, long-stalked grass full of
waste, but tender spears cut three or four inches from
the succulent tops.

"Don't believe in foolin' the goddam public," she
explained forthrightly. That same night Mama would
steam a mess and serve them with chunks of sweet
churned butter oozing down through the savory mound.

The early crop of peas was delectable, too. Pods
packed with peas the size of agates were full blown, and
so uniform and perfect in shape, they seemed to have
passed through an assembly line; even cooking never
affected their sweet flavor and we often ate them raw
like candy.

In the summer Ollie's buggy was laden with cabbage,
stringbeans, squash, corn, beets, carrots. With the
exception of Tony's, her garden truck grew bigger and
better than any around, and she defied anyone who
refused to buy, so proud was she of her yield.

It happened that Mama worked a small garden patch
and produced much of our summer vegetables. A believer
in fresh air and sunshine, she welcomed the hour she
spent there each day. But when Ollie got through with
her singular sales technique, Mama either forgot her
garden or lost the heart to bring it up. In a town where
everyone produced his summer vegetables, unloading
produce was as easy as selling cord wood during a heat
wave. Yet Ollie managed to do it.

The first time she stopped at the store she hitched her
buggy to the gas pump. Keevie ran out quickly. "Will
you please hitch 'er to the tree? Someone might drive up
for gas."

Ollie complied good-naturedly. "Okay, okay, boy, I do
that, I do that." She patted the horse's mane fondly.
"Gasoline won't do you no good, eh Prince?" There was
love and warmth in her eyes, a warmth that only shone
when she spoke to her horse or to Nellie, our beautiful

collie dog.

"Anyone who takes to animals like she does must have a good heart," said Mama.

Then Ollie turned back to the wagon and crisply went about the business at hand. She filled a shallow basket with samples of her vendibles; a head of cabbage, two tomatoes, two ears of corn, two potatoes still moist with fresh earth, and a few plump stringbeans. Each a beauty in its own right, they might have been specimens at the county fair; nor were the samples any better than the bushel baskets of produce in her buggy. Ollie thrust the lot directly on the counter when Mama started to say, "Good morn—" But Ollie cut in.

"You the new folks who bought out the old creamery? Mighty pleased t'meetcha. I says to my old man I has to meet the new folks, mebbe they'll be like Horace Fripps. He never turned down Ollie's produce. No sirree, he never did." Ollie babbled on without yielding. She picked up the head of cabbage and thrust it into Mama's hands. "Feel!" she ordered. "I got goddam good cabbage today, the best in Tolland County. You fix a barrel of good sauerkraut from goddam cabbage like this."

"You're right," said Mama, easily convinced even by a low-pressured job, "it's beautiful. Good and heavy, too."

"Y'betcha life. When I grows a head of cabbage I grows a head of cabbage—no lettuce leaves, mindja." Ollie snatched the cabbage from Mama's hands and picked up a tomato, which she turned from side to side as a jeweler displays a diamond to a prospective customer.

"Never seed tomatoes like this, I betcha life. Here, take a bite, you never tasted sweeter ones."

Mama bit into the tomato obligingly. "They really are delicious, and so sweet," agreed Mama, impressed. Ollie watched and glowed. "I ain't out to kidja." She snapped two meaty stringbeans that fairly oozed. "Ever seed stringbeans like 'em?" Mama admitted she hadn't.

"You must use plenty of fertilizer," said Mama.

"Don't know nothin' about this here fertilizin' business. I jest use plenty goddam manure and hoe 'em up good."

When Ollie left, her buggy was empty and the next two days we sat around the kitchen table shredding cabbage, salting it away in two huge earthenware crocks; we canned bushels of tomatoes, corn and stringbeans which we enjoyed well into the next winter, until Mama read about a family felled by botulism after eating a jar of home-canned spinach somewhere in Montana. The remaining vegetables were thrown into the dump. "It's best not to take chances," said Mama.

For fifteen years Ollie had been coming to the store, and over and over we heard in varying degrees—and anyone else who might be listening—the intimate details of her life.

"I got eight okay kids. They works hard on the farm and a couple of 'em work on the state road and they turns their full pay over to me every week like a clock. I ain't no mean grabbin' woman but I gotta collect the pay from the kids to keep the farm goin'. My sunuvabitch husband don't do nothin' but sit around on his ass all day long readin' the Bible. When his face ain't in his book he's givin' orders like a sunuvabitch foreman and beatin' the kids. Well, what d'ya think of a man like that? To hell with him, I says." For fifteen years we heard this with spicy variations.

Then one day Ollie walked into the store, a cold Saturday in November when she had nothing to sell—a strange time for Ollie to appear with a buggy empty of produce. Mama and I were busy opening cartons of groceries and placing them on the shelves. Ollie slammed the door behind her, rattling the panes. She spluttered and steamed like a defective boiler, her face livid with rage.

By the tone of her voice I knew Mama was startled. "What's wrong, Mrs. Wesson?"

"Plenty . . .plenty is wrong. . . .I took it long enough—now it's the end, I tell ya, the end. I gotta divorce the sunuvabitch, I gotta divorce 'im. Shoulda done it years ago. Now I can't take it no longer, I ain't young no more. Ayeh, shoulda done it years ago."

There was no mistaking Ollie's anguish as she let loose a string of epithets that could put a mule driver to shame. She kept on cussing, and rambling, then suddenly her voice lowered as she turned from me and spoke to Mama.

"D'ya know why I'm mad as a buzzin' hornet?" And without waiting for Mama to answer, she said, "I jest got off the train from Hartford where I went to see this lawyer feller. And d'ya know what he tells me?" Never was Ollie more bitter, more indignant. "D'ya know what he tells me!" she repeated savagely. "He says I gotta marry the lazy bastard before I gits me a divorce. Marry! Now what d'ya think of that? I'd ruther be shot dead before I'd marry that good-for-nothin' bum."

We never saw much of August Kleppinger, who lived two miles from the village, one mile in from the state road. August was well along in years, but he was agile and spry and could pound a nail along with the best, rarely turning down a job.

Every month he came in to stock his dwindling supplies and each time Mama was ready with a job or two. Sometimes a board in the floor that needed patching or a front step that pried loose, or a grocery shelf buckling from overweight. Whatever it was, August went right to work repairing the trouble spot, always turning out a first-rate job. Often Mama would say, "I hope August Kleppinger shows up early this month, the window sash is stuck," or, "We could use a new pantry shelf." And so each month we looked forward to his coming.

In time Rose and I got to know well his tiny one-room cottage. Many times Mama had sent us over when he was laid up with rheumatism or bronchitis, or when he hadn't shown up for his monthly trading. She'd pack a basket of food and a quart jar of hot soup and send us out to him, for she knew that August came when he was able.

This was one trip we were eager to make, for never had we seen a setting so delightful, so different. His little dwelling resembled a doll house, and his landscaping a child's wonderland. Set on a slight elevation, the cottage was surrounded by garden beds precise in their symmetry; the lawn was fine and thick and closely cropped. Two tiny chicken coops and a woodshed that looked like a doll's playhouse bordered the lawn. And hemming it all in like one neat package was a stone fence unlike any other anywhere around. August had built it with the skill and precision of an artisan, chopping up several huge boulders into small jagged stones. It stood two feet high, and when the sun shone it sparkled like a huge jewel. This was all that August owned and he had given it his time, his care and his love.

The first time we visited, he showed us around his little property with the pride of a collector. "This," he said fondly, pointing to the chickens and the shepherd dog trailing him, "is my small family, and a mighty good one, too."

"It's like a doll house," said Rose, entranced, "and you keep it neat as a pin."

August smiled and his face warmed up. "And why not? Reckon there's plenty of time on my hands and a man's got to do somethin' when he's past his workin' prime."

Rose hesitated, then blurted out, "Mr. Kleppinger,

aren't you afraid of living here all by yourself and so far from the main road?"

"B'gosh, Rosie," laughed August, "whut does the likes of me got to be afraid of? Ain't got no money or jewels."

"But—don't you get lonely?"

"Well . . .reckon I do, a mite." August looked into the hills as he spoke. "Sorta creeps up slowly sometimes and I starts t'thinkin—now what's an old buzzard the likes of me doin' here all by m'self. But it don't happen much. Like as not when I'm feelin' a wee bit sorry fer m'self somethin' turns up to let me know that the good God Almighty is up there lookin' after me. Come t'think of it, now, that's jest how it was today. M'rheumatism was actin' up, and first thing y'know I got t'feeling sorry for old August. Then d'ya know what happened? Well, I hears this light rap on the door and hobbles over to open it—as if the good Lord heerd my prayers—well, as I was sayin' I hears this rap and hobbles over to open the door, and standin' there is two of the nicest little girls comin' to visit an old man."

We were back in the little house, emptying the basket of food; the Mason jar of soup was heavily insulated with newspaper and still warm. "God bless your Ma," said August huskily. "Now how can an old man be lonely when folks is thinkin' of him?"

One day in midwinter, August walked into the store with a deep, bronchial cough. Mama brought him back into the kitchen, removed his mackinaw and poured a cup of coffee. "Something hot will help," she said, placing the steaming brew on the table. August drank the coffee slowly, wheezing with each mouthful. "Figgered I better hoof it to the village before I gits good and laid up. I know an ailment's comin' on when I get to feelin' stiff and sore all over, sorta like a warnin', and I starts fixin' m'self up for a spell in bed." August's voice was tired and labored and Mama knew he was sicker than he let on.

Before he left she prescribed a few of "nature's remedies." "Drink plenty of hot raspberry tea," she said, preparing a small sack of dried berries. "Take it before going to bed, it'll bring on a sweat. And drink plenty of liquids tomorrow to wash the impurities out of your system." Mama walked into the store and returned with a bottle of pine, honey and tar cough syrup. "Don't believe in bottle remedies myself," said Mama, "but if your cough hangs on you might take a spoon or two. You're all by yourself and can't afford to take any chances." She continued, as if to one of her brood. "Don't forget to do this and in a couple of days I'll take a walk over to see how you're doing. Better get well soon, Mr. Kleppinger, we need you around here. A couple of jobs are waiting on you."

August laughed weakly. "With all this doctorin' up, I'll have 'em fixed in no time."

But two days later, the day Mama promised to visit August, we awoke to a raging blizzard. All night the state road truck droned back and forth, sweeping the road, but the snow fell steady and thick, all but obliterating human effort, while a weird wind piled it high against the house. Across the road the snow swept high in front of the Town Hall's doors, and the tiny brick building that housed the town's records looked like the belly of a huge snowman. It was so far the heaviest snowfall, and frightening in its shroudlike beauty.

Mama looked out dismally. "Oh, my, today I promised to visit Mr. Kleppinger."

Keeve shook his head. "Today's out, that's for sure!"

Mama said nothing but kept looking skyward in search of some telltale signs to assist her.

"When will it stop?" Rose pressed her nose against the

misty glass. Mama shook her head anxiously. "I can see nothing . . . only snow. Her voice lowered to a whisper. "The old man is sick . . .it might be days before the plows reach him."

And as we watched the soft thick flurries piling up, fascinated by the clean, quiet desolation, as we stood there entranced by the spectacle, Mama suddenly said, "Children, take care of things. I must go out."

"Go out!" cried Keeve, "Why, that's crazy! Just look at it coming down!"

"That's why I must go, Keeve. The day he was here the old man was sick, too sick to carry enough supplies. I promised him I'd be around today. Can I stay home when I know that?"

"But what can you do?" Keeve was upset. "If you'd wait, maybe the snow'll stop, then you can think about it some more."

"Sometimes when you think too much about little things they grow bigger than their size." Mama tried to sound light-hearted. "Do you think I'd be foolish enough to go if I didn't think I could make it?"

We all implored her to stay, but we knew her mind was made up and there was little we could do but watch her as she dressed slowly and carefully with the same eye for detail Admiral Byrd might have exerted for a trip to the South Pole. Completing the outfit with a pair of rubber boots left from Horace Fripps, she started toward the door.

"I'll see you in a few hours. Don't worry about me, I'll be all right, I promise you."

She plowed her way through the driveway, tunneling, scooping, until she reached the freshly cleared state road, stopped to brush her coat and stomp her feet, then she was off, walking briskly down the road and through the underpass—and out of sight.

"In clear weather the trip takes about three hours,"

said Rose. "One each way and one to visit."

"We'll give her double that," said Keeve. "Maybe she'll make it in five. You can't tell . . .she may get a lift part of the way."

But in three hours we glued our faces to the window. There had been no let-up—the snow continued thick and settled heavily; the winds pummeled the drifts to fearful heights. And the minutes ticked away painfully.

Rose's voice wavered. "She won't make it. She won't." Don't be silly, Ro, she'll make it okay," said Keeve, turning away. "She still has plenty of time."

"I'm not waiting any longer," said Rose. "I'm going to call Ned Mobley. His truck can make it through the snow."

"I tried a few minutes ago but the phone's out of order." Keeve pursed his lips thoughtfully. "But we'll figure something out, don't worry."

Rose brightened. "I have an idea. We'll stop Kenny Fredlund when he drives by with the snow plow."

"Good idea, Ro. He'll go after Mama."

The strain relieved, Keeve fed the kitchen stove a couple of split logs. "Say, Ro, how about some supper? Mama'll need something hot when she comes in," said Keeve, more himself. "And you, Sarah, keep your eyes open for the truck while I go down and start Delco."

Cheered by Keeve's confidence, his brisk orders, Rose rushed into the kitchen and started the familiar clatter of dishes. In twenty minutes the table was set, the water boiling and hot canned soup pushed to the back of the stove to keep warm.

Though my eyes smarted from the blinding snow I kept a diligent watch at the window. All was still except for an occasional car driving by in gear, and the clanking of broken chains that pierced the gloomy silence like a wail in the night. The day stretched endlessly and now it was growing dark.

Delco sputtered out and again Keeve was down in the basement. "Yell if you see the truck," he called up.

The winter darkness spread quickly and nothing but the dim gleam of headlights breaking through the snow could be seen. Worse yet, it was now difficult to distinguish a passenger car from a truck from any distance, no matter how close. My fear, moderately concealed until now, broke through. What if the snow plow drives by before I can stop it? I thought desperately. For the moment the safety of Mama depended on me and I felt like the little Dutch boy with his finger in the dike. The glass pane was thick with the moisture of breath and tears and I cupped my hands to my face so that Franny, playing close by, couldn't see me.

Lurid visions of Mama sinking in the snow, numbed, exhausted, with nobody to help only heightened the misery. The snow continued to pile heavily . . . .Mama could easily be covered in minutes and lie there to die. Where was that snow plow that passed with monotonous regularity when you didn't need it? Where was it . . .where was it? I cried out to myself.

Another frightening thought gripped me. What if Fredlund, tired of the driving, blinding snow, had retired for the night? I heaved with muffled sobs. And my concern turned to anger. Why did Mama go? Did she think more of Mr. Kleppinger than her own children? I'll never forgive . . .

At that moment a feeble turn of the doorknob brought me stumbling to the door. There stood Mama, a picture of frozen exhaustion, her lips parted, her face blue with cold, the look of strain you see on the face of a cross-country runner.

Suddenly we were all about her, attacking like Liliputians—Keeve pulling off her boots, Rose and I removing layers of soggy clothing, Franny filling a bucket of cold water to soak her frost-bitten feet. Mama was too faint to talk and the four of us flitted around nervously, tripping over each other, trying to make her comfortable. Keeve and Rose proceeded to massage her hands gently and every minute or so, in plain delight, Rose bent down to kiss her head.

When Mama was sufficiently thawed she smiled weakly and said, "It was good, children . . .it was good I went. August will be well soon."

But Rose hardly heard. "Why did you go, Mama?" she said, tears in her voice, "why did you go?"

Mama drew Rose's face close to hers.

"Now what would Bernarr Macfadden say if I missed my daily constitutional?"

Rose burst into happy laughter and Keeve and I joined in from the sheer relief of it all. Mama was beginning to feel better. Everything would be all right. It was a good warm feeling.

14

Never Praise a Ford Till You're Over

Always, things happened without warning. Since there was little we children could do about it, we plunged into the thick of it, sometimes willingly, mostly protesting.

Like the time Papa decided to raise the roof—not the simple, angry outburst variety, but the real McCoy, and we barely cleared out of the attic room before it started. One bright and sunny morning in July at the ungodly hour of six, Rose and I were troubled by a faint but persistent wheezing, tapping, hammering, almost as if—perish the thought—people were pulling the roof apart. A weird dream, I told myself as I turned over, settling into sleep again. But sleep would not come; those strange noises seemed to be persisting and I pulled the covers over my head. I wasn't dreaming, it was now evident, and I trembled with chill though the morning was warm.

By now I was attuned to all sorts of clamor—noisy New York and the deceptive quiet of Coventry. Especially that first night in Andover that turned all other tumult into the purrings of a kitten.

"Only a five-minute walk to the depot," said Mr.

Fripps when he sold Papa the property. He failed to mention—and Papa didn't notice—the railroad underpass only a few hundred feet from the house. But Papa was impressed, we were impressed, and I tried to impress my New York cousins with our proximity to this remarkable fact, though it never had the impact I hoped for.

That first night we were terrified by a piercing wail that could come from no human being, and all too soon we got to know the warning whistles of freight trains approaching station crossings. Assured the world was still intact, we lay silently, listening to the rattling of freight cars passing by. Sometimes they screeched to a halt, and from the engine to the caboose there echoed a jerking, clangy clinking.

Anything after that seemed as tranquil as a field of daisies, yet these peculiar, unfamiliar sounds were bewildering, and stranger yet, they seemed to get closer and louder.

"Sounds like someone is tearing down the house," I mumbled to Rose, and as I said this my eyes were drawn, as if magnetized, to a large jagged opening in the roof, baring the early morning sun and sky. Still drowsy from sleep I jerked myself up, too dazed for comprehension.

"Someone *is* tearing down the house!" I screamed in panic, jumping out of bed, clutching Rose to save her from destruction.

Rose grunted her annoyance, turned over and stretched, feeling around for the covers I thrust on the floor. "Darn it! The carpenters are here."

"Carpenters!"

"Yeah. Papa said something about starting the second floor today."

"You didn't tell me," I said gloomily.

"What's there to tell? It's not *that* important," Rose said, as if tearing down roofs was standard operational procedure.

Dismantling a thirty-by-fifty-foot roof turned out to be no simple matter. Even for Mama, an ardent fresh-air disciple, the "clean, fresh air" we breathed for two weeks was more than she had bargained for. Aside from the thorough air-conditioning we endured, the house took on the rawness of a Maine lumber camp. Nor was our comfort increased when old Ned Raney, the carpenter in charge, would say, prying off shingles one by one, "I may be slow, but by God, I'm sure."

What he was sure about we weren't certain. As it turned out we were two days away from becoming the community swimming pool. That we were in the midst of a seasonal drought, he took as a personal dispensation from heaven. "God looks after sinners!" he'd say, looking skyward each day.

A roof-lifting was by no means an everyday affair, and "open house" was slapped on us in more ways than one. Each day customers beat a path through the sawdust to view the progress, generously sprinkling advice and counsel. And dear Papa, eager as he was grateful, revised his sketches daily until the final drawing was an architectural masterpiece of what a blueprint for gracious living should never be.

"Seems to me a low pitch is called fer, whut with the height goin' up eight feet," said one.

"Long as yer buildin', might's well shoot the works and put plenty of rooms upstairs. Could come in handy," said another.

"It'd take a special boiler room to heat the new floor. Best to close it off good'n tight and fergit about it."

"Beaver board makes fair to middlin wall siding...good and cheap, too." This we learned soon enough to our sorrow.

Papa was even less partial than selective. Happily he blended a bit of everyone's advice. Result: twelve small, unheated rooms, "closed off good'n tight." So good, in fact, we froze in the winter, and in the summer during the height of day, sweltered under the low peak of stored-up heat.

At night, to our great relief, the change was sudden. The cool New England air breezed through the multitude of windows and sleeping was sheer delight.

My architectural know-how was even less than Papa's and I was delighted with the profusion of rooms. For the first time we luxuriated in the privacy of our very own bedrooms, and compared to our earlier quarters this was the Waldorf-Astoria, for now there were rooms for the family and many to spare. One we labeled "clothes room," which Papa equipped with steel bars the width of the room, ample for the family's wardrobe. Another, the "storeroom," substituted for the rummage space of an attic. Still another, my "dancing room," Keeve equipped with stretching bars he sawed off a maple tree, and except for a portable Victrola, a few records and pictures of dancing stars tacked on the walls, the room was empty. We polished the rough flooring with beeswax and here I practiced every day. The cubicle we dubbed "office" was hardly big enough for the outsized rolltop desk and chair.

"At last," Papa sighed, "we have a place for our friends and relatives. Now everyone can come and be comfortable."

Word got around fast, somehow, and the turnover of our guest rooms may well have been the envy of every second-rate hotel in the borscht circuit.

During the roof-raising I was suddenly catapulted into the roles of waitress, cook, chambermaid. It happened one day when two good-looking young men walked into the store. Papa was scooping a handful of ten-penny nails from the bottom of a barrel.

One of them addressed Papa. "Could you use some extra help, sir?"

Papa eyed them intently. Help he needed and desperately; one of Mr. Raney's helpers was laid up with a sprained ankle. But for a moment he hesitated. Blazers and knickerbockers were certainly not working garb, by any stretch of the imagination. Nor did their urban bearing suggest any characteristics of the local swain; in every way they looked like college boys on a holiday.

"You boys had any experience?"

Quickly they exchanged glances. "We think we can handle anything you might require of us," the taller one said quietly.

Papa looked down at his bruised, taped fingers—a carpenter he was not. "You can learn," he said, "you look like smart fellows." Then out of friendly curiosity he proceeded to question them about their hometown, their destination, their reason for working. But their responses came slow and studied, vague and evasive, and when the tall blond one introduced himself as Tom Brown, and the shorter one as Jack Smith, you suspected they were a couple of aliases by the way they deliberated before answering. This, Papa seemed not to notice. Suddenly he said, "Well, boys, let's see what you can do." There was more talk about pay, room and board, working clothes and getting on the job at seven in the morning. It was now past two o'clock and Tom said, ever so politely, "Do you think we could get a bite of lunch?"

"You didn't have dinner yet?" Papa was appalled.

The noonday meal was dinner, the evening meal, supper. Lunch was something cold and dry you carried to school in your dinner pail.

"We lost track of time," said Tom, shuffling his feet.

"Well," said Papa grandly, "we'll fix that up in no time." When Papa said "we" it meant he, she or they. "Nobody goes to work on an empty stomach around here." *"Sarah!"* boomed Papa, spotting me behind the candy counter where I pretended to be working. "Fix these gentlemen a good meal and make a fresh pot of coffee."

Mama was out in the garden weeding. Rose was nowhere to be seen. There was no question about it. I was IT.

Until now my culinary prowess was limited to singeing chickens over an open flame and hard-boiling three-minute eggs. But when Papa ordered a job done, there was no getting around it, you went ahead and did it. There was something in his voice that made you feel mentally retarded if you didn't, so I scurried in and soon found that I could—and did. So well, in fact, I became Mama's official kitchen helper for the rest of the summer.

Tom and Jack turned out to be good company and we all adjusted quickly to the strange idea of boarders and more work. Their wit and humor more than compensated for the heavier load, yet there was something in their demeanor that troubled me. While never at a loss for subject matter, they rarely mentioned anything about their home life, and when they did it was so vague as to be spurious. Sometimes Mama brought it up but they artfully avoided the subject, and one time when I called Jack, though he was no more than six feet away, he didn't answer. When I called again he turned abruptly as if suddenly remembering something. It seemed a little strange but in a few minutes I'd forgotten all about it. Another time I said to Tom, "Golly, isn't it funny, your name being Tom Brown. I'm reading *Tom Brown at Oxford* right now."

"I'm not *that* Tom Brown," he said lightly, as he and Jack exchanged glances.

Yet for all their good fun there was something in their on-and-off manner that boarded on the mysterious. I kept my doubts to myself but they constantly plagued me. What, I shuddered, would we do if these boys were in trouble, were hiding from the police? No—it couldn't be true . . .it must not be true. These were good boys . . . my imagination was running wild. I wanted so to believe in them. And then when I contented myself with this thinking, I'd suddenly come upon them in animated whispering, and at my appearance the conversation would come to an awkward halt.

When they were on the job but two weeks Papa said, "They're fine boys. It was a piece of good luck the day they walked into the store." And two months later Papa bestowed on them his highest praise, "They know how to put in an honest day's work." The thought of this helped to drain my suspicions.

Then one day after the midday meal, Tom and Jack walked into the store to pick up a few Hershey bars as they often did before returning to work. Adjusting their seats on a couple of nail kegs they'd rolled against the wall, they sat quietly munching away at the chocolate as Rose and I were bagging Russell Sykes's weekly order. And just as Russ carried the last sack of supplies out the door, a chauffeured slinking black Rolls-Royce purred luxuriously up to the store.

There was something about liveried limousines that made you feel like Cinderella at the stroke of twelve. I looked down quickly at my favorite blue-checked gingham. Only that morning the crisp, starched tiers of ruffles which I'd eagerly pressed the night before stood out like tiny balustrades around a hacienda. Now it suddenly seemed soiled and wilted and I slunk behind the counter.

"It's your turn to pump gas," I called to Rose. But Rose felt it, too. After a harried inspection she carefully adjusted her white middy blouse and navy blue serge skirt.

"If you take this one, Sarie, I'll take the next six in a

row."

"Okay," I said, as much touched by the term of endearment as the plea in her voice, not to mention the princely munificence of the trade. I was about to walk out when Tom called, "What's the fuss about girls? I'll go out and pump it."

"Guess he doesn't want gas. He's coming in," said Rose as Tom jumped up—and just as quickly stopped, as if glued in his tracks. By the drawn look on his face it was apparent that something was up. In seconds the tall, immaculately groomed gentleman was in the store.

They stared at each other; an electrifying spark of communion passed between them.

"Glenn!" The man's voice shook.

I turned, expecting a stranger, but it was only Tom. Then suddenly the light dawned; like parts on an assembly line clicking into place, the little intrigues, the hushed whisperings suddenly began to make sense.

As the two shook hands, holding back the tears that rimmed their eyes, they fell into each other's arms, embracing quietly. Rose and I looked on the emotion-packed scene like gaping intruders, too shocked for words.

The next thing we knew Tom was back in the house, talking soberly to Jack as they packed their few possessions. All those wonderful weeks dissolved in minutes as Papa, back in the store, was figuring out what he owed them.

Then Tom was saying good-bye to Mama in the kitchen. "Now it's out and you know—we ran away from home. It's like a load's been lifted from my shoulders." It was easy to talk to Mama.

"You're such a fine boy, Tom, what made you do it?"

"Dad thinks I'm the family misfit because I like working with my hands. He lit into me once when he caught me taking apart the generator of my old runabout. 'Leave the tinkering to mechanics,' he said. 'Don't waste your time fooling around—your future is cut out for you—one that will secure your place in society.' He meant working in his bank, of course."

"What is so terrible about that?" asked Mama softly.

"I want to do the work I feel I'm cut out for, and I'd like to get there on my own."

"Did your father know this?"

"Yes, but he never paid any attention to it, figuring I'd grow out of it. Anyway, one day he found me tinkering with my jalopy again and he blew his top."

" 'Get rid of that piece of junk and report to the bank first thing in the morning!' I'd never seen him so furious. 'Either you do as I say or get out—one or the other,' he said. "He left me little choice and I was too proud to stay on—well, you know the rest."

"What do you know!" Mama was still overwhelmed. "But what about Jack—I mean Dick?"

"Dick and I met in college. We're two of a kind. Only one horrible difference, according to Dad. He lives on the wrong side of the tracks; his father's a carpenter and that makes him an untouchable in Dad's caste system. Perhaps now you understand why we ran off."

"I think I do, Tom." Glenn was still too new for comfort. "You're a fine young man and so is Jack. I knew it the first day you walked in."

Tom gripped Mama's hands and held them. "Thanks." He faltered a moment, turning his face. "Thanks for everything." It's meant a lot to me and Dick being here; we've felt happy and useful for the first time. You've been like a mother . . ."

Mama was misting up. "Keeve and the girls will miss you, Tom. We all will, I think you know that. You and Jack are good boys and someday we'll hear big things of you. You know the old saying, 'Good fortune is the comrade of virtue,' and someday I hope you'll be back to tell me it's true." For a full moment no one spoke, then Mama in an effort to mask her feelings, pursed her lips and said genially, matter-of-factly, "How does your father feel now?"

"He seems a bit more mellowed. He's even agreed to let me switch to engineering this fall, providing," and Tom laughed lightly, "I don't try any more 'childish stunts.' I'm still not sure whether he's waving the red or white flag. Guess I'll always be his little boy," he said, a shade of resignation creeping in.

A deep and warm friendship resists plucking as stubbornly as deep-set taproots. Each knew this leavetaking to be a somber finality, and each knew the other was bantering with words, attempting to hide the void gnawing in his heart. And then suddenly, as if to firm the hold, Tom's arms were about Mama and he was kissing her cheek. "Good-bye, Mama...and thanks." The words came out naturally, easy, though he had never called her Mama before.

Every few days when Ned Raney complained of his "rheumatism kickin' up" he'd suddenly take leave, and work on the upper floor all but slowed down to a standstill. He'd say, "I feels the ailment comin' on and I gotta go home for a spell and rub my joints with the ointment." This meant smearing a Raney concoction of goose grease, honey and wax into the painful sore spots. "Be back in the mornin' . . .works like a charm, lubricates every gnarled, tooth-achin' joint in m' body." This left the near-sighted Walt Wickham on his own, which resulted generally in chaos and disorder, and work the next day consisted of dismantling and re-doing. "Don't believe in arteefishal doodads like them theyah eyeglasses," said Walt one day as he crashed through the freshly laid, quarter-inch beaver-board wall.

The day Tom and Jack left, progress halted. Raney was home applying his ointment and Walt was nursing a smashed thumb. "Drat these fool nails, they makes 'em smaller and smaller."

A few times in desperation Papa prevailed on Cabe Johnson and Clyde Smith to lend a hand though they were busy working their farms. Now that the boys were gone it was clear that new help must be wooed at once or the construction would go on forever. Tom and Jack had worked out so well, Papa was on the lookout for other itinerants, expecting the same level of competence and ardor. But when work lagged seriously, Papa welcomed anyone—even an old man walking in one day asking for a cup of hot coffee and "rib-stickin' vittles," and except for the duffel-like bag slung over his shoulder, nothing about him suggested a vagrant. It was clear he was old by the shock of fine, white hair that capped his head like an Indian topi, but the startling disparity of a browned, leathery skin freshly shaven, the skin of a hardy lumberjack, seemed to give him an odd, ageless aura. His coarse shirt and trousers were rumpled with heat but spotlessly clean, and the jacket over his arm was neatly folded; not the slightest trace of a down-at-the-heel drifter. The strange totality of this figure conjured up visions of a deck-swabbing, seagoing jacky, and we were not too far off we soon learned. Many strangers passed this way and many stopped in but there was something different, something compelling about this trim, spry oldster.

Papa sized him up swiftly. As the old man was finishing his second cup of coffee, feeling in his pocket for his change pouch, Papa, in a gust of decision, offered him work.

"Work?" The old man looked up warily. "What do you have in mind, Captain?"

Papa quickly explained his troubles—Mr. Raney, the unexpected withdrawal of Tom and Jack. His voice took on a note of entreaty.

The man quickly withdrew his hand from his pocket.

"How long you suspect it'll last?"

"A couple of weeks. Maybe three."

"Well—mebbe I'll give it a try for a coupla weeks," he said, stroking his face in thought. "But not much longer—still tryin' to straighten out these crooked old sea-legs." Slowly he wiped his mouth with the back of his hand. "You really be needin' an extry hand?"

Papa assured him he did.

"Mebbe we can make a little deal. You need me—and to tell you the plain truth, Captain, I need you. Could do with a little extry seaweed in my pockets. Ayeh, mebbe we can do each other a bit of good." The decision came quickly.

Though Papa was more desperate than discerning, that night when we slept a new boarder we unwittingly slept a first-class craftsman who would more than earn his room and board and "seaweed."

Ned Raney was still home nursing his gout, a circumstance that pleased Dan immeasurably, for now he could take over—and this he did with the vigor of a foreman long familiar with the job. Walt came in the next morning and despite his sore thumb and the constant tearing down and dismantling, work progressed at a decent speed. And strangely, under Dan's skillful hands he did little bungling.

Each day Papa watched wide-eyed, contributing his share of labor, and Dan lost no time sizing up the finished work under Raney. "Should've put a good four or five extry feet under that roof pitch; it's sure goin' to suck that sun." Then he promptly deplored the workmanship, the no-account planning, the grades of lumber. "Christ sakes. The kitchen stove burns better timber than this here driftwood. You buildin' a barn or a house? Any lubber knows that first-grade lumber don't come gnarled up with loosened knots. It's like a sailor not knowin' a scuttlebutt from a poop deck." Dan was now head man and he lost no time issuing orders like a sailing master. Partitions were ripped apart, joists replaced, mitering torn out and rejoined, much of the beaver-board scuttled.

"The solid work don't show up like the trim. It ain't meant to any more than a line of strake; it's the covered up job that builds a house or rigs a ship, and keeps it runnin'."

Every time Dan uttered a new dictum, new lumber, new supplies were hauled in, and Papa said not a word but looked on contented as a cat with a litter of kittens, continuing to pay the mounting bills.

Papa's experience with skilled craftsmen was not new. "You work more like a pattern-maker than a carpenter." This was high praise from Papa. "And with many years of experience."

"No mistakin' that," Dan said with no trace of humility. "An' no wonder. Been a mighty fine cooper in my day. But I tell ya, Skipper, it don't come from schoolin'. Began swabbin' decks on a merchant ship since I was a tender lad of fifteen, and over the years one bloody thing led t'another and I find myself riggin' vessels, apprenticed to a mad sea-dog that hacked to pieces everything that waren't perfect. But he learned me good. Built many a small vessel and cruiser that's still choppin' the waves. Aye, Captain, vessels still as sturdy, as solid as the day they was rigged." Dan's voice trailing nostalgically, ended in a mist of silence.

His coming was a boon to Papa since his work was by far the best, and just as important for Rose and me, his yarns—utterly weird and unreliable—were delightfully amusing.

"Ever heerd of mermaids?" he asked one evening, between customers, when we were sitting on the store porch.

"Yes, but they're not real," Rose said. "Just a fairy tale."

"Not real? Christ sakes, the only ones I seen was

real."

"You sure you saw them?" Rose's eyes narrowed.

"Why, Rosie, my girl, jest as sure as I'm sitting here in the town of Andover, Connecticut, I seen 'em. Reckon you don't believe it but let me tell you how it come about," he said, wiping his brow that suddenly broke out in a sweat.

"This morning we was laying around the deck of the trawler Myrtle. Never a day so blazing hot—and the sea without a ripple—like a pane of glass. We was in a hot, dry spell and every day steamed hotter than the one afore it; the lubbers sprawled out like they was massacred, drunk from the sun and mebbe a little liquid tonic. Never felt heat like this. Never. Even the birds above looked ready to drop. I'm telling you it was sizzlin' hot. Then near about mid-noon there was this rumblin' in the skies, rumblin' that waren't rumblin', but rumblin' that was music. Was you ever you so hot and thirsty, not being near water and then of a sudden you find y're on top of a clear, crystal brook—a brook that's singing. 'Have a drink, have a drink,' like a mirage in the desert. Well, that's the feelin' that run through our groins when we heard this here rumbling. Just a bit of rain to cool, we prayed. Not for no one to hear o'course, but pray we did like sinners.

"Do you suspect we got answered? You betcha land lubbin' boots we did. Like nothing we never seen before! The rain bust out like thunderbolts; in no time at all it waled into a gulley-washer. Every blasted hand lit up and scuttled down into the hold to keep from drowning. Never—never in my days did rain pelt so hard on that old hulk; it lashed the fore, it lashed the aft until we looped up and down like a horse on a merry-go-round—all the time ladlin' up the sea like a fifty-gallon scoop. Ayeh, the storm were as hard as the sun were hot—and it kept on slashing and slopping with no let-up. I tell you, Rosie, it near washed us down into

Davy Jones's locker." Dan stopped to catch his breath.
"It sure did," he said, wiping his brow again.

"Then about the time dusk was setting in, the lashin'
stopped of a sudden and the soakin' was over—jest as
quick as that. Every lubber on the trawler scrambled up
from the hold and began balin' out water a foot deep,
thanking the God Almighty. They was smack in the
middle of this when one of 'em hollers out, 'Flyin' fish,
flyin' fish!' Dan thrust his right arm skyward. "As sure
as I'm sittin' here, them fish—the biggest I ever seen,
hopped up from the ocean like a diver comin' up for air.
Beauties they was, smooth lolloping beauties springin' up
all around us.

"You know what a sight like this can do to a young
troller sailin' his first vessel? When I sees these fish with
winglike fins leapin' out of the sea and into the air, I
stood there rooted to the old bucket, watching and not
believing. No, Rosie, not believing any more than you
young'uns sittin' here. Figured the sun was hotter than I
calculated and I was plumb crazy."

Dan lit a pipe and settled back against the
clapboarding; there was a strange far-off gleam lighting
his face, and as he drew brisk, vigorous puffs he eyed his
audience closely. Then he continued.

"As I was sayin'...I was staring at this
wonderment—and by now the sea were a gentle
ripple—rooted to the spot when my eyes was drawn, like
magnetized, to this one fish far out in the northing, a
fish so whalin' big it made gimcrack of these other
beauties. So sure I was seeing things, or mebbe dreaming,
I struck my head with both fists, tryin' to wake myself
up. Just then I heerd shouting from the lubbers and
they's yelling like in frenzy, 'Mermaids, mermaids, the
lady fish'! I was still staggerin' from the blows but I up
and cupped my eyes on this here fish out in the
distance. Dusk was settlin' quick and the early darkness

made it hard put to see clear, but I kept lookin' out there, straining my sights till I was ready to bust, and sure as I be sittin' here, so help me, I sees this fish with the shape of a biddy, hoppin' in and out the sea. If I had'na seen it m'self, wouldn't of believed it. It's the truth, sure as I'm drawin' breath."

Dan finished, exhausted, and as we sat there silent and wondering, a car drove up for gas.

The day Mr. Raney returned to work the impact was like a head-on crash of two gun boats. Fortunately, most of the new work was safely behind beaver-board and he couldn't estimate the "damage"; but what he saw he didn't like.

"Who'd you bespeak to handle this confounded job anyways?" he demanded of Papa. It's no less than makin' a fool of a man's sweat and labor."

And once when he and Dan clashed on methods of joining beaver-board, he abruptly threw his hammer up in the air and stalked out, but Papa stopped him before he got too far. What he told him we could only guess, but by his gestures it was clear he was salving his wounds—and they returned together. Many times after that Papa was forced into the position of reluctant referee, but nothing succeeded as well as the day Dan announced he'd had enough work, enough seaweed, not to mention enough Raney and would stay until the end of the week—only. "So's not to put you in a bigger hole'n you're in, Captain."

We watched him leave with almost the same affection, the same sense of loss that we felt with Tom and Jack's departure.

15

A Salve for Every Sore

The roof was raised, twelve new rooms were safely under cover before temperatures plunged, and suddenly time hung heavy for Papa. It was now between seasons in the clothing trade; usually during a slowdown he'd improve an old machine or develop a new one. And when we lived in New York it was the time for pattern-makers; it was also the time to take stock of materials, compile inventories, visit foundries for a better-turned casting, for new quotes, new tools, or perhaps to hunt around for a high-powered drilling machine. It was time for everything but the manufacturers who were up to their necks in stylists, new fashions, new headaches. This was the order. Unless you were directly concerned with fabrics and cutters you stayed away. And Papa stayed away.

But here in Andover it came together—the finished second story and the seasonal slack. Papa became restless and fidgety. Like a nervous housewife on a cleaning binge he painted the store walls, clamped new fasteners on every window, changed rusty door hinges—and then when he tired and needed rest, he charged downstairs and scoured the basement floors. Then he was up again moving counters and showcases and rearranging every item of merchandise. Suddenly auto supplies popped up in notions, hardware in groceries, suspender straps in patent medicines. A state of mild chaos prevailed; trying to fill an order was like your first day in a new job, especially one you never trained for.

Satisfied with the house and store, he tripped down to the spotless basement—fortified with Madame Melba on the Victrola—to assemble machine parts and paint flanges and castings. These he brought upstairs, placed in a hot oven gently like fresh cake batter, for quick drying—a process that made a crude oil refinery smell like Chanel No. 5. After packing away the last shining black coupling, flange and casting, the last nickel-plated bar, the last wooden roller; after piling up cases of assembled parts to be hauled to New York in the spring, he looked around the basement like a man satisifed with his work. Then he came upstairs to reappraise the clean, renovated store. Here, too, he looked around and was satisfied. There was nothing more to do. That night he retired early—a strange thing for Papa.

The next morning at breakfast he seemed preoccupied, which was not unusual for a man with an inventive mind; he was often this way when a new idea was churning in his head. He ate his breakfast in silence, helped Mama wash the dishes and then sat down again.

"What do you know, Estherel," he said suddenly. "Ned Raney is talking of getting a job in Florida for the winter. He says with the building boom going on down there carpenters are at a premium."

"Is that so!" said Mama, a little surprised. "He's a smart man to think of it. The good warm sun will help his rheumatism; it always gets worse in the winter."

Papa looked at Mama warily. "And what do you think he asked me? Estherel, you'd never guess what he asked me!"

Mama looked up quickly.

"Ah, such foolishness. He wants me to drive down
with him. Can you imagine that?"

Mama wasn't easily thrown off the scent. "What did
you tell him?"

"What else could I tell him? 'Impossible,' I said.
'Impossible.' " Mama said nothing and waited.

"How can I go with one business in New York and a
business here? How could I tear myself away?" Papa
kept up a steady banter disavowing so fantastic an idea,
all the while the gleam in his eyes growing brighter.
Mama kept listening quietly, almost as if she wasn't
hearing. But she was thinking.

"See, even you agree it's a senseless thing . . . sure,
that's what I told him."

Then Mama said unexpectedly. "What's so senseless
about it? It's time you took a rest—and a little vacation
in Florida won't do you any harm. The world will wait."

"But the business . . . what . . ."

"Forget the business. You said yourself it was dead in
New York. And here, in winter, it's the same story.
Don't worry; with the children, I'll get along fine."

Papa jumped up from his chair so quickly, it
overturned and broke a slat; he left it lying on the floor
and rushed over and hugged Mama. "You really mean it,
Estherel?" He grinned like a little boy with his first
baseball mitt. "To tell you the truth—now that I think
of it—it's not such a bad idea after all." And since Papa
wouldn't dream of going down just for the pleasure of it,
he said, "I might even run into a good piece of ground,
you never can tell. They say land is dirt cheap down
there; it's practically yours for the asking . . ."

They started out one bitter-cold morning when a
fine-grained snow lay fresh and menacing on the ground.
But Papa didn't see it. After he greased the transmission,

gave the Ford a painstaking overhaul, a fresh change of oil and a full tank of gas, he and Ned Raney set out for Miami like two boys on a fishing trip—despite the fact that anyone driving down to Florida during the twenties was regarded as one or more of three things: an oddball, a chronic rheumatic, or a brainless speculator. ("Why, most of the land be covered by ten good foot of water," the stove forum said.) Especially if you transported yourself via Model T which Papa did.

"With a little good luck," said Papa, "and a steady two hundred miles or so a day, we should make it in a week." Which meant a ten-hour driving day at twenty miles per hour. "Maniacs," he muttered when a car swished by at thirty-five miles per. Even in those days Papa obstructed traffic and the cops briskly waved him along.

Before he left Papa assured Mama, "Ned and I sat down and figured everything out to the smallest detail, we left nothing to guesswork. On a trip of this magnitude you don't fool around, everything must be precisely on schedule. We picked the best route and the best roads and with God's help and no machine trouble we should make it in good time—no more than a week. I'll write every night; you'll know exactly where we stop for the night and how we're doing."

We rushed to the post office each day to pick up the letters and cards that gave us a full-dress account of his progress. The first one, postmarked Philadelphia, read, "Arrived on schedule, on the dot of six p.m. tired and hungry but after a good meal and two hot cups of coffee (almost as good as yours, Estherel) we felt rested. The motor hummed like sweet music but I checked it again for tomorrow's trip just to be sure. Not a sign of snow here. It is obvious we are heading South. I would enjoy this trip much more if I knew you weren't back there in the cold."

The second arrived from Fredericksburg, Virginia. "We are averaging a steady twenty miles per hour and again arrived on schedule. We had a beautiful day, the sun was shining and driving was a pleasure. Raney is having a few mild rheumatic pains. He says he feels this way every time a change in weather takes place. And I guess he's not far from right for the papers say we're due for rain tomorrow. But I hope it won't slow us down. No trouble except for a flat which was caused by a rusty nail and which I quickly fixed. Everything is fine again."

Post-marked Raleigh, North Carolina, the third letter read: "Were we caught in that rain they predicted! To say we were slowed down is an understatement. At best, this time of year the roads are not in good shape. Some roads are completely washed out and every few miles there is a time-consuming detour where the road is even worse. Because of this we decided to travel an extra hour or two each night to make up lost time. Even so we don't expect to reach Miami on schedule.

"There is no comparing our roads up North with roads down here and if I had been told beforehand you can believe me when I say that I would have thought twice before starting out on a trip such as this. But don't worry, everything else is OK. At least the weather is milder and we don't have to bundle up."

From Columbia, South Carolina, the fourth day: We surely did not pick the best time of year for going South. All we've been getting is rain and more rain. But we manage to keep traveling since there is nothing gained by waiting. But you can bet your boots the next time I should decide to go to Florida it will be by train—if ever I decide to go, that is."

When Mama read the letter she sighed. "I have a feeling that Papa is sorry he started. When he talks about going to Florida again, it is only because he wishes he were home. If only it stopped raining and there is a change . . . well, let's hope the rest of the trip will be easier."

But the rest of the trip was not easier; and as for change, it was worse. The roads were a perpetuation of mud, deep beds of mud; and where it was possible he hedged them by swerving to level stretches of sodden grass, already rutted from many wheels. For hours, as the rain beat furiously against the windshield with the stunning force of a tornado, Ned Raney kept up a ceaseless vigil of clearing misted windows and wiping puddles that seeped in from the usual places plus a few brand-new ones. And so the two travelers kept pushing on, damp and chilled and miserable.

Papa's next letter said: "For six hours we have been riding—the net result, fifty miles. In view of this we decided to stop and rest up for tomorrow. Driving in weather like this is like trying to push back the ocean. Perhaps in the morning, with God's help, it will clear up. Then we can keep going. Ned Raney is not feeling so good. He's complained of pain in his joints since Fredericksburg and, of course, this rain doesn't help any."

According to Papa, the next morning they awoke to clear and rainless sky. "It was like God heard us, Estherel."

Mist was rising all over the countryside, warm and steaming like a giant cauldron.

"Ah," wrote Papa, this is more like it. With a little good luck we'll make up for yesterday's loss."

After breakfast they refueled the car, checked the tires, filled the radiator. To avoid even minor delays they bought a supply of food to last the day—and then they were on their way. Their spirits recouped quickly.

But not for long.

As they drove along they viewed, dismally, vast inundated stretches of land—the full-blown havoc of hurricane fury; stretches which once burgeoned with vegetation ripe for trucking, or overrun with wooded growth, were now flooded to lake proportions. Saplings, full-grown trees floated around like helpless bodies in a ship disaster; the road continued on in one big splatter of debris which forced them to stop and disperse every few minutes. And every mile or two red flags hailed them down while crews cleared the road of heavy timber, a dead cow or a wild pig.

Papa was now driving in second gear at a strolling rate of speed, his eyes closely glued to the road ahead. In this manner they traveled for hours and hours until they passed the Georgia state line.

For a moment Ned forgot his rheumatism. "Another miserable state behind us, b'God." What he'd been viewing the past two days was far removed from anything he, as a fourth-generation New Englander, had ever witnessed before.

"Never figgered we'd been gettin' into anything like this, Henry. The way I be feelin' now I'd just as ruther turn around and head back."

"We came a long distance, Ned. I think we'd be foolish to turn back now, and Florida's not too far away."

"Reckon you're right." Ned was quiet a few minutes. "Anyways, to tell you the truth, I'm lookin' to layin' in that Floridy sunshine. My bones is achin' somethin' terrible."

They inched on in silence; nothing could be added to the desolate picture around them. And so they drove for miles.

Suddenly Ned groaned aloud. "Look away down there, Henry. Appears like another long delay. Just look at that line of machines down the road. I reckon it's the biggest tie-up so far. Only the good Lord knows when we'll get a-goin' again. Sure don't look purty to me."

"We can't tell from here what it is. Let's hope the road isn't washed out. We've been lucky so far."

"That's about all we be needin'. A washed-out road."

The Ford crept on until Papa took his place behind the other vehicles. All over the road people milled and buzzed about.

"No . . . I'm afraid it doesn't look so good." Papa's usual buoyancy was beginning to wear down. He got out of the car and walked over to a small group of men.

"What's the story, gentlemen?"

"Road's flooded clean out since last night," said one.

"You mean no one got through since last night?" Papa asked in dismay.

"A few got through for five bucks, goddamit."

"That's a lot of money but it's not hopeless."

"It's hopeless enough if you got northern plates and have to shell out fifteen dollars to a coupla liver-faced crackers waiting to ferry you across. They're still fighting the Civil War down here."

"Fifteen dollars! That's highway robbery!"

"You called it by the right name, mister."

"There must be something we can do . . .who can afford fifteen dollars . . ."

"I guess they figure after you been waitin' around long enough you'll be in a sweat to get movin'. And they's right there. After waitin' around for a few hours a few has paid it to get hauled through. Trouble is most of us buggers headin' South ain't got it to throw away and we's waitin' around hopin' the water'll soak in before long."

"My God! That could take a couple of days. Maybe longer."

"Could be," said the man with Maine plates, chewing his pipe nervously, "but we ain't got much choice."

"Fifteen dollars . . . *fifteen dollars* . . .thieves, blackmailers, cutthroats."

"You can say that again," said Raney who was standing by. "I didn't pay no mind to the folks back home when they was tellin' me, 'Take it mighty easy down in Georgy, they don't take none to Northerners. They got speed traps in every town to snare 'em.' Speed traps! Why, you can't move more'n ten miles per, even when it ain't stormin'. Full of boulders and potholes and the road only wide enough for two cars to squeeze by. They should pay you for passin' through—the other way around. Can't understand why a soul'd be ticketed unless mebbe he was shiftin' into high. Can't say I wasn't told of it—except for these leeches they didn't tell me none about that."

"Well," said Papa. "There's nothing gained by standing here. Let's go down and take a look."

"Pleasure's all yours," said a man from New Jersey. "We saw enough."

All around people stood disconsolately talking to one another to pass the time while others paced up and down the road, nervous and worried. They were trapped in the heart of desolate country; not a house or gas station for miles around. Behind wide-spreading cypress trees mothers were urging their offspring to perform necessary bodily functions and few paid them heed.

Papa and Ned walked over alone. They came to the submerged road—the muddy waters still ripply from a freshly drawn vehicle. On the other side two men in dirty overalls sat on a log pushed up against a tree, only a pole's reach from their team, already heavily harnessed with plow gear, and from the traces hung heavy looped chains ready to latch on to the next victim and tow him through the motor-deep mud. Five dollars for "Georgians" or neighborly states and fifteen for damn Yankees."

The two smirking croppers leaned contentedly against the tree as they puffed away on their pipes, a gallon crock of liquor close by to sustain them. Every so often they called out jeeringly, "Time's a-goin' and the little ole sun'll be settin' befo' you' all know it. Don't be bashful, folks, jest speak up brightly."

"What riles me so bad," said Ned Raney, "is the gloatin' look on those miserable crackers' faces—like a hungry cat landin' a paw on a field mouse. They got no shame or mercy in they's stony hearts. And they ain't so smart either. You know, Henry, these Georgy crackers ain't got a mite of Yankee horse sense. They got pumpkins for heads. Now, if they was smart and reasonable they'd haul every durned vehicle that came along for two dollars a piece. This way every poor gudgeon'd manage to peel out a couple of bucks without knockin' him out too much. In the end they'd be makin' out a heap sight better'n they's making out now. The line's gettin' longer and longer and them crackers is just settin' and settin'."

"*If* they were smart," said Papa, "they wouldn't be sitting around fermenting in bad blood. They seem to enjoy watching the suffering of others."

"Ayeh," said Ned, "that they sure do."

"It's against the laws of nature for one human being to perpetrate an injustice on another human being."

"I go along with you some, Henry, but those critters don't act like human beings, they act like varmints."

"You heard the old saying, Ned, 'All fish are not caught with flies.' I say nothing is impossible in this world. Maybe, with God's help, we'll figure something out yet."

"Mebbe so, Henry, but it looks mighty bad. You can see for yourself. Plenty of water, and worse yet, plenty of mud to bed a car down. If there was a way I reckon someone would of thought of it by now."

Papa was forced to agree as he edged closer to the sunken road, all the while thinking hard; and this was good, for when Papa thought hard he pushed on till a germ sprouted and burst into fruition.

Ned watched inquiringly as Papa walked over to the left bank for a firsthand survey. He watched him stand there, quietly appraising the situation, then squat for a closer inspection like a man trying to recover a lost coin. Then Papa got up, slowly rolled his shirt-sleeves, removed his shoes and socks, turned his pants cuffs up to his knees, smoothing each fold with rigid deliberateness.

Papa's placid actions aroused interest and a few men came forward, openly curious. One called out, "No sense in getting all gooed up in that mire. Afraid it won't help none, mister. A few others tried it and got sucked down in the mud."

But Papa continued without hearing him. Nor did he hear the loud sniggering of the croppers, convinced another Yankee was making a damned fool of himself. "Here comes another city fella," one yelled in derision. "Come on in, the water's fine! A little cloudy, but fine for wadin'." They continued to guffaw until they tired, then one yelled out, "Who all is next in line? Step right up. Step right up." Business was slowing down; it was well over three hours since they had last hauled an automobile across, and now their jibes held more concern than amusement.

Behind Papa was an angry rumbling of frustrated men. "It ain't the money, it's the damn principle. Them robbin' thieves is stickin' us like clay pigeons. They know we're stuck and they's waitin' us out like we're ambushed. I'd as lief wait it out until mornin' and take my chances. Who else is willing?"

One man yelled out to his wife. "What do you say, Myrtle, you game?" Loudly she called back, "I'm with you, Jim."

"By God, then we'll stay!"

Curiously the men watched Papa tread up and down

the sloping bank, pounding the ground with his feet; they watched him jab the earth with a sturdy branch he'd whittled—jab it hard into the softened earth until it stopped abruptly. He continued, inch by inck, to tamp the earth and pierce the ground, and when he'd finished it was as perforated as a punchboard. Then he waded into the rim of the mucky water, walking its length. Back and forth he walked, each time moving in a few inches; sometimes he stopped as if to work out something in his mind. And when he'd reconnoitered the situation to his satisfaction he pulled out and once again turned around to appraise the watery impasse. Then he sat down on a rock and rinsed his muddied feet with a little surface water, dried them with his handkerchief and put on his socks and shoes.

The rumbling had long died down as the men watched Papa, some wondering, some eager. When he was through with his obvious course he walked over to Ned and a few others standing by.

"I think I can make it," he whispered.

"It's a long shot," cautioned a bystander.

"That slope's steep. If your right wheels get caught you can topple over," said another.

Paps said nothing, winked his eye and walked on.

"Well, the good Lord be with you. If you make it we'll be right behind you."

Walking back to the Ford, Ned warned, "I tell you, Henry, you be crazy to try it. Mebbe it won't work then we'd be in a fine pickle. Why, them crackers'd be so cankered for breaking up they's racket, they'd as lief tar and feather us. Don't want no tangling with them thievin' crooks. I'd ruther pay them off."

Papa's mind was already made up but he heard him out quietly. "The money's the least of it now, Ned, it's the principle. My mind's made up. Somebody's got to try and stop these good-for-nothing highway robbers. But

don't worry," he added, sensing Ned's fear, "I'll try it
myself. If I make it—and I have reason to believe I
will—you can meet me on the other side."

"Hell, no, Henry. You ain't going over alone. We
might's well be two damnfool Yankees as one.
Together—or not at all."

There was now a long line of cars parked behind Papa,
their drivers and families milling about. He started the
motor, let it idle gently.

"She must be warmed up good," he said to Ned as
people swarmed curiously to the tune of the motor. In a
few minutes he eased the Ford out of line, slowly
making his way down the road.

"A damnfool," said one loud enough for Papa to
hear.

"Maybe, but he ain't short on guts," said another.

The rest milled around, silently watching, anxiously
hopeful. Papa drove resolutely down the road, past the
long, desolate stream of cars. The engine aroused the
teamsters, who appeared surprised, then amused, never
losing the situation-well-in-hand look on their mealy
faces.

The motor was now warmed and purring smoothly, as
if freshly overhauled. The time was ripe for action. Papa
pushed the gas throttle down several notches and the car
lurched forward; there was no nonsense in the sound of
that engine. Then, approaching the soggy road, he thrust
the lever down three more notches, swerved sharply to
the left and plunged the Ford in the muddy snare.

A cheer went up and just as quickly died. The engine
sputtered and gasped as water deluged the wires, the
transmission. It seeped in from the right door, flooding
the wood floor. Raney's feet jammed the dashboard. It
must be now or never. Throwing caution to the winds
Papa ground the gas lever to its limit, pulled out choke,
called on God and pleaded with Lizzie to keep going.

And though the wet, sharply tilted motor had somehow defied all of Newton's law of gravity, Lizzie, out of sheer loyalty, obliged. She kept grunting and puffing for what seemed an eternity, and then Papa was safely on the other side.

A sudden thundering roar of voices and bleating of horns filled the air. As if on cue the drivers hopped into their cars, started their motors and suddenly the road was cleared of all humanity. One by one they swerved around, following Papa's path, tooting and yelling. The roar was sweet but nothing as sweet as the look on the teamsters' faces. Dangerously, with one hand on the wheel, Papa waved back to the cars as they passed, maintaining his steady twenty miles an hour, discreetly hugging the side of the road despite his sudden soar to prominence. Though the day had started dismally, it turned out good after all, and Papa was smugly contented. He breathed deeply of the warm, free air, perhaps thinking of Mama's little booster, "All's well that ends well."

When the last car had passed, and the last loving toot had died away and Papa had driven safely beyond the town's limits, Ned said quietly, with more than a little trace of respect in his voice, "By the light of God, Henry, you made it. Never thought we would. There for a spell when the motor was losing hold, it sure looked like we was a pair of goners. You should've seen them crackers jumping up, fixing they mules for action, their faces looking like we was putty in they's hands." For a few moments he was thoughtful, pondering silently on the hair-breadth escape, "Y'know, Henry, when you come right down to it, you was taking a mighty big gamble. Whut in tarnation give you the idea you could make it?"

"I'm no gambler, Ned. You know that. And I don't believe in taking foolish chances, but I had a pretty good

idea I could make it. You remember when I was
walking in that muddy water, and when I got down on
my knees to feel what was under it."

"I do—ayeh."

"I didn't let on, but what I found there settled in my
mind—shoulders as solid as bedrock, the slope not too
steep. It looked far from hopeless. What I figured was to
get my right wheels in water and my left ones on hard
bank. That would just about allow for a tight squeeze,
and with a bit of luck and a prayer I guessed I could
manage it. But then I looked up and saw those robbers
on the other side waiting to bleed us and I knew it
wasn't a matter of maybe, but a matter of must."

"Well, I'll be a—" Ned chuckled lightly. "Say, Henry, I
sure'd give anything to get a look at them thievin' crooks
right now!"

Papa was deep in his own thoughts. "Can you
imagine," he said, his pleasure outweighing his outrage.
"Fifteen dollars. Who ever heard of such nonsense!"

16

No Pains, No Gains

Hardly a ·day passed without a drummer stopping on his round of calls; the constant flow of tradespeople was enough to supply Macy's, Gimbel's, and us in the span of one week. After the first year Papa stopped hauling supplies from New York, except for occasional "finds" like a dozen "irresistible" solid-brass chafing dishes and six huge hand-decorated chamber pots he picked up at an auction—items we needed like a summer drought, though not entirely without merit, for they lent the store a certain touch. "They sure smarten up the shelves," observed August Kepplinger, fingering a chafing dish, "but what in tarnation be they for?" As it turned out—conversation pieces, for not one of them ever sold.

We got to know them all; the Salada Tea man, the Procter & Gamble, Natonal Biscuit, and (no partiality) Sunshine Biscuit men, the Hershey man, salesmen ad infinitum, along with the wholesale jobbers who handled every variety of tobacco, candy, hardware, dry goods, patent medicines, adequately filling in the gaps of the specialty men.

The better we got to know the drummers, the longer

they lingered. Covering a wide territory, one small town to another, week in and week out in hot summer and bleak winter, was not in the realm of unalloyed ecstasy; it was a tiring, tedious affair and when they stopped it was to rest and chat as much as to take an order. Sometimes Mama invited them back in the kitchen for a hot cup of coffee, but more often they relaxed in the store with a bottle of Moxie or sarsaparilla before getting down to business.

Best of all we enjoyed the cookie men, whose sample cases, a delight to behold, opened up into staircase tiers, revealing a tempting array of goodies. Fluffy cocoanut-topped marshmallow rounds, chewy raisin bars, Fig Newtons, peanut squares, Lorna Doones, chocolate puffs, molasses, oatmeal, sugar-and-spice cookies, jelly tarts, macaroons, milk crackers and soda biscuits, and honeyed grahams—all glued down to a series of tiny collapsible shelves. Plenty of samples to taste, too. They were packed tightly in ten-pound containers with glass snap-on lids for visibility, and as a slight extra service, for bug protection. Freshness never entered into it. Cookies were bagged, never boxed; so was sugar and rice along with other loose staples.

To display their wares, biscuit companies installed special cookie racks which held nine ten-pound containers, three on each shelf. We put them to other good use, too, partitioning the store, separating groceries from hardware.

They were a varied lot these salesmen; some came every week, some once a month. Formosa Tea was all business, Copenhagen Snuff a bore, Patent Medicines a self-styled doctor, Chiclets a punster, Hardware a tale-spinner, Auto Supplies a dreamer. Even Novelties & Notions came, loaded with juicy trade gossip, though his wares hardly moved.

Then there was Motor Oil and Transmission Grease,

fresh out of Yale and a snob of the first order. One day a worn Galli-Curci record was rasping on the old victrola when he walked in, and from that day forward our lives were drastically altered. Culture took over. Route salesman was merely "a menial task" to be borne until he'd apprenticed his three full years of meeting the nasty public. William Stotts ("My friends call me Billium") was now second in line for fourth vice-president in his uncle's company and he was learning the business from the very, very bottom up. And the way he said it you got to feeling like that very, very bottom. It was more the way he sized you up that made you feel like dust curls under his bed—his eyes scaled his nose, slowly advancing and retreating, and by its long, arrogant shape, this was no mean attainment. And whenever we could we'd run for cover. In a mad dash to the kitchen Rose would say, "The Cat's Meow is back," when she'd spot the oil emblem on his gray coupe, and Mama would come out and order the oil and grease.

This Saturday we were grounded to the store. Mama was visiting August Kepplinger, and Papa had just put on his favorite Galli-Curci record as loud as we could bear it—and that could mean but one thing; he was heading for the basement to assemble a supply of rollers, flanges and castings to haul back to New York Monday morning. He liked good music while he worked, especially Melba, Galli-Curci, and Caruso. At that moment Motor Oil walked in.

"Well!" said Mr. Stotts as if he'd blundered into an art museum instead of the flea circus he expected, "Galli-Curci!" in a tone that implied Louisville Lou was more within our range of development.

"We always listen to Opera," Rose said, mincing the truth.

Young Motor Oil stared; he seemed startled, almost shaken, and then an astonishing thing took place. Almost at once he seemed agreeable, as if at last he were meeting up with members of the human race. He began to smile and talk in an animated way, almost like Salada Tea, only more dignified.

After that, whether we liked it or not—and I must admit we did—we were thoroughly indoctrinated to harmonics and Culture. Each week he'd slide a new recording into his brief case—one week it might be Rachmaninoff's Concerto No. 2 in C Minor. "It's soulful, girls. Melts in your mouth." The next, Saint-Saens' Danse Macabre—"haunting, bewitching, stirs the senses." And so it went week after week. So enraptured was he with music, after playing something "soulful" like Petrouchka, he'd leave without an order—who could dream of offending Stravinsky?

Often he'd leave the record until the following week. "Pay special note to the cadence of the second glorious movement. The brilliance of its nuances inspires, enriches the soul; its balance of tone, quality of control, every sustained harmony and exploding coda is a composite of all that is beautiful in this worn, weary world. Listen carefully, girls, listen and listen, then tell me what *YOU* hear."

We would if we could, but who could follow that?

Our lesser musical endowments were supplied by the Record man who arrived promptly each month with the latest hits, leaving these goodies, more within our range of appreciation, on consignment. If we sold them, well and good; if not they were exchanged for new stock. Sometimes when we inflicted too much wear on a record, playing it until it scratched like a shovel scooping gravel, we bought it out of sheer guilt.

Al Jolson records sold quickly, especially "April Showers," "Sonny Boy" and "Mammy," songs that still prick my memory like a first date. State songs sold well, too. Topping the list were "California Here I Come,"

"Chicago," "Alabamy Bound," "Sidewalks of New York," and "Way Down Yonder in New Orleans." Much later came the less musical opus "Connecticut is the State for Me." It seemed that popular music devotees harbored no geographical prejudices and song writers drew inspiration from their home states instead of the heart.

For days after the Record man's visit we cranked the Victrola incessantly, blaring out new tunes until we memorized every last one—except when Papa was around. "You call that music?" he'd bellow. And to offset this musical demise of his family, he'd buy more and more recordings of Caruso, Madame Melba, and Galli-Curci—all huge twelve-inchers, dwarfing the eight-inch spindle, that went on and on—failing miserably to arouse so much as a slight appreciation for grand opera, or even a faint stirring.

Eventually, the popular records sparked a new love in my life—the Dance. When the store was emptied of customers, I'd swirl and twirl and leap to the strains of rhythmic music, vowing to myself that life would be bereft of meaning unless I turned my full energies to this calling—aiming, of course, to follow in the hallowed footsteps of Pavlova, but in a pinch would settle for Ruby Keeler. Dancing, any form of dancing, was now the new order. Then all at once my inner rumblings, my pent-up teenage emotions spouted steam, releasing me suddenly from adolescent constraint almost as if I'd emerged into broad daylight after a long confinement.

When I was about five the flame was kindled—the day Mama accompanied me and Rose to one of the more fashionable apartment houses on Nineteenth Street. A lacy, grilled elevator jerked us up to the fifth floor and we waited breathlessly until a woman, who had called on Mama earlier in the month, regaling her with the unusual opportunity being offered us, opened the door and ushered us in, a warm smile lighting her face. She was pink and soft and radiant, and a mass of golden hair swirled high on her head like a Renoir model. A tantalizing scent hovered all about her and I was all but hypnotized. Mrs. Fire, she was called, a strange name for so serene, so exquisite, so beautiful a woman, I thought.

We followed her into a richly draped studio that looked like a private ballroom and she proceeded to introduce us to a line of youngsters and their mammas who were already seated on gilt Louis XIV or XV chairs. Looking eager and elegant in their Sunday best, the little girls were all similarly attired and coiffured; their hair hung in long, stiffly coiled curls that reached far below their shoulders, and immediately I was stung with embarrassment, since Rose was sporting a Buster Brown cut, and I, tightly drawn pigtails. Nor were we dressed in knee-length black silk socks and organdy dresses, but in long white cotton-ribbed stockings, skirts and middies. The way they stared we might have been wearing red-flannel underwear.

The boys looked and dressed alike, too; navy blue Eton suits and white starched shirts—but with one marked difference. They were sullen and glum, as if they'd fought Mamma every inch of the way up and lost.

My discomfort quickly dissolved when Miss Victoria, Mrs. Fire's assistant, swept into the room looking like a page from *Vogue* magazine. The contrast between the two was startling. I quickly noted (with pleasure) her silky black hair was combed back tightly, too, but there the similarity ended. Instead of a pigtail, one soft glorious bun coiled at the nape of her long, swanlike neck. There was no mistaking the intensity smoldering in those large dark eyes, nor the fiery temperament emphasized in every lithe movement.

She greeted us glowingly, her words dripping with accent, telling us we were a "see-lact" group of children (by what means I never knew) to be trained as a dancing unit designed to step up a children's theater project already in progress. When a play called for sprites or bunnies or nymphs to flit on and off stage on cue, we were to supply the appropriate diversional background. This, she told us, was a "very beeg" opportunity and that such an offer did not come knocking every day. Though there'd be no training fees, neither would we be paid for performing, and again she insisted we were a choice group indeed and so-o-o-o lucky to be "choosed." "But," she emphasized, her eyes flashing, "if de offer is not acceptable, you must weethdraw right now. Thees minute. Not wan week from now."

Rose and I looked at Mama hopefully and we squirmed with delight when she accepted—as did all the others—pleased that her little girls would benefit from so rare an opportunity. And when at last we left with instructions to appear the following Saturday in bloomers and middies, the boys in knee pants and white shirts, we knew a new exciting career was in the launching.

And so the weeks flew by, each schoolday dragging drearily until Saturday morning when we again reveled in arabesques and pirouettes, the girls awkwardly glorying in every movement, despite the weird snickers and shrieks pelted at us constantly by the boys. That they were actively plotting to be kicked out of class was no big secret, nor their ideas on "fairy" dancing even lightly concealed. They came only because a determined squad of mammas marched them bodily to class each week.

Lovely, voluptuous Mrs. Fire soon found to her dismay that holding grudging, energetic boys in line was no simple matter; every attempt at control was met with snickers and amusement. Each week she'd warn, "If you boys don't behave today there will be no class next week." But every week the boys behaved in their usual manner and every week she resorted lamely to her threat.

It was Miss Victoria who took over—stilling the rascals at once, for even they were charmed by her vibrance, her throaty voice drenched in Spanish accent; her rich contralto singing, and dancing as she half-called, half-sung in rhythmic tempo, "Wanna-two-tree, wanna-two-tree, wanna-two-tree, w-a-n-n-a, t-w-o, t-r-e-e—stop de nonsense, bend de knees, boys, keep de hands op, la, la, la, la," rolling her r's like a steady volley of artillery. She was a delight to work with, and in three months when she and Mrs. Fire decided we were ready to execute our divertissements before a trial audience, parents and relatives were invited one evening to view their budding Pavlovas and Nijinskys.

"By no means are you ready for the theater," warned the soft, curvy Mrs. Fire before the performance, "but it is most important to expose your development." Then she added cryptically, rolling her baby-blue eyes, "If you behave like the little ladies and gentleman you really are, Miss Victoria will present you with a special treat at the end of the program."

Visions of swirling gobs of charlotte russe and cream puffs swept us vigorously through battements and attitudes almost without flaw—Melvin Kahn, chief boy rebel, fell during a leap but hopped right back into line again like a trouper—and as it turned out to everyone's surprise, the boys danced as they had never danced before; either the promise of a treat or the smell of an audience produced a magical effect. Not a smirk or a smile or a blustering giggle, nor a trace of horseplay clouded the performance.

Beaming relatives filled the studio, overflowing in the rear and onto the sides; at every pause they applauded thunderously—and that sound was like strange and exciting music. When at last the silk magenta curtain came down, that strange, exciting music continued to linger.

In a cubicle off stage a few mothers were waiting to tear off our costumes and herd us into empty chairs waiting out front. This we had not rehearsed, and when we were seated but a few minutes, the curtain rose again, and standing there in the center stage, poised like a proud duchess with a headdress of fine Spanish lace, was the dark and queenly Miss Victoria, one hand on her hip and one high above her head. At the sound of a shattering chord she burst into action like a lithe and supple doe, then—her eyes flashing—a fiery and irrepressible tigress, all the while clicking her heels with swift staccato taps, twirling and swaying and whipping, pulsating her castanets with passionate grace. Then suddenly all movement halted abruptly and her head flung back in majestic sweep; the effect, like a shaft of lightning, overpowered the audience and she was cheered back for six glorious encores. We sat entranced, all sixteen tyros. Never before had we witnessed such an exhibition of professional skill, and now cream puffs were but a dim memory, for this we knew was the promised treat of the evening. And as further tribute to Miss Victoria, not a single hungry, pastry-loving face revealed a trace of disappointment.

Mrs. Fire performed, too, in a wispy, cloudlike costume, but of her my recollections were of a vastly different sort.

A few weeks after the student performance, when we were about ripe for the theater group, my dancing career came to an abrupt demise. We arrived for class one Saturday when Mrs. Fire was just emerging from a steaming bathroom, pink and sweet and scented, a negligee wrapped snugly about her. In itself this was not uncommon, since the apartment combined both home and studio, and often she dawdled leisurely with her toilette while Miss Victoria put us through the warm-up period.

This time, however, she greeted us before slipping into her practice tights, and it startled me when the boys suddenly doubled over with convulsive laughter and the girls tittered uncontrollably. Lamely she tried to bring order, clapping her hands, stamping her fuzzy, slippered feet and yelling "Silence!" But the shrieking and giggling continued. Bewildered by this outburst, I thought everyone had taken leave of his senses—until Mrs. Fire turned around, desperately looking for Miss Victoria—and there in all its natural glory, two ripply pink buttock cheeks emerged unexpectedly through her negligee which had burst down the middle.

"I want order!" she shouted. "I demand order!" But laughter had now turned to hysteria and there was no stopping.

"Stop immediately or there will be no more classes." Stop an avalanche halfway down a mountain!

It was clear she was oblivious to her state of undress, and in my five-year-old innocence I felt it my moral duty to acquaint her with this fact, though the chore was a delicate one. Above the racket I tried to make myself heard but my small voice went unheeded. Then I walked up to her and tugged urgently at her gown.

"Mrs. Fire, Mrs. Fire, your hiney is showing."

Mrs. Fire glared down at me and screeched, "My *What?*" Her words flailed as a whip and I hung my head in absolute dejection.

"My *What?*" she repeated, shaking me gently.

"There's a hole in your kimono and your hiney is showing," I repeated miserably, and burst into sobs.

This tearful little tableau seemed to affect the youngsters for they suddenly quieted down as if one. Even the boys. By now Mrs. Fire's name was a perfect blend with the look in her eyes, and she turned around slowly in disblief. Then her eyes met flesh, and as if struck by a hot iron, she emitted a blast of fury that terrified every child in the room.

"Get out! Get out! Every last one of you—and never come back again! Do you hear me? Never come back!"

We heard her all right. Rose and I darted out the door so quickly we forgot to wait for Keeve, and we raced home as if the devil were tailing us.

And that little episode spelled finis to our sprouting careers, for to ease Mama's anger at our crossing First and Second Avenues without Keeve, we amply impressed her with our hairbreadth escape, embroidering the facts more than a little. So much so, that when classes continued (despite Mrs. Fire's pronouncement to the contrary) Mama refused to let us return. "With such a temper who knows what might happen next!"

17

All Are Not Saints That Go to Church

And so dancing flew out of my life until the Record Man walked in; though he revived the spark, it was some time before I started again. Mama approved, but Papa roared the first time the subject came up. "What kind of nonsense is this? Who ever heard of dancing for a living? Typing, shorthand, yes! But dancing? Is this a job for a respectable girl?"

Mama was firmly behind me. "Don't be foolish, Henry. Learning to dance does not mean she will be a dancer. There are few Pavlovas in this world."

But Papa didn't hear. "Did you become a dancer? Did my sister become a dancer? What will my family say? What will the world say?"

Mama was now laughing. "Don't worry what the world will say, Hreshkoo." To further punctuate her point she added, "You know the old saying, 'All are not saints that go to church.' "

And Papa, though not fully placated, would glumly drive me to Willimantic for my lessons. It was through Peg Connors, a sophomore, that I first heard of Mrs. Rider, a popular dancing teacher. I envied Peggy's performances—slim, graceful Peggy who could turn a rugged buck and wing into Les Sylphides and make it look right—and I could hardly wait till I met her scintillating teacher.

When finally I rapped on her door, I was greeted by a middle-aged woman with a mop in her hands—the maid, I suspected.

"Come right in," said the woman limply, and at once I felt a surge of pity. Her figure was proportioned like an oil drum battered in the middle, and her voice droned like a sluggish Model T pulling uphill. To see that she was exhausted required no perspicacity.

"I have an appointment with Mrs. Rider," I said. "I guess I'm a little early."

"Oh that's all right. Just come in and make yourself comfortable." And she rushed off before I could say anything more.

I walked into a small drab parlor where another girl about my age was curled up in a huge overstuffed chair, reading. At my presence she glanced up quickly, then buried herself in her book again as if I hadn't existed, like a speck of dust she might have flicked off her dress. The whole atmosphere could thwart any budding Pavlova and I tried to focus my mind on Peggy and her sparkling performances in the weekly lyceums, and the bright thought that she, too, came here for her lessons. Then, as I sat nervously thinking, the woman who greeted me at the door appeared again, but this time no mop was in her hands and a limp, black dress with a wide-flared skirt replaced the gray dust wrapper.

"Come into the studio, Sarah," she said pleasantly, but by now my disillusionment was shattering. For this was not the maid, but Mrs. Rider herself. She was smiling now, and slowly the tired wrinkles dissolved into a faded, pretty face. Pointing to the girl in the chair she said, "This is my daughter Rachel." But daughter Rachel kept on reading and did not look up. Mrs. Rider laughed dryly. "Rachel wants to become a research chemist. She thinks dancing is a waste of time, don't you, Rachel?"

Without waiting for a response we moved quickly into the studio, through a narrow gingerbread arch hardly big enough to clear a couple of jetés, and while this in itself was hampering it was nothing compared to the ever-present goggled Rachel who managed to be sitting in that same overstuffed chair with the same thick manual every time I arrived. She rarely raised her head but when she did it was long enough to squelch me with a withering look while she twirled some trinket, which for all I knew could have been a Phi Beta Kappa key. So disdainful was her look as I attempted an elevation or a rhythmic time step that I felt like a Jezebel-in-training, or at best a watered-down Sadie Thompson.

I managed to learn the rudiments of ballet and tap-dancing but after a few months I began to tire of the morbid, danceless setting and Rachel's subtle, shifty needling, and I was determined to look for a real dance school—one totally drenched, totally steeped in the Dance. And this I soon found, on lower Main Street, a huge studio dedicated to serious students and young hopefuls, and operated by a Mr. Valez, a lean, sleek Latin and his lovely wife, Estelle, lately from Sheboygen. Ah! I beamed, this was it! The handsome Mr. Valez I envisioned as the male counterpart of the beauteous Miss Victoria.

Instead of the drab little room at Mrs. Rider's, here the walls danced gaily with vivid murals painted by the talented Mr. Valez; winged horses, fauns, Degas-like ballerinas, flamenco dancers—and these fanned me with a challenge, a stimulus and a new determination. I bit into the bridle, charging into the groundwork like a bulldozer before a mountain of rubble. And this was easy, for intense activity raced all about me; students working out in every corner of the studio took on the excitement of a three-ring circus, providing a new, exhilarating dimension. In one corner, ballet students stretched and pivoted on bars; in another, heels and castanets clicked to soft, fiery music; in still another muscles toned up in limbering back-bends, hand-springs, high kicks and splits, each group utterly oblivious of the others. I was mesmerized, as any neophyte would be, and the day came when I, too, was part of the clicking, twirling, stretching, gyrating mass, and in my too ardent fervor pulled a tendon that laid me up for a week.

A few months after studying with Juan and Estelle, I was bestowed the supreme honor of performing a Spanish dance in the spring recital with none other than Juan Valez himself. When I heard the news, the words pealed in my ears like the crash of heavenly cymbals; nor shall I ever forget that performance—the performance that would beyond a doubt snare the Great Ziegfeld's attention. My entrance into the scintillating world of Broadway would now be but a matter of time.

Throughout the dance—as soon as the orchestra struck up—I was seized by a mild state of euphoria, except during the finale when the suave Mr. Valez lithely twirled my ninety-five pounds over his head like a wound-up top, then with marvelous dexterity gently pivoted me to the hard floor of reality. I took my bows amidst ringing applause and then, head high in triumph, slipped off the stage with Juan still bowing.

Papa sat somberly at the wheel as we drove home from Willimantic. I expected a rush of praise at my bright achievement, my first performance of any account, but there was nothing but silence that lasted well past the town of Columbia, a few miles from home. Then Mama spoke up and I turned to her in proud expectation. Now it would start. But all Mama said was, "My! What a dangerous dance, Sarah. I was so sure that man would drop you on your head, I shut my eyes until it was all over. You should thank God you were spared."

And Keeve said, "Boy, what a fancy costume. You looked like a lady bull thrower—I mean, bullfighter. Not bad, kiddo." Rose threw more heart into it. "You weren't nearly as stiff as I thought you'd be."

Papa alone said nothing but his silence was loaded. Not until we reached the house did he begin, and then in a dead calm. He strode into the kitchen, slumped heavily in a chair and stared at the stove with an odd, fixed glare. "Very nice . . . so now my daughter has become a dancer . . . oh, this is very nice"—the tone a low rumble of thunder before a storm. "What I saw with my own eyes tonight I never believed could happen in my house, in any decent house." He continued in a low rage as if the neighbors in Bolton Notch might hear, and by the way he amplified each horrendous thought he might well have added "trollop" or "streetwalker"—but this he refrained from saying, perhaps from fear the suggestion might take. With each sad *tch-tch*, he repeated, his voice rising, "And *in my house!*"

So ended my big night, the night that was to have launched my *career*. Instead I stumbled blindly to my room dissolved in tears, crushed to the marrow. Mama, who knew when to be quiet, came quickly after me, to assure me that all wasn't lost.

"Papa doesn't mean what he says, he's just not used to the idea. Have a little patience, Sarah, he'll get over it, I know he will. It's like the old sayings, "Every tide has its ebb," and "Every day brings a new light." This means people, too, and why should Papa be different from the rest? It will take a little time but you'll find a new school, maybe in Manchester or even Hartford.

A few months later that day came about, but not until she went to work on Papa—subtly, outright—finally convincing him that there were dancers and *dancers,* the stage and teaching variety, and that his daughter would concern herself solely with the latter; on this she pledged the "health and happiness of the family," which even Papa couldn't resist.

Then one morning in late October Papa deposited me in front of the awesome Robely School of the Dance on sedate Farmington Avenue in Hartford, some twenty miles distant, then drove off to replenish Bendix springs and timers and gaskets, and fresh produce—always fresh produce Saturday mornings, insisting that already he was hours late for the choicest of Front Street's marketables. This was nine a.m., a full hour on a strange street before class would start, on a raw and windy morning. No ray of sun to lift the gloom from that red-brick converted mansion-studio, and the chill nipped through my meager coat and Rose's new sweater which at the last moment Mama insisted I wear. I walked up and down the street eight or ten times, nervously waiting for a more decorous time to make my entrance.

Then I was being ushered in by a dreary uniformed maid who promptly informed me, as if I didn't know, "You're much too early. Class starts at ten. But come in anyways and sit down." She didn't look the type that would care about Papa and Front Street so I kept my silence and meekly walked into the sleek empty ballroom that looked like a fashionable mausoleum and sat down on one of the gilt chairs lined up precisely on a spotless waxed floor. The walls were hung with huge mirrors, instead of hand-painted murals, shamelessly looking on. With pumping heart I sat, my feet rigid for fear of scratching the shining, mirrored floor, until a few minutes before the hour when, in twos and threes, a group of modishly attired girls appeared. There was light easy chatter as they filed past me into the dressing room, barely noticing my presence. I wanted to run out but as I got up and reached for my coat, there were rapid footsteps from above and then a ruddy-faced, middle-aged man was walking down calling out his greeting cheerfully, "Oh, yes you're the new girl."

The contrast between Mr. Robely and Juan Valez was like a slim-ankled trotter lined up against a plow horse. He was short and round and pot-bellied but I quickly reminded myself that Ned Wayburn, my dream idol who conducted a famous dancing school in New York City, was no glamor boy either, yet my one desire in life was to train under him. Especially after reading his literature—which I sent for annually and devoured—that pointed with pride to students like Ruby Keeler, Gilda Gray, Ann Pennington, and every other outstanding actor or dancer. Why can't you be famous, too, his pamphlets read?

While Mr. Robley spoke, he carefully appraised me like a chunk of gold ore under assay; all the while the weight in my stomach squealing like a fiddle tuning up. What did you expect, I jogged myself, a Nijinsky? Even Ned Wayburn is old and heavy—what did you expect?

I quickly learned, however, that what Mr. Robley lacked in personal appeal he made up in expert dancing. Despite his rotund bulk he danced as if suspended in air, his body a mass of unexpected grace; a prodigious teacher, too. Before we worked out a new step on the floor, he'd roll out a mammoth blackboard, proceeding to fill it with numbers, dots and dashes, humming and tapping as he went along. Then facing us, he hummed and clapped the beat until the rhythm slowly filtered in and we all hummed and clapped in unison, and twenty feet started tapping out routines to music. From simple to complicated routines I could hardly wait to get home and perform for my audience—Mama. Dancing was sheer joy and progress in the staid dancing establishment on Farmington Avenue was rapid.

At last I was beginning to get somewhere.

18

Never Howl Till You're Hit

One day while Keeve was setting type on the multigraph I walked into the room and hovered over his shoulder.

How costly that casual visit would be, I had no idea.

I was feeling a tinge of unrest, though progress in the Robley School continued on a decent level, and hardly a day passed without a workout sandwiched in between waiting on store, helping Mama, homework, and a few other pursuits. By the time my junior year rolled around, my week ran something like this: Monday—7:30 p.m. adult class; Tuesday, free (catch up on homework); Wednesday, 4:00 p.m. children's class; Thursday p.m. coach dancing line in Rockville revue; Friday, homework; Saturday a.m., go to Hartford for lesson. This schedule varied with the seasons, but with the Rockville Revue now only a memory, time hung heavy on my hands, and this I voiced to Keeve.

"I'd like to do something new . . ."

"Like what?" said Keeve, intent on his work.

"Well—like starting a new class in Will—"

"Willimantic?" Keeve not only caught the ball, but

221

snatched it. "Sounds like a good idea, Sarie."

"I was just wondering how I'd get started."

"What's the big deal about getting started?" said Keeve.

"Where would I begin?"

Keeve was filing the last line of type. "Wheew! That finishes that," he said, whirling around on the swivel stool. "You know, kiddo, you have a great idea there."

When Keeve called me "kiddo" I knew an idea was rolling around in his head, ready to bounce into action. But I wasn't sure I wanted it to. He stopped a moment, staring in thought, but just a moment.

"I've got it, Sarie. Forget about it. Just leave it to me and in no time you'll be running your school. Of course, you'll have to help a little here and there, like distributing the circulars I'll print on the multigraph."

I cringed at the thought. "But where?" I asked, trying hard not to show ingratitude.

"To a public school."

"A school!"

"Of course a school! Hand them to a couple of teachers and I bet they'll be glad to pass them out. I figure it this way. If you get rid of fifty flyers you're sure to get one kid out of ten. See what I mean, kiddo? Right off, you start with five pupils. With a little luck maybe ten." His ideas popped out with the assurance of a second lieutenant feeling his fresh authority.

Keeve and I functioned on two plateaus: I, on the just-thinking-about-it level; he, on the let's-get-started-before-it's-too-late level. I was listening to a surge of ideas that left me bewildered, yet I felt my excitement rising with so glowing a picture. Even allowing for a sprinkling of stardust, point by point his breakdown held logic and reason though loaded with overtones of Madison Avenue. Anyway, resisting a good sales pitch has never been my strong suit. I never had what Keeve calls the guts to say no.

"Yeah—it sounds pretty good," I said, paper and pencil in hand. "What'll I say? Let's see now . . .a class in dancing will—"

Keeve stopped me short. "Forget about it, kiddo, just leave the details to me and you worry about the routines."

That was the thing you liked about Keeve, always pitching in, eager to pull the load off your shoulders. No one I knew had a brother like him.

My gratitude overwhelmed me. "Gee, Keeve, you're swell. I don't know how I can ever thank you."

But he knew.

The rest of the afternoon I typed letters, pick-and-peck method, for Keeve's enterprise—the mail-order business.

True to his word, three days later Keeve handed me a neat package of circulars. "Well, Sarie, You're on your way to the big time. Take a look at this." He carefully pulled out a sheet and handed it to me. "Just take a look," he repeated excitedly over my shoulder.

I took a look and reeled into the closest chair. "Oh, no!"

"What's wrong? Just tell me one thing that's wrong."

"*It's all wrong!*" I read the bold black print back to him.

HAVE YOU LEARNED TO DANCE? If not, a bright future awaits you. COME TO THE NATHAN HALE HOTEL this FRIDAY after school 4:00 P.M. for a FREE DANCING LESSON in tap and ballet. A New World Will Open Up For You.

"Name one thing wrong. Just one. The trouble with you is that you haven't been around. How else can you stir up a little interest?"

"Let's start from the beginning. In the first place I'm not the Ned Wayburn School of Dancing. In the second place, who ever heard of a free sample lesson? Who do you think I am, the Cookie man? If I can't run a school like the others I won't start. Anyway," I said, my eyes puddling, "I want to teach children who love dancing, not those who come because it's free."

"Silly girl," said Keeve, softening the pitch, "who else will show up but kids who love to dance? Who else would bother? Anyway, let's face the facts. Who knows you in Willimantic? Nobody. You have to try a gimmick to attract kids, and once they come, you're set."

"It's cheap and undignified."

"It's all the way you look at it. Don't forget it's a two-way street. You've got to give them a chance to look you over, too. Where do you get the dignity stuff? You're a young kid, completely unknown, and you expect kids to flock to you? The only way you can get dignity is to show them you have the stuff. If you don't, kiddo, no fancy words can give it to you."

He was right there. Why would a youngster come to me instead of an established school?

Keeve, quick to sense a change, continued to play down my fears, his arguments so compelling and reasonable it now seemed the right, sensible thing to do.

"Try it," he said. "If it doesn't work out, what have you to lose?"

"If it doesn't work out . . . I'll never set foot in Willimantic again."

I listened as Keeve poured on the instructions. He had it figured out to the last detail, and the next day I strode nervously through the Natchaug grammar school yard, rehearsing my speech over and over before walking into the building. Some ten minutes later I found myself in the room of a fifth-grade teacher and shyly mumbled my request. She was a sweet young thing with a freshly marcelled wave and to my great surprise she agreed to pass them out—not only pass them out, but assured me it would be a pleasure. "I'll turn the rest over to Miss Baker's class."

By now I was in a state of elation and hurried over to the Nathan Hale, the newest, most modern hotel this side of Boston, found the manager and poured out my magnanimous plan, explaining the trial lesson would most certainly blossom into a regular weekly class. Could I rent a large room? And what would the cost be per week?

As he listened, he looked me over so intently I expected any moment he'd ask to see my teeth, or at any rate my birth certificate. But he didn't. "So you're the little teacher," he said, a weak smile parting his lips. I nodded, reddening, expecting defeat. "By gosh, girlie, we never did anything like this before, but I reckon there's not much harm in giving it a try. About the rent," he said thoughtfully, "we'll talk about that after we see the size of your class."

"Could I see the room, please?"

"Room? Why, there's only one room big enough—the main dining room. Think that'll suit you?"

I looked at him and stared, open-mouthed. This was far more than I expected.

"But there's just one thing," he said, "you'll have to clear out at 5 p.m. sharp. That'll just about give us time to set the tables straight for the early guests."

When I found my voice I thanked him heartily, then hurried out to catch the first bus home before he changed his mind.

I poured it all out to Keeve. "Just imagine teaching in that gorgeous dining room. I couldn't believe it!"

"Sarie, that's only the beginning. You're just starting to go places and don't forget it."

Immediately I began mapping a program for the trial lesson which must double as a lure to hold the few on-the-fencers who might show up. "If only just five or six will come," I said hopefully.

"Don't worry your little head about that. If nothing else, the prestige of a fine hotel like the Nathan Hale will haul 'em out."

"You really think so?"

"Do I really think so!"

Buckling down to homework was impossible. My mind could function on nothing but the Friday class at the Nathan Hale, and the five or six or (with a little luck) eight shining new faces. Over and over I revised the form of instruction, the welcoming speech. This first lesson must be planned to perfection, the lesson that would determine my future success.

During school hours on Friday—The Day—I watched the minute hand on the clock, listened to teachers I didn't hear, fumbled through recitations I didn't study. My mind raced wildly with greetings and steps and opening remarks, but most of all with visions of a flowering career. Yet during it all a vague gnawing at the pit of my stomach kept reminding me that no one might show up at all...no, this couldn't happen...forget it, you silly fool, this just couldn't happen—even to you.

When at last the bell rang on the final period I jumped as if the sound was the starting shot at the Winter Olympics. There was time, plenty of time, but I was the first one out of school and hurried down High Street, my hands clammy with sweat. More than a little terror gripped me; pounding away at my heart like an automatic trip hammer was the vagueness, the utter uncertainty of it all. I tried to regain my composure by inhaling deep draughts of fresh air, for I must above all create a dignified, poised posture. I must rise to the occasion, Keeve insisted before I left. He went on to talk about situations that separated little girls from women, only he put it in terms of boys and men.

As I walked my eyes were drawn to a clock in a small

barbershop attached to a frame house with a sagging porch. Only three o'clock—one full hour to go. I could hear the barber laughing heartily as he lathered a customer and I envied all the people in the world who were happy with their lot; especially those who never heard of dancing careers.

I kept walking in a circuitous route to pass the interminable hour, all the while trying to remain calm, but I was frightened to death. Then, too tired to take another step, I plopped down on a stone wall jutting out from a house, and as I sat there wearily passing the time I looked up and down the street. There was something depressing about the gloomy frame houses, all pleading for fresh paint and a few trees to lessen the drabness. Even the glow of the late afternoon sun only added to the gray harshness—and on the few people that walked the street.

My strength partially returned, I rose, starting slowly for the Nathan Hale Hotel. I was now on Main Street approaching the hotel, and though a full block away I could see a crowd milling around, blocking the main doorway. Just my sweet luck, I thought, something big *would* be happening on *The Day* . . .a wedding. . .a convention . . .maybe a fire . . .anything! But as I drew closer the mob appeared more like children, some as young as seven, I judged, others fourteen or fifteen. Perhaps a school function. Then I stopped short.

"Oh, no!" I groaned as a passer-by turned and stared. Could this mass of kids be the turnout for a free dancing lesson? The five or six or eight children? In a haze I started a head count but gave up after thirty. No, no, it couldn't be . . .it's only a horrible coincidence . . .other things are going on . . .this is a big hotel. Sure—other things. I took a deep breath. You could count on the law of averages, Keeve said. Fifty circulars, five or six kids . . .one out of ten, maybe two. With a little luck,

three—never more. "Never more," quoth the raven,
"never more."

At least sixty or seventy milled about in front; only
God knew how many inside. How silly can I get? These
kids aren't waiting for me . . .ha, ha . . .there for a
moment . .ha, ha . . .

The boys, rumpled and dirty, started grappling with
each other to pass time; the girls, wilted and grubby,
after a day at school, giggled shrilly as an urchin with
tousled hair and patched overalls managed to emit a
nasal bark. "Step right up, folks, step right up for yer
free dancin' lesson. And pitching like a carnival barker,
"H-u-r-r-y, h-u-r-r-y, h-u-r-r-y! Don't cost you nothin',
folks, just walk right in, just walk right in!"

I pushed my way close to this monster of eleven or
twelve.

"Got any sisters or brudders who wants a free lesson,"
he asked, still forcing a twang.

"You sure it's free?" I managed to say. "How do you
know?"

"Everybody at the school knows. All the kids."

I tried again, smothering thoughts of mayhem.

"You must like dancing to come down here for a
lesson."

"Who, *me?* Suddenly he lost his bark. "Waddya take
me for anyways, a fairy?"

"Then—why are you here?"

"Just for the bangs."

"Just for the bangs?" I mumbled. "Just for the
bangs?"

"Sure. Just like the rest of dem."

Even at this moment Keeve's words flashed
back . . .with luck even ten might show up. Take my
word for it, kiddo, nobody'll show up who's not
interested. A sudden surge of heat enveloped me like a
wall of flame; my cheeks burned and my body broke out

in a sticky sweat. By now, a larger crowd, fired by mob curiosity, formed a lively border around the dance lovers, awaiting action, any action.

I don't know how long I stood there, but the sight of the manager's face pressed ominously against the glass door, bolted me into action like a shooting iron pressed to my ribs.

I clapped my sticky, palsied hands, my embarrassment matching my panic. "How many are here for a dancing lesson?" I said when I finally drew their attention.

"Me!" roared a thunderous chorus.

"Raise your right hand," I said, testing my voice.

The hands flew up. Enough for an all-out welcome for visiting royalty.

"Raise your right hand again," I said, because I couldn't think of anything else to say.

Again, defying count, the hands flew up. This time more vigorously.

I waited a moment, summoning what could be mistaken for composure. "I can only take twenty. The rest of you will have to leave."

Then the shouts and roars began. People poured out of stores, traffic halted as drivers jumped out to aid the victim, and then a cop was on the scene. "Break it up, kids, break it up," he said, swinging his club dangerously, but no one heard him above the din of "Pick me! Pick me!" Right there I wanted to die as quickly and gracefully as the law allowed, but first I felt duty bound to explain this human eruption to the officer.

"Okay, girlie, but I'll give you just two minutes to settle this. You're obstructing traffic," he said scowling.

I thanked him for his generosity. All I needed was twenty seconds. I beckoned to a neatly dressed boy who seemed as misplaced as a petunia in an onion bed, and indicated to nineteen others surrounding me—regardless of sex, age, or degree of dirt—that they had emerged the chosen ones. At this a sullen howl went up, and while the line filed through the door, I waited, expecting to be pelted, but nothing happened and I rushed in eager to be out of range of the mob—and the management, whom I deftly avoided by looking neither to right or left. Once inside the dining room, I shut the French doors solidly behind me.

A strange quiet seized the group as they stared at the spacious, polished room, the rich brocaded drapes, the ornate trappings and paintings, but most of all their eyes were drawn to the tables formally set for the dinner hour—the shining silver, the mass of shining silver, gleaming royally against the snowy white cloths. Everyone seemed more than a little awed by the spectacle.

I snatched at the lull to recoup my wits. The real me, the hidden subconscious me, strained to cry, "Out, creatures, every miserable one of you!" But the conscious me, the dancing me, said hollowly, "Form two lines, please."

But no one turned. They were still gaping at the tables. *"Form Two Lines!"* I shouted, clapping my hands. "Form two lines!" Life returned. The odd mixture of ages and sizes shuffled clumsily about until two jagged lines were formed. Some whispered, others giggled. A few boys still gaped at the table.

Abandoning my prepared speech, I proceeded with the lesson, my sole desire of the moment to get this thing over as painlessly as nature would permit. Starting with the basic single shuffle, one-two-three, one-two-three, one-two-three-four-five-six-seven, I clapped out the tempo, thinking murderously to rhythm, "Oh, my God, oh my goodness, would that Keeve were here now."

Two boys seemed to be shuffling slowly back to the tables. Twice I brought them forward. In a few moments they had again gravitated to the rear, but now it didn't matter. If they learned or didn't learn, nothing mattered less, for now I was dead certain that Willimantic would never see me again.

I continued teaching, mechanically repeating the single shuffle over and over and over until rhythm thumps tapped in unison—then continued on to the double shuffle, combining the two. For a moment the unexpected response erased my anxieties and I felt a degree of well-being. Perhaps, I told myself, a judgment formed too hastily was like convicting a man without a trial. These kids could be earnest, even talented; the thought strengthened me, though now my immediate concern lay with the management outside the closed door. Inside, the scene appeared to be moving favorably. Blessed with nature's instinct for survival, my resilience stretched and contracted like a rubber band. In this semi-deluded state I was ready for the finis of the step, the Break, which when added to the basic shuffles, amounted to normal progress, in this or any other group.

I was calling for quiet to illustrate the Break when a jingling clatter, like falling silverware, tinkled through the room, and as I looked back I saw one of the boys, who kept wriggling to the rear, thrust a piece of silver in his pocket.

Tact, I believe, is a virtue entrenched in the molecules from birth, or painfully acquired at a mellow age in the accumulation of civilized processes. Not graced at birth, and being of tender years, I rushed back, grabbed the pint-sized Fagin and extracted a silver fork from his pocket with a fury amounting to relish. All the despair of the day was brought down on his tousled head. I shook him as if all of Tiffany's stock would drop from his torn overalls, and to further complete the job at hand, I searched his meager person as a cop frisks a gunman.

"Beat it, you—you . . .beat it!" I sputtered, stooping to pick the silver from the floor. He gladly obliged, as did several others at the same moment, possibly fearing an attack. The rest remained, obviously cheered by the outburst, and this roiled me even more.

Somehow, even at this moment, Mama's words, "Everything happens for the best," rushed back to comfort me. Mentally, I brushed my hands decisively and called the dwindled class to order, mustering a firm voice. This time there was no hesitation; the lines scrambled into prompt formation. But now it was too late; the hour was giving out.

So was I.

"Who expects to continue with the class?" I asked in a voice that would scare a mongrel.

For a moment, stone silence. Then a voice spoke up—the only clean boy in the neat suit. "I do."

"Anyone else?" The room was quiet except for the awkward shuffling of feet.

"Class dismissed," I said almost happily. I wanted to get out too, but the neat little boy stayed behind.

"I'd like very much to join your social dancing class," he said smiling politely.

"Social dancing . . .not tap dancing?"

"Oh, no, not tap-dancing. Mother wouldn't approve. I came to enroll in your ballroom dancing course of study."

"Course of study?"

"You see, Mother says that social dancing is important to the development of one's poise and self-confidence. She thinks the other is vulgar."

I wanted to laugh and I wanted to cry but my lungs refused to oblige. Instead, I recommended another studio in town, and he left thanking me ever so much for a most interesting lesson.

Wearily I looked about at the terribly empty room with the terribly beautiful appointments. Somehow I managed to straighten the victimized place settings at a moment when I would have happily indulged in a bit of hysteria had I been less concerned with avoiding the management—a feat I gracefully maneuvered in one fast sprint down the lobby and three long leaps out the door.

19

Every Day in Every Way

In a week my wounds healed substantially, thanks to time and a stack of Mrs. Foster's unsold magazines, and once again Keeve and I resumed friendly relations.

"Sarie," he said remorsefully, "it was a dirty piece of rotten luck, that's what it was. You can't even count on the law of averages any more." A strange note of doubt softened his voice and I sensed a twinge that could pass for compassion.

To atone for this "rotten luck" Keeve insisted on "blowing" me to a day in Hartford. "We'll do the town up brown, kiddo," he said, meaning a second-run movie before morning prices changed, and lunch at the Waldorf Cafeteria. "Order anything—sandwich, apple pie—anything."

Keeve allowed a discreet week to pass before reverting to business as usual. Exactly one week from the unmentionable day he returned from the post office, gripping a long thick envelope. Rose and I were sitting on the porch steps reading a new batch of coverless magazines.

"Hey, kids, listen to this." A familiar glow filled his voice, and Rose and I looked up warily.

234

He raced on. "Here's something that'll change your lives. It'll put color in your cheeks and marrow in your bones." He tore open the glossy, well-illustrated leaflet and thrust it before us. A biceps-bulging, bushy-haired Tarzan clad in a pair of leopard tights and an I-did-this-all-by-myself stance amply filled the page.

"Do you know this man?" Veneration lit Keeve's face.

"No," said Rose, thumbing through the magazine.

"Do you know that most men his age suffer from heart trouble, diabetes, hardening of the arteries?"

"They do?" Airily, Rose continued to leaf the pages.

"Most men of fifty-five are victims of general decline. Now look at him. Does *he* look ready for the grave? This man," he went on, flourishing the sheet before our eyes, "is *the* Bernarr Macfadden, a perfect specimen of the human race. This very same man was a physical wreck at twenty—with one outstanding trait—will power. Now look at him. What he can do, anyone can do."

"You don't mean me, do you?" Rose snickered. "Who needs muscles?"

My burns, while healed, still left a slight scar. I buried my head deeper in the magazine, on guard against Keeve's onslaught.

"Very funny, Rosie. Good health is for girls and women, too, venerable smart one." Keeve was talented at finding a vulnerable spot. Only last week Rose signed up for the annual tennis tournament.

"You'd like to become a first-rate player, wouldn't you?" he plowed on, melting any likely resistance. "Any fool knows a top-rate tennis player must develop wind and endurance. Most would-be's exhaust themselves after the first set; that's when they start losing out. But those who keep fit by constant training go on to become champions. It's just as simple as that."

Rose listened, and her silence, which Keeve took as assent, propelled him to drive on.

"See, kiddo," he said, his voice mellowing. "What have I to gain? *Nothing.* I'm only thinking of *your* good." A clincher that succeeded in making us feel like heels, ingrates.

"Look at Sarah." I still made a pretense at reading. "I don't have to convince her. As a dancer she knows the value of a sound body and a sound mind. Don't you Sarie?" he said by way of command, not question.

Perpetually motivated, Keeve acquired an adeptness in transferring his urges and ideas with a vigor that weighed us with feelings of guilt if we turned him down, and though Rose instinctively put herself on the defensive she would finally agree, though not without a worthy struggle.

But I, like a spineless flunky, recognized the impregnable opposition and catapulted before the battle began. A perennial recruit, I was now hearing the bugler's blare and I stepped saluting into line.

Neither Rose nor I uttered a sound. To reveal a spark of interest would be throwing oil on a blazing flame.

"Well, how about it, kids?" asked Keeve in his kindest, wind-up voice.

"Okay," said Rose, "we'll give it a try."

And Keeve, confident she spoke for me too, lit up like a sparkler. It soon got to Mama who glowed even more than Keeve, though this was not unexpected. So it was we succumbed, in varying degrees, to the Body Beautiful overhaul.

With the precision of a Prussian officer, Keeve mapped out a schedule which he tacked over the kitchen sink.

7:00 AM—Rise
7:10 AM—Cold water rubdown
7:30 AM—Brisk walk
8:15 AM—Breakfast

The next morning, when we ignored the call, Keeve

blustered into our room. "Okay, kids, let's go," he said trying to pull the covers from our viselike grips.

"I'm too tired. Not today—tomorrow," said Rose.

"Just keep on sleeping. It's okay with me. If you want to be fat and puffy at twenty, it's your funeral. Just keep on sleeping." With this he stalked out of the room and down the hall.

I lay there feeling guilty. I nudged Rose. "Maybe he's right, Ro. If we don't exercise we *could* get fat and flabby as he says," I said torn between sleep and conscience. Wearily I dressed and walked downstairs.

Keeve beamed. "Thatsa kid, Sarie, I knew you'd show good sense. Now hurry up and fill the tub with cold water, jump in for a minute, then rub yourself briskly with a Turkish towel till your body tingles and you're feeling like a millon."

"A tub of cold water? Never!"

Twenty minutes later I emerged from the bathroom, feeling more like a raw carrot than "a million." Keeve eyed me discreetly but said nothing, then he called, "Ready, Mama?"

The three of us marched off like soldiers on a drill. I thought of Rose, not without envy, lying in bed risking her youth and figure. As we proceeded up the State road, Keeve said, "Let's see now . . . .Bunker Hill's the steepest road and we can work up a good sweat. Yep, we'll start there."

Before turning into Bunker Hill, Keeve demonstrated the new breathing process. "Walk briskly, swing the arms loose in natural rhythm, breathe deeply like this: Inhale one-two-three. Hold, one-two-three. Exhale, one-two.

"Only one-two to exhale?"

"Right. Develops lung intake." Keeve's orders were short and crisp. "Let's stop talking and start breathing."

I felt like asking what he thought we were doing, but skipped it.

Bunker Hill was long and steep, dividing into three breaks like landings on a staircase. The first was the longest and steepest and for a starter, Keeve said, we'd climb it only twice, increasing it daily until we reached five, then take the next hill when our lung power developed. He said it like a general directing a surprise attack within enemy range.

Thus the New Order was launched. It started with walks, fresh air and exercise, but it didn't end there.

One evening as we sat down to an oven roast flanked by browned new potatoes oozing in succulent gravy, and our favorite sweet-and-sour spinach-and-rice-dish, Keeve eyed the food suspiciously.

"Mama, do you know this meal is potential poison?" We all looked at Keeve as Rose tapped the side of her head. "And I'm not kidding. In the first place, meat—any person who knows anything about anything will tell you that meat is acid-forming. And what is meat, anyway, but dead animals? And these potatoes, peeled and robbed of Nature's minerals—and this overcooked, doctored-up spinach. Why, what you're serving is a fatty, starchy, devitalizing mass that deadens the body's functions almost as much as arsenic—only the process is slower."

"You don't say so, Keevie." Mama was a picture of despair as she looked at the steaming, tantalizing devastation on the table. "Maybe we shouldn't—"

"Maybe we shouldn't what? Maybe we shouldn't eat this supper?" interrupted Rose, clutching the casserole closely as she heaped a generous serving on her plate. "Brother, if this meal will kill me, I'm a willing victim."

"And this bread," continued Keeve as if no one had spoken. He lifted Exhibit A—a slice of white bread—"the curse of civilization—the typical diet of the white man—meat, potatoes, white bread and chocolate cake. This, not war, can be the ruination of man."

"Who can be so sure," said Papa, helping himself to the roast. "A new idea is not always a good idea. Sometimes it takes years of experimenting . . ."

And Mama, always on the lookout for the Better Life, said, "Maybe Keeve's right. Every day you hear new ways to help people and we should be thankful for these new ideas and try them out."

"But why should we be the first guinea pigs?" said Rose, spokesman for the resistance.

"We're not the first," said Mama. "Look at our cousins, the Bamburgs, they've been vegetarians for years, and happy and healthy with never a sick day."

"You bet," said Keeve, refueling. "Bad food habits are handed down from generation to generation. You've got to be one of two things—or both, to resist them—strong enough or smart enough. That lets some people out." Keeve pointed airily to Rose, who was now walking out.

For a moment Mama said nothing. Perhaps she was thinking how well her food habits went over with the family—especially with Papa. "Maybe the change shouldn't be too quick, Keevie. Once in a while a nourishing top round beef roast with good fresh vegetables—or a little fresh broiled trout when the fishermen from Columbia—"

"You've got to make a clean break like a chain smoker kicking the habit. You make up your mind to do it at once. In the end it's easier."

For the first time Mama showed concern. "So what do we eat?"

"Don't worry, Mama, leave it to me. I'll figure it out. But first of all we eliminate meat com-plete-ly."

"Maybe just a little chicken soup once in a while . . ." Mama was holding on.

"Chicken soup! Least of all, chicken soup, which anybody knows is nothing but glorified urine. Like I said, we quit eating meat, fish or foul." The words came crisp, like a doctor's orders. "Substitute cheese, eggs, nuts, legumes for meat proteins. Stop cooking vegetables. Cooking devitalizes, and the only part worth saving, the water, nourishes nothing but the sink drain."

"But—but how?"

"Simple. Use them raw in salads. With a little thought and imagination you can use every vegetable in its natural organic state. Now, the next step is to eliminate white food products. Utilize whole grains as Nature intended them to be used, and serve plenty of milk, the one perfect food rich in essential nutrients. And fruits, of course. Fruit and vegetables contain the newest nutritional discovery—vitamins, A, B, and C."

Keeve's presentation, infused with vigor and spirit and a few well-memorized passages, rang with an air of authority. Though we looked forward to the prospect of bidding good-bye to tasty, temptingly prepared cooked and baked foods the way a pussy cat looks forward to meeting a mountain lion, his glowing account of The Change so wheedled us, we were sure the day would come when we'd be more than compensated for this new Spartan existence.

"Look at Charles Atlas, Annette Kellerman, and thousands of others," he'd say whenever Rose or I bewailed the chopped dandelion greens set before us.

"You look at them," Rose would say balefully, but Keeve paid no heed.

It so happened our good health could well have been the envy of the "thousands of others," and when we'd confront him with this apparent state of the flesh, he argued it was our old age we must be concerned with, the long-range picture, and not the immediate present—the occupation of fools. Did we want to be fools? Of course not! So—what were we waiting for?

Thus we were launched on old-age security long before the government heard of it—Mama excitedly, Papa cautiously, Rose balkingly, and I, submissively—but nonetheless, launched.

Mama quickly learned to combine varieties of raw vegetables, fruits, nuts, eggs, cheese—every kind of cheese—into salads, and since this was the main course, she was most painstaking in the preparation. Like exquisite designs, they sparkled with the love and care she poured into them. To compensate for tedious sameness she strove for color and decoration and most of the day was spent washing greens, slicing tomatoes, grating carrots, cabbage, beets; shelling peas, stringing beans, shredding lettuce, endives, spinach, romaine; chopping nuts, figs, dates, prunes; cubing, slicing, segmenting. And she worked away at these objets d'(culinary) art in a grim attempt to lure the wary palate.

From early morning to late evening Mama was busy. Her vegetable garden sprang an edible jungle, her flower bed sprouted weeds. She rarely stopped to chat with the townspeople who came to the store, which was not like Mama at all. No sooner was one meal served and cleared away then she was shredding, slicing, chopping away at the next.

"It certainly takes time," said Mama wearily as she bandaged her bruised, acid-stained fingers, "but after all, what is time when you are doing good for your family?"

"Grass—cow's food," muttered Papa as he dug into the raw chopped spinach garnished with slices of hard-boiled eggs—the mouth-watering Rumanian-style spinach and rice only a memory now.

Though Papa grumbled at first he slowly resigned himself to the new regimen. "At least he didn't turn out to be a gangster," he'd say ruefully. He deferred to this strange new order until the morning Mama served him a cup of steaming fluid. Absently he sipped the brew, jumped up from his chair, splattering the brown liquid over the table. "What next!" he shouted. "Is this meant to be coffee?"

"This," said Mama, "is the kind of coffee human beings were meant to drink. Only, thank God, it's not coffee."

"Then what is it?" demanded Papa, sniffing the brew from a safe distance.

"A coffee substitute blended from toasted ground figs and whole wheat cereals. It won't keep you awake, it won't make you nervous, and besides, it works as a physic," Mama said, exactly as Keeve had told her.

Papa flushed with anger. "Since when do I complain of insomnia or constipation? And if I'm nervous, does it surprise you with all this damn nonsense going on? I ask very little out of life. All I ask is a good cup of coffee and what do I get? Something that tastes like dishwater!" Papa strode into the store, throwing up his hands. "What will come next!"

Mama looked at him with understanding. "Changes don't come easy for older people," she said, sighing.

Early the next morning Papa walked grimly into the kitchen speaking to no one, and set about measuring coffee, chicory and water in the white agate percolator. When the pot bubbled, floating the steaming fragrance through the house, he poured himself a cup. I joined in the mutiny and poured the usual trickle of coffee into a glass of milk. Mama looked on but she knew well the sageness of the proverb "Silence is golden." With the spirited restraint of victor over vanquished she poured foaming fresh orange juice into eight-ounce tumblers and set them before us. Four-ounce glasses, Mama reasoned, provided you with only half the vitamins cf an eight-ounce glass, which any fool could tell was twice as good.

Papa drank, his eyes focused on the juice and she

proceeded to serve breakfast—steaming bowls of puffy whole-grain cereal (fresh from the fireless cooker where it steamed all night) submerged in hot milk—soft-boiled eggs and whole-wheat bread toasted to the proper degree of brittleness for proper digestion. Sated with vitamins, minerals and real coffee, his anger melted by the time she poured his usual second cup. He walked over to Mama in genial truce and kissed her forehead. Still silent, he finished his coffee and walked into the store humming.

"A person must know when to give in a little," cooed Mama. The next morning and every morning thereafter she perked Papa's coffee, though not without the daily reminder it was never too late to avoid becoming an addict.

By now the cupboards and pantry were emptied of all "devitalized" cereals, white flour, white rice, white sugar, spices and condiments. In its place stood gleaming Mason jars filled with whole-wheat flour, brown sugar, honey, natural rice, whole-grain kernels which Papa brought home in fifty-pound burlap sacks. Figs, dates, nuts, prunes, raisins were substituted for cake and candy, and most of this was merged through the meat grinder to insure equitable distribution of nutrients.

No sooner were we adjusted to our new way of life, our vegetarian cousins—the Bamburgs from Norwich—Mike and Tillie and their husky twelve-year old Aaron paid us an unexpected visit. It was a great day when they found other members of the family who were not only kin, but kindred in spirit, too. The "ism" of vegetarianism seemed to cause as much ruffle as the "ism" in Bolshevism, and was looked upon with as much favor. A vegetarian found little rapport with carnivorous members of society and each viewed the other with an air tinged with pity. "How terrible!" each said of the other. In this light, the discovery of new recruits was due cause for rejoicing.

Mama worked a littler harder preparing the supper meal. She looked at Tillie's rosy, rounded cheeks and marveled; no trace of cosmetics sullied her skin. She looked at Mike, ruddy and muscular, and remembered he was not always this way. A number of years back the New Order turned out to be desperate medicine. Even Aaron was solid and healthy. Looking at them, she smiled happily and needed no further convincing.

This was the first time Mama was called upon to serve a company meal and she took special pains to make the salads a little more beautiful, to serve a larger variety of steamed vegetables and to cut the Cheddar, Edam, and Roquefort cheese into more tempting designs. Repeatedly she brushed back wisps of hair from her tired, flushed face.

"Delicious," beamed Mike, helping himself to a second serving of raw beet salad garnished with sour cream. "You'll have to make this, Tillie." Mama responded as if a medal for outstanding service to her country had been pinned on her apron, and when she topped the meal with whole-wheat honey cake and fig coffee, the Bamburgs ate and applauded heartily. Nor did the weight of the cake deter them.

Tillie looked at Mama, a new glint in her eyes. "Do you know, Esther, you can turn fig coffee into tea. Instead of cream, serve slices of lemon."

"You don't say," said Mama as Papa gurgled audibly and walked into the store with Mike and the boys.

Rose and I cleared the table and washed the dishes while Tillie and Mama huddled, their voices rising to a pitch of excitement as if each had stumbled into a cove of treasure; they gleamed as they spoke of the prospects of our Better Life. Mama's fervor was shifting into second gear, ready for high.

"But one thing is important, Esther," said Tillie. "If you don't want the family to complain of the same salads and steamed vegetables you must offer them variety."

"Yes?" Mama hung on every word.

"Serve them chops and cutlets, perhaps some chopped liver or meat loaf."

"Chops and cutlets!" said Mama, dismayed. "But I thought—"

Tillie cut in, laughing. "Of course we are, Esther. It takes a little experimenting but you can cook dishes that taste just like meat if you combine them with the proper vegetables, nuts and cheese."

"You don't say!" said Mama, who could generate respect for any kind of talent.

"Of course! Nearly everything."

Tillie was partly right. A bit of autohypnosis coupled with a wild imagination could induce anyone to believe he were dining grandly on roast venison or chopped liver.

"Yeah," said Rose quietly, "especially porterhouse steak medium rare."

It might have been the Bamburgs' visit or the heartburn he suffered in New York the previous week, but Papa, as if suddenly inspired, turned to the New Order with a zeal that even stunned Mama—except for his coffee which he doggedly clung to, as if to insure his place as head of the house. Mama never knew nor did she ask, thanking God for small favors. But join the ranks he did and for her that was enough.

Despite the Change, of which our relatives and city friends were duly forewarned, the annual visits continued. Not only did we provide cross-ventilated rooms for good sleeping, but Papa installed kitchen equipment in the old Delco room to encourage meat-eating guests to cook their meals in privacy.

Since little recreation was available locally, our guests'

leisure time was spent bathing in the river, hiking in the woods and over country roads, walking to the post office to listen to country gossip and wait for mail, but most of all hurling innuendoes about the change. A gentle but well-aimed bombardment sallied back and forth like a shuttlecock each attempting to shift the other to his way of life.

From our relatives, "At least you might let these poor, undernourished children eat with *US*. If you won't think of yourselves, think of them. Do you call grass nourishment? Who put these dangerous ideas into your head?"

Mama, not to be outdone, would retort quietly, "We don't know the meaning of indigestion—maybe less greasy meat and spicy foods might stop the heartburn you complain about . . ." And so it went, one making no impression on the other.

Rose and I managed to remove ourselves from the range of volley but it was a little more difficult to resist the pungent, juicy whiffs of steak broiling over charcoal, the savory aroma of chicken stewing or meat roasting. Cooking odors hovered thickly like fragrant miasma, and building resistance was like pushing back a tornado with two bare hands. However, we made the grand effort and managed to work up a magnanimous mixture of pity and tolerance—much like a pious pillar of the church who shrouds his not-too-pious rumblings in charitable gestures, pouring it lavishly over our poor, dear misguided relatives painfully ignorant of the facts of life, namely, whole-grain cereals and vitamins A, B, and C.

In a few months Keeve's name appeared on every health-promoting list in the country; an onslaught of new theories, new approaches swelled the daily mail. The Body Beautiful started with Bernarr Macfadden, but it didn't end there. A mass of leaflets profusely illustrated almost swamped us. Down came seductive, glamorous movie stars from the bedroom walls; up went bulging biceps, tensed muscles, and bosomy females of the rigorous cult.

But new theories require research—and research requires people. If no one volunteers, what then? Enlist them, to be sure! Who? Mama? She was elbow-deep in current research. Papa? Lately he seemed touchy, especially about new thinking. Rose? She shows no appreciation for the better things. Sarah? Ah, yes, Sarah! Just thirty minutes more . . .

And thirty minutes more each day I bent and swayed to the rhythm of a phonograph record while a too cheerful voice urged me on.

"Wake up, ladies! Wipe those naughty sleepers from your eyes. Ready now? S-t-r-e-t-c-h. Come, ladies, this exercise will bounce that youthful spring right back in your step as you lose pounds, pounds, pounds. All set to go? Won-der-ful! Down one, two, up one, two, repeat one, two, ten times, one, two." I figured he must mean me though I was sixteen and slim as a reed. Keeve patrolled, beaming. When at last he said, "Atta-girl, Sarie, you can quit now," it was like a dispensation from the Pope, and after that I worked twice as hard at whatever it was.

When autumn came our morning walks were already infused with a new vigor. My wind power increased threefold; I could easily breathe one-two-three, one-two-three, one-two as we bore down on the first two hills five times daily in training for the attack on the last third.

My progress did not go unnoticed. "Someday you'll be in shape to enroll at Sargeant's Physical Training School." Once before I told him of my plans for ballet school. "Sure, kiddo, you can do anything you like in your spare time."

On bright, clear weekends, our walks stretched into

hikes. When we'd hit the top of Bunker Hill, by now a minor feat, a stretch of rustic splendor spread before us like a bright horizon and we continued on, proceeding down the narrow dirt road that wound refreshingly under leafy canopies; compared to the daily walking menu, these hikes were dessert. We packed lunches and walked the seven miles that led through Coventry, winding around to Long Hill, down past the church, railway depot, and home. Often we picnicked beside a racing, tumbling brook which seemed to beckon us as an old friend.

These days we discarded the breathing exercise, the brisk gait. Even Keeve agreed you had to change pace occasionally. "It charges you up like a new set of spark plugs."

Some days we stopped to visit with Mrs. Green whose house perched majestically on Bunker Hill like a shrine on a mountaintop; the panoramic view of neighboring villages looked like an aerial shot in the Sunday rotogravure section—vast countrysides dotted with barns and farmhouses, brooks coursing through clumped masses of trees, and as if in accent, the Congregational church's white steeple.

Except for a hay wagon, a stray cow, or the mailman sputtering up in low gear, we encountered few people. Sometimes we met Ed Green in his shining black buggy or the Cartwrights who summered in a weathered Cape Cod dwelling set back on a clearing halfway up the hill; townspeople used roads to get places, not for exercise .

Spry and healthy and well along in her seventieth year, Mrs. Green would look for us each day, beckoning vigorously.

"Sakes alive," she'd say, leading us to the parlor, never understanding what possessed folks who walked for exercise alone, yet grateful that we did, "you must be plumb tuckered out after all that trudging."

We munched on juicy winesap apples, swayed on rockers covered with starched huck toweling yellowed with age, and gazed in awe at priceless treasures, whose origins dated back hundreds of years, simply placed about the room. Antique collectors besieged Mrs. Green but she refused to sell.

"These pieces were handed down by my mamma and her granny, and granny's mamma and her granny, and I suspect they'll continue to be handed down," she'd say, a determined twinkle in her eye.

She chatted about her children, her grandchildren, the weather, crops, the village news, but mostly about her house plants which she tended with gentle passion.

"I have a new baby, come see it," she'd say, satisfied each topic was picked clean like chicken off a bone, and out we tripped behind her to a sun-splattered room that looked like a toy greenhouse. Plants, seedlings and herbs, ranging from baby sprouts to tall, lush specimens spilled over tables, sills, chests, and each she referred to lovingly by a strange, botanical term. While most were unfamiliar, a few we knew by simple common names, and in time learned to equal the little old lady's fervor, patiently waiting for the burgeoning of a seedling to a full-grown plant, delighting in each fresh growth.

On days when "village news" lagged, Mrs. Green would show us through her heirloom-filled house, one room a visit, zealously and conditionally, as if to say, "Children, continue to be good and you'll get a bigger and better lollipop." When finally the house was shown in its entirety, it was like an award earned for good conduct.

For some weeks now the Green farm had supplied us with milk and we welcomed the definite reason to stop. Each of us carted two two-quart milk cans filled with fresh, foamy milk still warm from the cow's udder. Mama used it extravagantly, converting most of it to pot cheese, sweet and sour cream, sometimes butter when the supply accumulated too quickly. With the opening of school, trips were earlier, visits shorter. We returned home in time for a mineral-studded breakfast which never varied. Before the morning walk Mama continued to fortify us with large glasses of orange juice, insisting the timing was essential for proper digestion.

The rugged pattern—vegetarianism, hikes, exercise, routine—was now set like hardened clay in a mold, and now that we oozed with health and vitality, Keeve decided he must look to other areas, namely the mental.

"Not only must you work at keeping your body in shape, but your mind as well." He had just finished reading about Emil Coué of France, father of the cult of autosuggestion that was currently creating a stir around the country.

"This Coué fellow says you can do anything you set out to, providing you firmly believe you can do it. It boils down to developing strong faith in yourself, and in time this will conquer mind over matter. That, believe it or not, is all there is to it."

Mama's face was a study in awe. "Can a person really accomplish this?"

"Why, it's so easy, you wouldn't believe it. Just listen: all you do is repeat eleven simple words, twenty times on rising, twenty times before sleep. These periods respond productively to your subconscious; your thoughts absorb and register in some mysterious way. If you have strong faith in these thoughts they will go to work and before you know it they're part of your conscious behavior. Understand?"

Rose was apparently sparked by this studied account. "What is the subconscious?"

Keeve thought a moment. "Well, Ro, let's see. Do you know that your mental processes are active twenty-four hours a day?"

Rose shook her head.

"It's this way. When you're awake you're conscious of feelings and impulses, but not during sleep. Yet they go on, often governing your conscious thinking. For example, your subconscious holds on to knowledge gained over the years, and plays a big part in memory. Dreams, also, are an outlet of the subconscious. A fellow by the name of Freud says that someday men will understand the mind as well as they do the body."

Mama listened and beamed. She was proud of Keeve. Almost as proud as the day when as a little boy he asked to eat his lunch in the pure, fresh air—before she discovered Sport. She knew he thirsted for anything printed and availed himself of every book with a guarantee of satisfaction or money back offer, yet his amazing horde of information never failed to astound her. She looked lovingly at the colorful array of self-improvement and body-building books lining the Nabisco bookcase, in company with complete-in-one-volume classics—Shakespeare, DeMaupassant, Browning, Emerson; Roget's Thesaurus, Book of Etiquette (two volumes), a huge dictionary, a set of World Histories and a twelve-volume set called *The Outline of Knowledge.* This and Joe Miller's jokebook, George Ade's *Fables in Slang,* Milt Gross and an odd assortment of titles.

About the time Papa acquired a 35-millimeter motion-picture camera, projector and silver screen to demonstrate his labor-saving models to the clothing trade, a large thick volume titled, *Behind the Motion Picture Screen* suddenly appeared. A vast new unexplored territory opened up—Hollywood, and Keeve lost no time pursuing it.

"First things first," he said, posting a special delivery letter to Charlie Werner in New York, his straight-A-in-English friend from Stuyvesant High, urging him to write the scenario for a smash movie hit. "We got to save production costs in the beginning, Charlie, so give it a rural setting. All profits we share fifty-fifty. Remember, we want a good story so take your time. How about two weeks? Rush it back special delivery."

Keeve promised Rose the roles of leading lady and assistant producer, provided she agreed to head up the costume department. My role in the production would be minor, but a major one in the props department, he assured me. "It's the man behind the scene that counts, kiddo. Actors come a dime a dozen."

Charlie got right down to the scenario and rushed it back in ten days. When Keeve read it he moaned, "He should have taken the full two weeks." By his tone I knew we were not destined for a glamor career.

"You can't expect to get a real screen writer, a studio, actors, props without dough," he said sadly, placing the volume on a closet shelf.

Mama marveled about the Coué fellow. "Such an idea! Only eleven words." She wondered, innocent of any trace of doubt, how this could be. "So what are the words?"

"As I said, they're so simple you wouldn't believe it, and it works like magic. Now listen carefully," said Keeve, weighing the words slowly, "and remember them, 'Every day in every way I'm getting better and better.' "

"Just that?" asked Rose.

"What did you expect? Merlin the magician?"

And so it was that Coué's method of autosuggestion rounded out the New Order. Counting on my fingers, morning and night, I breathlessly repeated the words that would change my life. *"Every day in every way I'm getting better and better,"* tingling with the thought of the new miracle soon to befall me. Every day in every way . . .every day in every way . . .every day in every way . . . .

20

No Wisdom Like Silence

The best thing about a small-town store was that you could always expect the unexpected. Every time the doorbell jingled it aroused a mixture of curiosity and excitement second only to the arrival of the daily mail.

And so it was one Saturday morning. I was busy filling the tobacco case with fresh stock when the door opened and in walked a strange woman, a strong essence of jasmine floating in with her. It was crystal clear this was no villager coming in for her weekly order. Dripping with make-up, her satin knee-length dress sashayed voluptuously with silk tassels, and her bobbed, blond hair—bleached, I was certain—peeped out under her tam which perched at a daring angle.

I stood gaping behind the tobacco case until a husky voice boomed out, "Oh, hello there, girlie, didn't see you."

"Can I help you?" I said, edging closer.

"Quite a burg you got here. How many people in it?"

"Four hundred."

"Four hundred! Suddenly she emitted a throaty giggle.

"Guess the town pulls in their sidewalks at night." She continued to laugh and I stiffened slightly. We endured this scintillating repartee constantly from passing motorists.

"We don't have many people," I said, infinitely grateful to Mama for her ready proverbs, "but what we lack in quantity we make up in quality."

She chuckled again but this time with good humor. "No offense, dearie, was only kidding. Small towns are okay with me but from the looks of it this here town is not the one for our show." Then she added as if I should know, "I'm Marjorie Ray from Hartford."

"Show? What show?"

"An all-girlie musical revue. I train them, manage them and book them and I do a lot of traveling around. I got to be sure a town's right before we hit it."

"You mean dancing girls? Real chorus girls?" Destiny had stumbled into my life.

"Guess you'd call them that, but let me tell you something, darling, they're good girls, every last one of them." There was never a doubt in my mind.

"Oh, my! This town would love that," I said, meaning me. "This is a wonderful town, Miss Ray. Our Town Hall could easily hold over two hundred people." I forgot to add if we included the vestibule and cloak room. I pointed breathlessly to the white clapboard building across the road. "People will come from all around for something as special as that."

"You think so?" The heavily rouged impresario seemed deep in thought. "We put a lot into every production and we can't afford to go bust. Every show has got to pay off."

"It will. I'm sure it will."

Her interest seemed aroused. "You really think so?"

Again I assured her.

"Well, you may be right," she said slowly. "It might

be worth a try . . .yeah, it might just be worth a try."
Then Miss Ray was triggered into action. "Let's see, we'll
book the show a month in advance, we'll plaster the
town with posters, and on every telephone pole this side
of Willimantic and Manchester. We'll do the same in all
nearby burgs, and we'll work up a ballyhoo with spot
announcements over the radio. Yep, p-lenty of ballyhoo.
That's what brings 'em out." And as an afterthought, "I
think we'll run the show for two nights to accommodate
the overflow. We generally do one-night stands but we'll
make an exception in this case. Yes sirree, it might just
go!"

I was carried along in the excitement. "Why sure,
you'll probably be asked to come back year after year,
especially if you offered round and square dancing after
the show. Everyone would be sure to turn out."

"Good idea, dearie, we bring along our own musicians
anyway. They'll play for dancing, too."

Things were popping—and popping fast. All aglow
within, I could picture the extravaganza going over like
the fabulous Ziegfeld Follies, every bit as glamorous,
with a genuine orchestra, not just a fiddle and piano;
frothy costumes, ushers, and most of all a packed house.
Not many events could boast a full house—but this was
not any event. It was something the town would talk
about for days and weeks, maybe months—this I was
sure. And maybe in a year or two I'd be booked in the
troupe as a specialty dancer.

Miss Ray broke into my reverie. "I'll see that you get
two complimentary tickets for being such a help,
darling."

As soon as she left I rushed to the clothes room to
find a dress suitable for this rare occasion. I found it.
The same dress I wore to every other occasion.

The next week Marjorie Ray was back with a thick
roll of posters—gay, rollicking girls in abbreviated

costumes dominated the sheet. It read: Marjorie Ray's
All-Girl Fast-Stepping Revue. Georgeous Chorus of 16—
Specialty Numbers—Novelty Dances—Round and Square
Dancing After the Show—Come One, Come All. She slid
one out and tacked it in the most conspicuous spot in
the store. She put another in the front window. "Now,
dearie, would you tack a few more in the center of town
where folks can see them. I'm covering Coventry,
Columbia and Hebron; we'll have them all out today."

Would I tack them! I called back to Mama to tell her
I was leaving for a few moments and out I rushed to the
post office, the railroad depot, and back to the Town
Hall. I tacked them up in the most prominent places,
including every telephone pole in sight. I was beginning
to feel personally responsible for making this production a
success and brought the poster to every customer's
attention, pointing out how lucky we were to have a
show of this kind actually coming to our town.

Reactions ran the gamut, though men leaned heavily
in favor of the whole idea, especially the stove forum.
"Sounds mighty like a sweet bit of spice to stir up tired
blood." "Look Out, Broadway and 42nd Street" . . ."I
reckon we're about ready for a good leg show, heh,
heh." And in no time the whole town joined in the talk,
openly ventilating their views. Some agreed with the
stove forum, saying it was just what the town needed.
Others insisted it was just what the town didn't need.
Wasn't it enough the young generation was already
defiling the moral fiber of this country with their
bathtub gin, their lewd talk of free love, their wild
automobile rides—some even hitting fifty miles an
hour—brazenly making love in rumble seats. And now, a
sex show, and in our quiet, respectable town? Never!
Artfully forgetting that sex activity flourished not only
in rumble seats but in safe, respectable old-fashioned
haylofts.

And one of the more proper ladies who never so much as laid a power puff on her red, oily nose said, "There oughta be a law against chorus hussies invading a good, clean village." There were many who shared her view and I didn't dare admit I was the steam behind the engine. Not even to Mama. Especially Mama, who often said there was no wisdom like silence. One day I finally blurted it out to Rose, who said I put my big mouth in too many things, and this time I was inclined to agree with her.

It turned into the most heated topic in months, and some of the town's upright and virtuous discussed it only in whispers. But news had a way of leaking out and into the store via the stove forum. When Miss Ray came to make final arrangements, I gloomily poured out the worst, but to my great surprise it phased her not in the least .

"Cheer up, dearie, that's the kind of talk I like to hear. Get those farmers curious and talking and they'll come out to see for themselves. It's good publicity and just what we're after." Marjorie winked good-humoredly as she walked out.

Finally, the night of the opening arrived, and a Stutz, an Essex, an old Packard, and two model T Fords drove up early, depositing a stream of girls. As they disembarked, loaded with costumes and makeup kits, Marjorie rushed from car to car booming out instructions. I had been dressed and waiting for two hours and dashed across the road offering my help. "Sure, darling, you can help with the costumes." And then she was off. Though my experience with costumes was limited to a granny frock in a school play, I ran into the dining-wing which now doubled as a dressing room, well aware of the maxim, "Opportunity only knocks once."

As the troupe filed in I was surprised to find them

looking like any other group of wholesome young girls.
Weren't show people supposed to be coarse-talking and
heavily made up? These girls were nothing of the sort.
Moreover they were pleasant and friendly, and when
Marjorie introduced me around as the "little gal who
worked so hard," establishing me as some kind of pro,
my day was complete.

It was now close to curtain time and a few faint
voices began to filter through from the front; my
thoughts were full of the hall which soon would be filled
to capacity. This was real show biz, there was no
mistaking it, and I tingled with opening-night jitters no
less than if I were one of the performers.

Chatting noisily, the girls clustered around in groups,
attired in brief costumes, long fishnet hose,
patent-leather shoes reinforced with heel-and-toe metal
taps, readying for the opening number, their chief
concern a lively, unified performance. As the self-styled
press agent I looked on with envy, for *my* one big
concern lay with the size of the audience, and it hung
heavy, especially because in some strange way the quality
of the production was linked to my activity. For
according to Marjorie there was nothing like a full house
to make you look and feel like a true pro, on stage or
back in the wings. And while everyone within a radius of
ten miles had heard of the show and a full house for
both nights was assured, one couldn't take anything for
granted.

A line of sixteen girls patiently awaited their cue as
Marjorie bustled about the stage giving final touches to
the scenery—painted umbrellas against a background of
huge raindrops—appropriate for two chorus numbers,
"Let a Smile Be Your Umbrella on a Rain, Rain, Rainy
day," and "April Showers." Every few minutes she
peered through the red velvet curtains appraising the

audience, smoking one cigarette after another. Since it was now curtain time and still no cue from Marjorie, I left the girls, peeped quickly through the curtains—and just as quickly withdrew. For what I saw left me stunned. Moving about the vestibule was a handful of men minus their spouses, and every one a member of the stove forum. Sitting quietly at a table near the door was the ticket-seller, Marjorie's gray-haired mother. She looked very tired.

Then Marjorie appeared in the dressing room. She held up her hand. "Quiet, girls, quiet. Folks are slow coming. We'll wait twenty minutes more for the hall to fill up." With that she walked abruptly away.

For a minute the girls were silent. Then Mitzi, a pretty little redhead, spoke out, "We should've known that farmers only get out Saturday nights." And Bee, a tall brunette who was constantly straightening her seams, tried to console us. "Don't worry, they'll be coming in as soon as they finish their chores." Then they all sat down quietly and waited.

On and on ticked the huge hall clock and the hour hand pointed to nine. The same group of men—all seven of them—were milling in the rear, now huddling together as if to outmaneuver a vice squad. Then Marjorie stepped in and took over like the real trouper she was. Out in front of the curtain, in the voice of a side-show barker, she called, "Come on in, fellers, come on in! I invite each of you to take orchestra seats right up here in the front." There was a shuffling of feet but no one moved.

"Come on, boys, I'm not about to bite you. Honest. Hey, there, you in the red-necktie. Start the march!" For a moment no one made a move, then Chris Gilbert, red-faced and grinning, walked down and the rest filed behind him.

"Now, that's more like it, boys. Didn't hurt one little bit, did it?" The men smiled sheepishly and Marjorie,

beset as she was with disappointment, drove on brightly,
"How's about a little hand for the gals?" Applause
echoed thinly through the empty hall. Then
motioning to the girl manning the curtain, she called,
"Okay, boys, here we go!"

The five-piece orchestra burst into "April Showers" as
the line of girls tripped on stage, kicking, bending,
twirling. The weight of sixteen bodies cavorted through
their paces, making the stage floor bounce. Never before
had it taken this form of punishment and I prayed
nothing would happen to make matters worse. Then
Marjorie, in step with the rhythm, walked on stage
belting out "April Showers" with the Al Jolson schmaltz.
The girls, interlocked, swayed from side to side in
rhythm, all the while out in front the men squirmed in
their seats looking like little boys caught at the cookie
jar. It was a dazzling sight and I was giddy with pleasure,
forgetting for a moment the disaster.

Other soloists came on singing and dancing—the most
dazzling, Marjorie's baby-faced protege, Marlene, who
performed three novelty numbers. And then Candy, the
high-kicking acrobatic dancer, convoluting her slim body
into ball-shaped backbends, splits, cartwheels, and other
lovely derangements to the grinning delight of the seven
men in the front row. Another solo, "Carolina Mammy,"
by Marjorie, and then the gay-colored finale; the entire
company costumed in red, white and blue against a
backdrop of Old Glory stretched across the wall. This
brought applause, the loudest applause yet. It came on
even stronger when one of the girls, dancing through a
medley of patriotic songs, tripped and fell.

Now the boys were warmed up to the occasion.
Cabe Johnson, who came without Ermie, yelled "Encore,
encore," but there were no encores. Marjorie stepped out
in front of the curtain, raising her hands for silence.

"Boys, there'll be dancing after the show, as

advertised. Since you left your ladies at home we'll supply the partners. Soon as the girls get out of costume they'll be out to trip the light fantastic."

The men cheered and Jeff Miller roared "Yippee!" as they quickly piled the long benches in the rear and readied the floor for dancing.

For an hour and a half the orchestra played while the men danced with the girls, a look of boyish mischief on every face. A look that said "I know I'll get it from the Missus, but as long as I'm here, wow! Baby!

Jeff, puffing with pleasure, called out as he was leaving. "See ya again tomorrow night."

"Not while Maud's breathin'," called back Chris, wiping the sweat from his face.

Back in the dining room Marjorie said, her voice tired and hoarse. "Tomorrow'll be different, gals. Saturday night is the big night in a hick town." The girls were silent; the only sound the swishing of tissue and the rustling of costumes, but I knew what they were feeling and I was more silent than the rest.

In one way Marjorie was right. Tomorrow *was* different. Not a soul showed up.

21

All Fish Are Not Caught with Flies

For several months now Papa would sit down more often and retire earlier. The strain of running one business in New York and one in Andover was beginning to show. More than once Mama urged him to sell his "machine" business and settle down with the store.

"How could I do such a thing? After all these years you want me to sell a business that is as much a part of me as my right hand? How could you even think such a thing!" Papa was outraged.

It was easy for Mama to think such a thing. She had lived patiently through an inventive trial-and-error period that began forty years back, the day Papa walked into a clothing manufacturing plant as a salesman offering a new smokeless iridescent lamp. He found the sales office empty and the door to the factory, with a Positively No Admittance sign, wide open. So Papa walked in.

He saw men shuffling heavily from one end of a long wooden table to another, unrolling massive bolts of cloth, straining and limping under the weight, spreading plies of material in preparation for the cutting. He watched the men at work, and the more he watched the more incensed he became. When he walked into the house that night he sputtered out to Mama what he had witnessed.

"You never saw anything like it. The men almost fell down from exhaustion—it was a terrible sight. There must be a more civilized way for men to do their jobs instead of slaving like a bunch of pack horses. A man must maintain a little dignity no matter how menial the work." Papa looked up dreamily, "There surely must be a way."

For weeks he was troubled by the thought of men sweating and laboring under mammoth bolts of cloth. And again one day he said to Mama, "A man is not a horse—he has a God-given brain and he must use it. There must be some other way for men to lay cloth on a table, roll it back and forth, and measure plies in the same operation. A machine perhaps . . .nor should it require more than a gentle push at one end . . .perhaps a ball-bearing roller could stop short and sail back on its own momentum . . .perhaps . . ."

As the vision continued to haunt him, night after night he worked, drawing sketch after sketch. Then one night he called loudly for Mama to come quickly. "Estherel, I think I have it! I believe I have something that will work."

The next day Papa brought his plan to a pattern-maker. Could he make wooden patterns of castings from these sketches? He went to a foundry. Could they mold iron castings from wooden patterns? How about tracks? For this machine must glide—smoothly, firmly . . .

Then one day Papa was ready.

He walked into the same clothing factory carrying his first rolling machine and sought out the plant owner. "This," he said simply, "will change the entire complexion of your shop."

The owner glared down at the crude machine, his thick fingers clutching a cigar. "Who needs fancy ideas! Machines yet. For twenty years I made a living without machines. So what's wrong with that, I ask you?"

"Mister, it's easy to see that a smart man like you don't have to be told that times are changing, that men want machines to help them with their burdens."

"Who heard of machines! Maybe you, but not them shlemiels in there." He directed his stubby hand to the loft.

"To me they're not shlemiels. They're human beings like you and me, trying to make a living for our families. A few weeks ago I walked in here and watched them work. In a civilized world like ours labor should be made simpler for the working man."

"So you got ideas what we should do? Baby them? Maybe give them a bottle. Waddya think they're here for, anyway?"

"To work, sure. But think how much more they could produce for you with a machine working like three men."

"A machine working like three men? Naah! How could a machine . . ."

Papa had touched on a sensitive spot and proceeded to exploit his meager advantage. "Give me a chance to show you what I mean. At the end of one week, if you're not completely satisfied, I guarantee it won't cost you a cent."

"So all right, bring it in. What have I got to lose? But remember, I ain't promising nothing and I ain't signing nothing."

Papa rushed out. In an hour he was back with several lengths of tracks and a sack of parts. As he proceeded to secure the tracks to the coarse wooden table the men edged forward curiously. They watched as he assembled the machine part by part. And when the machine was finished they watched as he snapped a huge bolt of cloth in place and sent it rolling on its maiden run, his heart racing. The machine glided gracefully down the length of track, clicked at the other end, and lurched smoothly back in place. He sent it down again and again . . .and again. The plies piled up evenly, thickly. Curiosity melted into wonder. "Y'mean to say this machine lays plies by itself?"

"All you do is give it a little push at one end? Nothing else?"

"Maybe there's a catch to it."

"Here, try it yourself," said Papa to the man beside him. The cutter gripped the handle and gently repeated the movement. Again it rolled smoothly, clicked at the far end and returned.

"How do you like that?" the cutter said softly. "It's like playing with a toy . . .just like a toy."

Through the labyrinthian grapevine word spread through the industry. "There's a new machine out—a rolling machine—that saves your strength, your health . . .no more lifting weights that give you hernias . . .there's nothing like it on the market . . . ."

Workmen were easily convinced but not the foremen who were suspicious of anything that might infringe on their cloth-and-scissors sovereignty. Plant owners stood firmly with their foremen. Only when the men clamored long and persistently were they persuaded to step down from their perch. Then, almost at once, the orders started trickling in.

"How about an installation today? The men are on my back! How soon can you deliver?"

The trickle coursed into a slow but steady flow, and Papa, inventor, salesman and installation man, was busy from early morning till late at night. "He hardly sleeps," sighed Mama, concerned with the sudden turn.

In three months Papa found larger quarters, hired two

men and promptly taught them to drill holes in castings, paint flanges, and build machines. "It's a pleasure the way they learn," said Papa to Mama one night. "They're just as adept at assembling as I am. Who ever dreamed I would run into such good luck!" And Papa was right. With clocklike precision machines were built and stored neatly in the rear cf the shop. When an order came in it was quickly filled.

Ben Brand was the first to work for Papa. He walked in one morning as Papa was baking some freshly painted castings.

"I saw your machine at L and M Clothing," he said, carefully looking around, "and I think you have a substantial idea there—an idea that could spread through the trade like wildfire."

"You think so?" Papa asked, surprised and pleased at his interest. "Who knows? Only time will tell."

Brand walked slowly to the tools, examining them closely.

"Fine equipment," he said, with more than a stranger's curiosity.

"It's the best I can afford," said Papa removing a sheet of hot castings from the cast-iron stove. "I'm a one-man company."

"With your brain, coupled with your potential, there's no limit how far you can go."

"I'm in no rush. Some things are more satisfying than money."

"Like what?"

"Like the happiness within me when I know I can ease the workingman's burden. To me, that is more satisfying than money."

"Mister, if I may say so without offending, you talk like a childish idealist. In this world ideals don't put money in your pockets."

"As I said, money isn't everything. We all end up in

the same place if we have a big bank account or a small one."

"That's foolish talk. Everybody knows that money makes life a little easier, and who can deny that when life is easier a person is happier?"

"You can be right. I'm not claiming to have all the answers, but of this moment I have very little money and I consider myself a fairly happy man."

"Bah! You got to be realistic in a realistic world. As far as I know that does not constitute a sin."

"Who says it's a sin?"

"Take this little set-up," said Brand, driving on. "Can you visualize it as something more than a two-bit business within the confines of these four walls?"

"To tell you the truth, sir, I don't look too far ahead. Sometimes I think it's not too smart."

"Aha! That's your trouble. You can't envisage a growing thing. I'm telling you, Henry—and I hope you excuse the familiarity—if we teamed up together you'd be stunned at your growth in the span of one year."

Brand's fire caught hold. "Maybe so," said Papa. "A man with your foresight and business acumen could be an asset to any firm."

"If those aren't idle words, what's the harm in working together?"

"You want to work with me? You'd be willing to take such a chance? You see" —Papa gestured around the room—"my business is small . . .I can't make any rosy promises."

"Who needs promises? Only a moment ago you said I had foresight. So, my friend Henry, if you're willing, let's consider it a deal."

"I would be foolish not to be willing," said Papa gratefully, extending his hand. "I hope you will never have reason to regret your decision."

"That I won't," said Ben Brand, "you can be sure.

But first you'll excuse me for a couple of days while I take care of a few personal matters. After that you'll see things start moving like you'd never believe possible."

And Brand proved right. Papa was amazed at the way he caught on to the business. In a few days he could assemble a machine as accurately as he, and in less time. He dealt with the foundry shrewdly, maneuvering quotations on steel bars, parts, like a seasoned speculator. When Papa purchased he paid the current market price. "If that is their price, that is their price," he'd say with finality.

Not Brand. When a figure was quoted, it posed a springboard from which to start bargaining.

"What can you do for me in hundred lots? In five-hundred lots? How much off for cash?" And so it went. In time he managed to slash sharply the cost of each machine.

"He's not only a hard worker but a gifted man, too," said Papa one day. The money he saves me alone pays for his wages."

Just as Brand predicted, the little machine shop buzzed with productivity. Systematically, with orderly precision, machine parts were bundled in burlap and stored in wooden cases, ready for quick assembly. Orders came in steadily and were filled within twenty-four hours. There came a day when the demand exceeded the supply.

We must find a boy to help around the shop," said Brand, "a boy who could do the shop work while we spend our time more productively soliciting orders and demonstrating rollers."

"Maybe you're right," agreed Papa, and Ben lost no time installing his nephew Alex. In a few weeks he, too, grasped hold of the work and the little shop hummed busily under Ben's feverish drive.

The pace established, business reached an

unprecedented peak within six months; now a crew of young men took over the drilling, painting, bundling, crating, with Alex at the helm. Ben insisted on relieving Papa of the assembling, urging him to spend more time on new ideas.

"Anybody can assemble, Henry, but only you can create."

"A fine man, a thoughtful man," said Papa, and started creating.

Mama, too, felt the upsurge. We moved into a new apartment on fashionable Seventeenth Street, a few doors from Stuyvesant Park, and Papa furnished it with a decor befitting the prosperous businessman. We still own the little ebony desk and a few peices of sterling silver that symbolized Papa's sudden affluence and good fortune. And so our lives took on a brighter hue; for the first time in her life, Mama greeted each day with a feeling of well-being. A cleaning woman came in regularly and an abundance of good food filled the larder. This rare state of leisure permitted Mama to air us daily in the nearby park, and this alone contributed to her great sense of serenity.

After three years of prosperity and near-blissful existence a new pattern, unheeded at first, was taking hold—creeping in slowly as the late afternoon tide, then breaking abruptly. In the shop Ben Brand preoccupied himself more, talked less. Vigorously he made notations in a small ledger, sometimes little drawings. Papa looked on happily and didn't see. He, too, was more preoccupied, less talkative; a new idea was gestating slowly and there was little time for talk. But on the very day of completion he presented it to Ben in full-dress detail, complete with sketches, and Ben lapped it up as a thirsty hound laps water.

Papa beamed. All this he regarded auspiciously as Ben's interest grew more intense, more personal, affording him more time for creative thought free of business pressures. And Papa made the most of it, perfecting another new idea which soon would be ready for the pattern-maker.

Then it happened—as suddenly as a thunderclap on a hot summer day. Ben walked into the shop one morning, hung up his coat, and without even a thin "good-morning" began swinging his words like small hard jabs to the jaw.

"We're living in a cold, hard world, Henry, and every man must think of himself—otherwise who will? Do you follow me, Henry?"

Papa looked up quickly, waiting to hear more.

Ben came straight to the point. "What I'm trying to say, Henry, is that I've been offered an option in a flourishing concern."

"You're not serious, Ben—"

"I'm afraid I am."

"Are you so unhappy with me?" Papa eyed him dismally. "You earn as much as I do."

"While this is true, Henry, you can't blame a man for striking out on his own when the opportunity suddenly presents itself." Ben mumbled on vaguely about the "big opportunity" but Papa didn't hear. He was thinking back to the day Ben first walked into the shop, his enthusiasm, his interest in working with him. Was this the same Ben that wanted out? Papa was stunned and bewildered; when finally he spoke he entreated, offered a full, legal partnership, but Ben remained firm and refused. And then, as if to heap kindling on a smoldering fire he added, "I forgot to mention that Alex will be joining me, too."

For weeks Papa walked around with pain in his heart, and anger, too. He would show Ben Brand—and all the world—that no one man is indispensable, and again Papa was in business alone, the new creation shelved while once more he flung himself into production and selling.

"Who needs him?" Papa tossed airily, but his voice was husky. Mama wasn't fooled. She saw the hurt, felt the hurt and tried to console him.

"Henry, the first time I met this Ben I knew he was not a man of character."

Papa looked up, questioning.

"The way he turned from me when he spoke, like he was trying to hide something. A man should look you straight in the face if he's a decent man.

"I never dreamt he'd walk out on me," muttered Papa, not hearing. "Never did I see a more devoted man."

"Sometimes even a crook can show an honest face." Mama, more angered than hurt, was concerned with Papa, not the departure of Brand. She watched him leave for the shop each morning like a man not fully roused; for several weeks now he said little and ate little. But then a strange new turn took place. Like a sprinter straining every sinew for the last few laps, he threw himself bodily into what seemed a fierce personal resolve. Almost at once he expedited the shopwork like a bright young foreman, purchased deftly at the foundry as shrewdly as a Yankee trader, and tallied more sales than ever before. Mama brooded as she warmed his food on the back of the stove night after night but wisely kept her silence as she knew she must. "Everything passes," she said quietly.

And she was right. Before many months had passed he was happily assembling the new machine, perfecting every detail. And so it went until the dark day Papa walked into the private office of M & S Clothing Company. Mr. Moskowitz, the M of M & S, greeted him warmly, for only a few months earlier, after purchasing three rolling machines, his shop spurred to peak production. Papa knew this and lost no time in the usual small talk; he was excited and proud of what he was

presenting that day. If Mr. Moskowitz was happy with
the rolling machines, he would be smitten by this newest
idea. He beamed with the glow of creation as he slowly
removed a band from a sheaf of pamphlets fresh with
the smell of printer's ink, and placed one before Mr. M.

"I want you to be the first to try our new laying
machine. I'll install it tomorrow. Keep it a week and at
the end of that time if you're not completely sold, I'll
gladly remove it," said Papa, jotting down the order,
which he was certain of getting, while Mr. Mosowitz
studied the leaflet. Carefully he read it through, and
looked hard at the illustrations. He turned it over, read it
through again, then looked closely at Papa.

"Why, I have a machine just like this."

"Impossible. This is new, brand new. No one has seen
it. How could you have it! You've made a mistake."

"Come into the plant and see for yourself."

Papa went. And Papa saw. Mr. Moskowitz was not
mistaken. The machine was there—big and shining—a
machine so like his own, only he could see the
difference; cruelly, the bold, gilt lettering BRAND
MANUFACTURING COMPANY glared back at him.

A full year passed before Papa was again himself.
When at last he could talk of Brand's treachery, he
muttered a vow he doggedly kept, "Never again in my
life will I take another man in the business." And
through the years, though Mama never tired pleading,
protesting he was hurting no one but himself, he never
did.

22

Things Are Not What They Seem

Often the store weighed heavily on our spirits, for hardly a night passed without interruption. With store and living quarters combined under one roof, people came to expect service seven days a week, early morning till late at night. Even through the night.

Time and again we were wakened by motorists stuck with empty tanks, stalled engines, or flat tires. "It's worse than being a doctor," groaned Keeve, dragging himself out of bed. But far and above the nuisance there lurked the pervading fear that a night intrusion might turn into a holdup. The papers bristled with such accounts and they did not pass us unnoticed.

The first few times our sleep was shattered by persistent motorists we all jumped out of bed and ran to the windows, our hands cupped about our eyes in pitch dark, trying to identify the night caller. If Mama knew him she'd call to Keeve, "It's all right," then dress and walk down, waiting, while he pumped gas or found a motor part. She discouraged any spurts of small talk and hastened the villagers on their way with a polite but firm good night, then wearily climbed the squeaking stairs and again to bed.

273

Sometimes startled into waking by a reveler soaked in prohibition moonshine, calling in garbled, fuzzy tones, we lay silent knowing Mama would pretend sleep no matter how hard the thumping or bellowing. We held our breaths until the tipsy carouser left muttering and cursing; these nocturnal invasions became a frightening aspect to our life in Andover, especially the first few months. In a short time, however, noises in the night became more irritating than alarming and Mama was more concerned for our interrupted sleep than the danger. Slowly a feeling of safety settled over us, especially during the winter when travel virtually ceased, and we slept the nights through, the feather bedding tightly around us, only our noses up for air.

At the end of the second year, with the holiday spirit melting quickly like a light snowfall, Papa took leave of us the day after the New Year. He had been home for two weeks; his sudden departure left a loneliness and a void, and that night we retired earlier than usual.

I tossed and turned in bed and finally dozed off, only to waken suddenly to a sharp thud as if a heavy tool had smacked against something metallic. Startled, I listened for more but there was nothing, only a vague, intense quiet. The noise woke Mama, too, and she called, "Keevie, you in the store?" A long silence, and she called again. Still no answer. It was now clear that Keeve was not in the store but snuggly asleep under the bulky covers. I raised myself as much as I dared, straining for sound, but there was only silence—a silence that seemed too quiet, strangely quiet. I waited to hear Mama call again but nothing came and I laid the noise to something rolling off a shelf. With this peaceful thought I soon forgot the incident and fell into a deep sleep.

What seemed like minutes later I woke again, but this time in a haze of panic. Mama's voice, shrill and agitated, sounded through the house, and her call was like the triggering of a switch for at that moment everything began to happen; the short, clear ring of the cash register, the thump of a fallen case, hasty, clumsy shuffling. Then complete silence. Dead silence. Trembling and terrified, I pulled the covers over my head. Through it all Rose slept like a baby, buried blissfuly under the feather quilt. I poked my head up for air in time to hear a sharp voice, clearly Mama's, but strange and commanding. "Keeve," she roared, "hand me the Winchester!"

Low, muffled voices, Mama's and Keeve's, hurried movement in the store, then suddenly a shot shattered the black quiet, liberating footsteps, frantic footsteps. Another shot pierced the stillness, then a sputtering motor lurched up the hill in stripped-gear, straining around the bend and out of sight.

Mama and Keeve rushed downstairs and when I could calm my chattering teeth I slipped into my cloth chinchilla coat and felt slippers and walked down. Mama and Keeve were talking in low, agitated tones as they examined the window through which the hoodlums had entered. Still trembling, I looked around. The store was in complete disorder; on the floor, apparently dropped when the shots were fired, lay a spilled case of groceries and scattered cartons of cigarettes. In the corner by the door a stack of tires six feet high had dwindled to one. Two smaller display fixtures, a stock of unopened candy and cigarette cartons were missing, as were most of the fan belts hanging from the ceiling. Wide open was the American Can cash register, the till cleaned of bills, but strangely no loss of silver. "kind-hearted bums," Keeve sputtered, "the silver would jingle." There was no mistaking the smooth operation, for most of the loot had been cached away in their waiting car before they dropped the case that woke Mama.

Keeve undertook to estimate the loss. "They got the new Goodrich tires and tubes, left the retreads—the stinkers.

All the cans of motor oil and the cases of
groceries...oh, boy!" Keeve was suddenly dismayed.
"I should've had those cases on the shelves by now.
Wait'll Papa hears this." His fury doubled as he vented
this new anguish on the crooks. "Those dirty, stinking
robbers. We should've aimed at them instead of the
sky!"

Papa was so stunned at the news he was ready to
move us all back to New York, "where at least people
are honest." It was two days before he calmed down
enough to assess the debacle, and then he began
fine-toothing the store for missing items, thanking God
between intervals the family was well and unharmed. The
loss, around five hundred dollars, was a big blow. We
were not insured against theft.

News of the robbery swept through town like an
autumn blaze. Excitement, speculation ran rampant.
Locally, a real break-in was news. You might hear of a
few chickens skulked in the dead of night, or a jug of
dandelion wine "borrowed"; even in the store we
watched and kept our silence while a son of a
respectable citizen slipped candy bars furtively into
pockets. The loss was minor, Mama insisted. "Stay close
to them so they won't be tempted."

Eager for sparks, much as an arsonist joins the fire
department, self-styled private eyes, the constable, a host
of would-be sleuths swarmed into the store surveying the
scene, deliberating on the possible culprits. Even the
state police appeared from nowhere, and this alone made
news. You rarely saw a trooper; they manned the
narrow, dirt side roads, and until you were pulling over,
on the receiving end of a ticket, you scarcely laid eyes
on them.

A point of vital evidence, the broken sash, was
examined with the seasoned scrutiny of the prosecution
ogling exhibit A at a murder trial. "Could've been the

work of pranksters; then again it could've been the work of slickers," they concluded sagely.

Then suddenly Mama confused the constabulary by discouraging them from pressing; she had some ideas, she admitted, but refused to divulge them.

For a full week everyone enjoyed the terrible injustice, *tsk-tsking* dolefully as at a funeral, but then the big furor died down and the villagers returned to their farms and soon forgot.

But not Mama and Keeve. Often they huddled together, speaking softly, like conspirators, stopping abruptly when anyone appeared. Knowing how Mama tried to hide her worries from us I laid it to concern, for now the break-in was rarely mentioned, and then only when some new piece of merchandise was discovered missing.

One day, however, Keeve opened the subject unexpectedly. We were busy in the store taking inventory of hardware and auto supplies. He sat down on the counter, his chin cupped in his palm, thoughtfully. "Kids, you should've seen Mama handle that Winchester! Like a pro. She aimed for the sky just to scare the bums but she could've let them have it just as easy."

I started as if smacked. "Mama?"

. "Mama fired that rifle?" Rose's eyes were hugh saucers.

"You bet she did."

"That's funny," said Rose, "we thought you did."

"Me? You fooling, kiddo?"

"But . . .Mama! Are you joking? Keevie, come on, tell us!"

"Would I joke about something like this?"

"I still can't believe it."

"She didn't want you kids to know."

"Mama . . ." Rose said thinly, "anyone but Mama."

"That's where you're wrong. Let me tell you something about our mother you never knew," said Keeve, hardly able to contain himself. "In Rumania she was a girl crack shot."

"But," countered Rose, "she came to America at the ripe age of thirteen."

"You're right. By that time she was trained as the best shot in the village."

"Trained! Who trained her?"

"Uncle Joe."

Keeve, satisfied he had delivered his coup de grace, sat back and watched quietly as it settled. Joe's reputation as a sharpshooter and crack shot was more than hearsay; these were facts and not to be disputed. He was the family legend—brave and fearless, and someone you didn't rush out of your way to tangle with. His devotion to the army was as strong as a clergyman's to the cloth and he could outshoot, outdrink any member of his cavalry, we heard again and again.

"I could drink any soldier in the United States cavalry under the table and never get drunk. A pocket flask was part of my rigging like my gun."

"You could do this?" Mama's dismay at his talent was no secret.

Uncle Joe's eyes narrowed to merry slits as he rubbed his fingers slowly through his thick mustache.

"Only once did I come near trouble—the day I got my third stripe. I was brushing down my fine stallion, Blackie, when I figured it called for a little private celebration. Just as I'd pulled the flask from my hip pocket, up walks my captain suddenly from nowhere.

" 'Sergeant, what in hell you doing with booze on your person!' Holding the bottle in one hand, I saluted with the other. 'Drinking it, sir,' " Joe's passion for the United States Army and the truth were unequaled.

" 'You know the rules about liquor on duty! What's

your excuse?'

" 'None, sir.'

" 'Hand over that flask!'

" 'Yes, sir,' I says as I pulled out the cork, put the flask to my lips and drained it down to the last sweet drop. The captain turned purple like he was ready for a stroke. 'What is the meaning of this action?'

" 'I was following orders, sir! You asked for the flask. Not the contents.' "

This was Uncle Joe, six foot six, and more like William S. Hart than Hart himself. A child could easily worship this tower of man, who after mustering out of the army turned to the law, first as deputy, then sheriff.

Keeve's announcement about Uncle Joe needed no further expansion.

"What ever made him do such a thing?"

"Mama was five when Grandpa died and after that Uncle Joe sort of took over. It was natural he'd want to protect the family, wasn't it? Well, he trained them all to shoot, including Mama, and in a year or so she was holding a gun, shooting at targets."

"Why?" Rose was still incredulous.

"As I said, for protection. They lived in a village close to a forest, and in Europe that means wolves, plenty of wolves. It was a matter of self-preservation."

Rose and I listened. There was little more to say; it was all true, so true. Our sweet, gentle Mama a Rumanian Annie Oakley with a trigger finger. Shocking, unbelievable, but there it was out in the open and there was nothing we could do but accept the dreadful facts.

Keeve looked at us soberly. "Mama never wanted to spread this around before, but she's changed her mind since the looting."

When Mama walked into the store we looked at her as we never looked at her before. Inside, I felt a gamut of respect, fear, awe—feelings one reserves for a kind ruler with an iron hand, but not a mother. It seemed that almost at once she had begun to take an inordinate, undisguised pleasure in regaling anyone who entered the store with stories of her exploits, a display deeply counter to her nature and principles. "Let others praise you," she'd say, discouraging self-glorification in any form. "If you're good, you don't have to tell people, they'll find out soon enough." One couldn't be sure about his own mother! A sharpshooting heroine is one thing, but when that heroine is your own mother, it's as Keeve would say, "a green horse of a different color."

The imposing Winchester, a gift from Uncle Joe, now hung conspicuously in the store. It continued to hang grandly for all to see, while Mama made it clear she prayed she'd never be obliged to use it. "I'd be very unhappy if some fool got the notion to break in again," she said twenty times if she said it once.

The first shock of discovery over, life went on as usual only now we were cushioned in a wonderfully safe feeling we'd never known before. Blissfully I fell asleep each night, confident that Mama would handle anyone who had the impertinence to disturb our peace again.

Some years later I spend an evening with Keevie and his family in their New York apartment. Nostalgically we reminisced about our days in Andover, the book I am writing, and I brought up the robbery. "While writing the chapter I vividly relived that frightful experience."

"I'll never forget it either," said Keeve.

"I still can't get over Mama shooting the rifle and revealing a side I never knew."

"Shooting what rifle?" Keeve looked at me strangely, then suddenly doubled up with laughter.

"Sarie, Mama never shot a gun in her life."

"But *you* told me . . ."

Still laughing, Keeve said, "Don't be *naïve.*"

"Then who—?" My voice sank to a whisper. "Then who really fired the shots that night?"

"I did. It was the first and only time I pulled a trigger, and boy did that backfire. It knocked me over."

"But what about those fantastic stories Mama told people. About Uncle Joe—and her sharpshooting exploits—"

It was something we both concocted."

"But why?" I looked at Keeve, hardly hearing, plucking my memory for something that might throw a little light on this revelation. "You know, Keeve, you can't begin to imagine the feeling of comfort I had after that."

"Then Mama was successful," said Keeve, his face softened by memory. "She wanted you kids to go to bed at night and sleep."

I looked at Keeve with an understanding suddenly born. And slowly, through a misty haze, I seemed to hear Mama's words filtering through—those firm but gentle words, "Remember, children, everything happens for the best."